The Making of
Rebel Without a Cause

The Making of
Rebel Without a Cause

Douglas L. Rathgeb

foreword by Stewart Stern

McFarland & Company, Inc., Publishers
Jefferson, North Carolina, and London

The present work is a reprint of the illustrated case bound edition of The Making of *Rebel Without a Cause, first published in 2004 by McFarland.*

All photographs provided by Photofest unless otherwise noted.

Frontispiece: Nicholas Ray and James Dean on the set of *Rebel Without a Cause.*

LIBRARY OF CONGRESS CATALOGUING-IN-PUBLICATION DATA

Rathgeb, Douglas L., 1945–
The making of Rebel without a cause / Douglas L. Rathgeb ;
foreword by Stewart Stern.
p.   cm.
Includes bibliographical references and index.

ISBN 978-0-7864-6115-8
softcover : 50# alkaline paper ∞

1. Rebel without a cause (Motion picture)   I. Title.
PN1997.R365R38   2011   791.43'72 — dc22   2004013464

British Library cataloguing data are available

Cover: Background photograph by Mark Durr

Manufactured in the United States of America

*McFarland & Company, Inc., Publishers
Box 611, Jefferson, North Carolina 28640
www.mcfarlandpub.com*

For Jean
and in memory of Richard Smith

ACKNOWLEDGMENTS

This book is the result of the many hours spent poring over, organizing and interpreting materials from the Warner Bros. Archive at the University of Southern California and numerous other sources from outside the collection. It has undergone significant changes since I began writing it in 1993, and it owes its existence not only to my efforts, but a number of others.

Thanks first to Leith Adams and his successor, Stuart Ng, for accessing the archive's wonderful materials and assisting me in their use, with a special thanks to the Cinema-Television Library's Ned Comstock, one of the best film researchers on the planet, for his efforts and encouragement.

I received early encouragement as well from Dana Polan of the University of Pittsburgh (and now at USC). In his efforts to help me on *Rebel* and mine to help him on his excellent BFI study of Nicholas Ray's *In a Lonely Place*, I believe we forged a mutual admiration society. Thanks also to Bernard Eisenschitz, whose superb biography of Ray is still definitive, and who answered many key questions in our brief but meaningful correspondence on the great director. A special thanks also to Sylvia Bongiovanni, president of the We Remember Dean International fan club (now JamesDean.com), who first put me in touch with Stewart Stern.

I cannot thank Mr. Stern enough for his contributions. His heartfelt Foreword (and letters in the appendix) attest not only to his skill and grace as a writer, but to his love for this film and the people who made it. His editorial skills are equally sharp. Numerous areas of *Rebel*'s production history would have remained hazy and inaccurate if Mr. Stern had not contributed his efforts to clarifying them and his own role in making the film. What began as an off-again on-again professional association of sorts has developed into a warm and genuine friendship.

I would like also to thank Mr. Allan L. Alexander, Irving Shulman's son-in-law, for his assistance. When Mr. Shulman was ill and unable to speak with this writer about Mr. Shulman's experiences working on the picture, Mr. Alexander provided valuable information.

And now a little something from the Strunk and White Department, with special thanks to Jean Lucas, my much better half. Her disdain for the passive sentence fell upon me time and again until I finally got the message.

Lawrence Epstein has been my good friend for almost 40 years. He has bull-dozed writing out of me, shamed it out of me, done whatever was necessary to keep me from losing my identity as a writer. This book owes a lot to his persuasive abilities, his patience and his love of the written word. He hasn't raised stupid children, either. His daughter, Rachel, was the agent for this book.

Thanks to Lindsay Kefauver and the University of Tennessee for photo permissions, and a huge round of applause to Photofest for supplying the majority of photographs for this book. Nobody *anywhere* does it better.

Douglas L. Rathgeb
Carmichael, California
June 2004

CONTENTS

Acknowledgments   vii

Foreword by Stewart Stern   1

Preface   3

Prologue   5

Part I: Preliminaries

1. Nicholas Ray   11

2. "The Blind Run"   16

3. James Dean   20

4. Weisbart and Uris   23

5. Story into Script   28

6. Lindner and Shulman   32

7. Changes   34

8. Stewart Stern   40

9. Dead End   42

10. A Critique   46

11. Los Angeles and New York   48

Part II: Pre-Production

12. A Private Hell   53

13. Screenplay by Stewart Stern   55

14. Start Notice   58

15. Casting   63

16. Mr. Warner   67

17. Free-for-All   70

18. Locations   74

19. Mr. Warner Returns   77

20. Majors and Minors   79

21. The Excitement Gathers   81

22. Cold Feet   84

23. Rehearsals   87

24. Blackboard Jungle   92

25. Exit Stern   99

Part III: Production

26. On Location   105

27. Transformation   111

28. Red Channels   114

29. Hard Work, Hard Feelings   117

30. Lost Time   120

31. The Mansion   124

32. Fury and Sound   127

33. Looping and Ad-Libbing   130

34. Stern's Argument   135

35. Lonely Street   138

36. Night Work   141

37. Reckless Violence   144

38. Two Endings and an
    Argument   147

Part IV: Post-Production and Beyond

39. Two Assignments   155

40. Inquisition   158

41. Rough Cut   161

42. Final Preparations   165

43. Previews   169

44. Death in the Afternoon   173

45. Damage Control   178

46. Reaping the Whirlwind   181

47. Premiere   185

48. Box Office   188

49. Shulman Strikes Back   193

50. Oscar and Beyond   195

Epilogue: *After* Rebel   197

Appendix   203

Notes   209

Bibliography   227

Index   229

FOREWORD
by Stewart Stern

The Seattle Arboretum is a verdant strip of fragrant rustic woodland that overlooks Lake Washington's ship canal. Its damp dirt trails roll over grassy ridges and descend into moist valleys of fern and cat-tail, wind through black groves of Douglas fir, rhododendrons thirty feet high, weeping cherries, magnolias, borders of azaleas of outrageous size and hue. I walk those trails in the mornings when I'm the only one I see. I go there to greet the trees — I know them all. They've become the living homes for the souls of dead friends I miss. I put them there so I can visit them, all within view of each other, from grove to grove. Famous and revered ones like Beatrice Lillie, Eva Le Gallienne, John Houseman have their trees close by my parents' and my sister's. My buddies' from the Battle of the Bulge. My teachers', favorite aunt's. Little Dynamite, the calf I had in my thirteenth summer, she's there too. They're all there in the drench of winter and the trembling spring; their ghost breath quakes the leaves and moves the branches. But the tree I never pass without stopping my walk, even for a visit as brief as a breath, is a towering big leaf maple with a restless canopy as dense as a lion's mane and a coat of moss shrouding half the trunk that's so spongy when I put my weight on it that it nearly shoves me away. I call it "The Rebel Tree" because it's where I put the souls of the friends who made that film. It's full of them: Jimmy, Natalie, Sal, Nick Ray, Dave Weisbart, Jim Backus, Nick Adams, Ann Doran, Bill Hopper, Ed Platt, Virginia Brissac, Marietta Canty, Ian Wolfe, Rochelle Hudson, so many, many more whose names I recite when I lay my palm on the moss and remember, or kiss the bark in gratitude and grief no matter how we raged when we all had life for raging, no matter how we loved, or might have, given time. I write their names down here at the start of Douglas Rathgeb's book just so they'll know it's here and that they had a hand in it, just as they did in the movie, and to wish Doug well for them and me, for the time he gave, and the care he took, and his fine fairmindedness.

PREFACE

The study of American film has, for the most part, been the study of a product rather than a process. Of all the works published to date on film, only a handful have examined the production process of an individual film in any detail. Like the jaded consumer who wants his cell phone but doesn't care how or why it operates, film scholars seem to look at production history as a kind of blue-collar stepchild to film analysis, secondary to studying the finished film.

At best, this is a limiting approach to the subject. Because film *is* a process, and a thoroughly fascinating one, whether it is undertaken by an individual filmmaker with a hand-held camera and an all-amateur cast and crew or the vast artistic bureaucracy of a major Hollywood studio. Looking at a film as product alone is like studying a lake by looking only at its surface.

I would even hazard the guess that the various human, technical, financial and meteorological dramas that take place during any film's production reach or surpass the drama provided by the film itself. You really have not "seen" *The Wizard of Oz* or *Casablanca*, for example, until you have read Aljean Harmetz's illuminating production histories of them.

Even the most wretched and abused films can have fascinating production histories. Who would not want to be a fly on the wall during the filming of *Plan 9 from Outer Space,* if only to observe the interplay between its hopelessly inept director, Ed Wood, and its faded star, Bela Lugosi? Tim Burton's film of that production gave us only a glimpse. And what of the disastrous *Cleopatra*, which brought 20th Century–Fox to its corporate knees? Or *Citizen Kane*, with the angry Mr. Hearst hovering? Or *any* film made by Howard Hughes?

Unfortunately, many production records are long-lost. The majority of the Hollywood studios (Disney and Warner Bros. being the major exceptions) treated their archival materials with the same scorn and neglect as film scholars have treated the production process. Many of MGM's records, for example, were trashed and are presumably buried under a freeway. The production records that have survived studio indifference either by special care or sheer luck are still waiting for rescue, still waiting to see the light of day as books.

When I found the records for *Rebel Without a Cause* in 1992, they were waiting

3

patiently for me in two neatly-arranged cardboard boxes. The files, which included production records, publicity releases, scripts and newspaper clippings, were part of the Warner Bros. Archive at the University of Southern California's Cinema-Television Library in Los Angeles.

But even that was not the beginning. The project actually began in 1990 when I discovered a book titled *James Dean: Behind the Scene*, a collection of never-before-published photographs and studio memoranda from Dean's three films. One of the authors was Leith Adams, then the Warner Bros. archivist at USC.

The photographs were intriguing, but those studio documents mesmerized me. Here was a tempting sampler of primary source material about one of my favorite films. Here was every single piece of information that Warner Bros. had assembled on a film that began as a humble "B" feature and became an American classic. If I could only get closer....

Fortunately, I was already in the process of switching coasts and careers, and in my second year of library school at San Jose State University, I was ready to reach for the prize. After several interviews with Steven Hanson, the director of the Cinema-Television Library at USC, I was taken on as a library intern. Two days a week for four months I sat at the reference desk or worked on the clippings files, and one day a week, on my own time, I sat in a paneled reading room with the archival materials from *Rebel Without a Cause*. No candy store could have been as sweet.

In those many months, and in the many months and years that followed, I came to know *Rebel Without a Cause* perhaps as no one had ever known it. I came to understand it through the processes that took it from idea to script to finished film. And I understood that the process was as important and as satisfying as the product. I believe that I have a better understanding of film as an art form because of that experience, and I believe that anyone who reads this book will see clearly and with admiration the industry, the creativity and the humanity that made *Rebel Without a Cause* possible.

PROLOGUE

1955

The images are indelible.

Dressed in blue jeans, white T-shirt and red windbreaker, Jim Stark sits behind the wheel of a stolen car, coolly smoking a cigarette and waiting for the start of the chickie run.

Sitting in a police station in her red Easter coat, Judy scowls at the Juvenile Officer, rails against her insensitive father and bursts into tears.

Frightened by an apocalyptic display in the planetarium, Plato says of the lecturer, "What does *he* know about man alone?"

These are the prototypical American teenagers of Nicholas Ray's *Rebel Without a Cause*. Because the images have become so ingrained in our consciousness and our culture, we may forget that the film once belonged to a particular place and time: America in the mid–Fifties.

Dwight D. Eisenhower was President then. The nation was politically and socially conservative, the economy sound and growing. The Korean War had ended two years earlier, but the Cold War showed no signs of waning and the threat of nuclear annihilation was still a daily reality. Senator Joseph McCarthy had fallen from grace during the Army-McCarthy Hearings the year before, but fears of an organized communist conspiracy still ran high.

People were moving out of the cities and into the suburbs. Spurred by the development of the Interstate Highway System, sprawling communities like Levittown on Long Island seemed to spring up overnight. "Little boxes made of ticky-tacky," as Malvina Reynolds described them in a song, lined street after identical street all across the country.

Rock 'n' roll had barely arrived, but television was already an institution. Milton Berle, Ed Sullivan, Davy Crockett and *The Honeymooners* captivated the nation through another "little box" that was fast becoming the focal point of American living rooms.

People still went to the movies, but Hollywood needed increasingly exotic lures to draw them from their televisions. Technicolor, 3-D and CinemaScope provided

5

the thrills that Americans couldn't get at home, but somehow it wasn't enough. The movie industry was in a slump.

Despite the threats of communism and nuclear annihilation, America was comfortably complacent: weekend barbecues, the Sunday paper, shopping trips, long, meandering drives in the country. For the nation's middle-class adults, who still remembered the Great Depression, life had never been better. For ever-increasing numbers of their teenage children, however, the Good Life was flawed by powerful feelings of alienation and anger.

More and more, teens seemed to express those feelings through violence and crime. According to an article in the September 17, 1954, issue of *U.S. News and World Report*, juvenile delinquency had increased more than 40 percent between 1948 and 1953, right along with the post-war prosperity. More than a million teenagers a year now came to the attention of the police.

A rising divorce rate, television, teenage drinking, even comic books took part of the blame for teenage violence, but too much of it had no explanation. Especially difficult to understand was criminal activity among the most affluent and privileged of America's youth. The spread of delinquency from the urban lower class to the suburban middle and upper classes was an ominous trend. Yet, these "concealed delinquents," as *U.S. News* called them, seemed mainly the problem of parents and child psychiatrists, not police or social workers. Like Leopold and Loeb, the rich, spoiled thrill killers of the 1920s, such teenagers were exceptions, anomalies, oddities. Despite the threat they posed to post-war society, they were not a concern of America's growing social consciousness movement.

The motion picture industry had begun its own such movement in the late 1940s. Films like *Crossfire* and *Gentleman's Agreement* had addressed the problem of anti–Semitism, while *Pinky* and *Home of the Brave* had attacked the roots of racial intolerance. But no one in Hollywood seemed eager to champion the cause of middle and upper-class teenagers who were perceived as hopelessly jaded, psychotic, or rebellious.

No one except the director, Nicholas Ray.

Rebel Without a Cause will remain a masterpiece,
because it is the American cinema's only Greek tragedy.
                    — attributed to William Faulkner

PART I

Preliminaries

1

NICHOLAS RAY

On an early September evening in 1954, Nicholas Ray hosted a small dinner party at his home. Ray, who lived in Bungalow 2 at the Chateau Marmont Hotel on Sunset Boulevard, usually entertained on a grand scale. His Sunday afternoon socials were widely-known and immensely popular with the Hollywood community. Tonight, however, his only guests were two old friends: MCA president Lew Wasserman and Wasserman's wife, Edie.

Earlier in the day, Ray and Wasserman had attended a screening of Ray's still-unreleased film, *Run for Cover*, his eleventh feature, and his second since leaving RKO Pictures in February, 1953. The screening was work; the informal dinner, highlighted by an episode of *Dragnet* on television, was supposed to be play, entirely free of shop talk. But on this occasion, Ray and Wasserman found themselves speculating about Ray's next project.

Ray's options should have been numerous and attractive. Freed from the restrictions once imposed on him by his RKO contract, he could hire on with any studio he wished for the length of a project, then move on. For a director as well-established as Ray, there was no limit to the artistic possibilities. But by early September of 1954, Ray had reached yet another crossroads in his personal and professional life. The end of his troubled marriage to actress Gloria Grahame two years earlier still haunted him, and the work on his latest film, *Johnny Guitar,* had at times made him physically ill. If he were to make another film now, he told the Wassermans, he would have to believe in it strongly.

When asked what subject he would consider important enough, Ray answered, "Kids. Young people growing up. Their problems." Wasserman knew of a property at Warner Bros. called *Rebel Without a Cause.* Its subject was troubled youth. Perhaps Warner Bros. would permit Ray to direct the picture. Ray agreed to consider the idea, and Wasserman quickly contacted the studio.

Warner Bros. had owned the film rights to a book titled *Rebel Without a Cause* since 1946. The author was Robert M. Lindner, a thirty-one-year-old prison psychologist who specialized in the study and treatment of juvenile delinquency. The book was a case study of a disturbed youth (known only as "Harold") whom Lindner had counseled at the Federal Penitentiary at Lewisburg, Pennsylvania. Lindner's

Rebel Without a Cause (subtitled *The Hypnoanalysis of a Criminal Psychopath*) was a routine prison-and-poverty tale with a psychiatric emphasis, but it had caught the attention of Jerry Wald, one of Warner Bros.' top producers. Wald's job was to sell the idea to studio executives and find a director, screenwriter and actors to realize the project. Wald had already persuaded the studio to pay Lindner $5,000, with the promise of an additional $4,000 if the picture generated a sequel.

Between 1946 and 1949, Wald made a number of attempts to film Lindner's book. Several studio writers, including Peter Viertel and Theodor Seuss Geisel (who later adopted the pseudonym Dr. Seuss), drafted story treatments and scripts during 1946 and 1947. With Wald's encouragement, Irving Shulman, author of *The Amboy Dukes* and one of the studio's newest contract writers, offered twice to rewrite Viertel's revised script. Lindner submitted his own script (co-written with H. L. Fishel) in 1949.

Wald supported each effort with his (even then) legendary enthusiasm. He pleaded and argued with the front office, cajoled directors, recruited actors, fired off memo after memo. It was to no avail. Perhaps prison pictures had become *passé*. Perhaps the right actors were unavailable (the studio offered Marlon Brando the role of Harold, but he refused; Skip Homeier tested but did not sign). Whatever the reason, not one of the studio's directors would accept the assignment, and Warner Bros. put *Rebel Without a Cause* on a shelf.

Lew Wasserman (shown here accepting the Jean Hersholt Award from Alfred Hitchcock in 1974) gave Nicholas Ray the project he'd been looking for.

Now, almost six years later, as the various *Rebel* scripts collected dust and turned a deeper yellow in the studio's Story Department, Warner Bros. was still trying to market Robert Lindner's book. Milton Sperling, a producer, and Walter MacEwen, an executive assistant in the Story Department, had each checked out Viertel's version the previous July. David Weisbart, the studio's newest producer, had recently checked out the Lindner script.

The prison picture concept had indeed gone stale, but the title still offered some exciting possibilities, perhaps for a low-budget exploitation film. Although films about teenage violence routinely created problems with industry censors and any number of civic and religious groups, the studios still recognized juvenile delinquency as a lucrative topic. Marlon Brando's portrayal of a hoodlum biker in *The Wild One* (1953) had stirred widespread controversy, but the picture had made a healthy profit for Columbia Pictures. Even MGM, a studio whose concept of teenagers usually stopped with Mickey Rooney and Judy Garland, was now making a film of Evan Hunter's controversial novel, *The Blackboard Jungle*.

Soon after his dinner party with the Wassermans, Nicholas Ray visited Warner Bros. Pictures, the very private kingdom of Jack L. Warner. Warner was the prototypical studio czar. Only he decided how important or unimportant a Warner Bros. picture would be: big budget or small; name actors or unknowns; color and wide-screen or small-screen black and white; prestige picture or the lower half of a double bill. Warner would also decide whether Ray was good enough to join the studio's elite corps of directors, which currently included George Stevens, Elia Kazan and Alfred Hitchcock.

At Warner Bros., the word "talented" was synonymous with "bankable," and at the moment, Nicholas Ray was both. His biggest success had come, ironically, with *Johnny Guitar*, the film that had made him ill. The critics had given it a mixed reception, but audiences were flocking to it.

Ray's success as a director was due in part to his versatility. Before *Johnny Guitar*, he had directed *On Dangerous Ground*, a film noir starring Ida Lupino; *Flying Leathernecks*, an action-filled war picture with John Wayne and Robert Ryan; and a psychological Western, *The Lusty Men*, with Robert Mitchum. All had fared well at the box office.

If there was a dark side to Ray's talent, it was an intensity that hovered at the edge of emotional instability. As Ray's friend Rodney Amateau once described his demeanor on the set: "Nick suffered for everybody. He was so emotionally charged that he couldn't turn it off and on like a light switch. Every film was a difficult film for him to make. He couldn't direct somebody crossing a street without getting involved." Ray's ongoing struggles with manic-depression and alcohol made the pressures of directing even more critical.

Ray was also at odds with the artistic constraints imposed by the studios and with the moguls like Jack Warner who wielded such absolute power. John Houseman, one of Ray's closest friends, observed that Ray "was at his best when he filmed stories of people oppressed by society." Ray saw himself as one of those people, a sensitive interloper attempting to create art in a world teeming with boors and petty tyrants. His lack of a protective shell doomed him in that battle. Unlike his other good friend, Elia Kazan, who Houseman thought was "tough as nails," Ray was almost without defenses. The studio system would eventually eat him alive.

The motion picture industry, of course, was a going concern. The studios trusted directors for their reliability in the same way that banks trusted the Solid Citizen. They valued craftsmanship over art. They punished, and occasionally banished, anyone who was oblivious to the bottom line. Ray followed the rules, but he did not accept them. It was the renegade artist in Ray more than anything else that made him appear "brilliant but unreliable" to Hollywood's moguls and their legions of accountants.

Ray's directing style was similarly threatening to a system that favored conformity and control. He gave extraordinary freedom to his actors, worked closely with his screenwriters, was open to suggestion from anyone on the set and was singularly low-key during rehearsals and the rigors of shooting. He did not raise his voice; he did not badger or humiliate his cast or crew; he did not use a bullhorn. This, too, was contrary to Hollywood's experience, and this, too, worried the moguls. Ray's radical style did not mesh well with the corporate gears.

Ray's background *was* somewhat radical. Schooled as an architect (a protégé of Frank Lloyd Wright), he developed an early passion for the theater, first as a performer and later as a writer. During the 1930s, he worked with the Group Theater, a revolutionary acting company in New York City. The Group Theater introduced him to another writer, Clifford Odets, and to Elia Kazan, who was to become his first mentor in Hollywood. The Group Theater was experimental in its approach and leftist in its politics. It was also a spawning ground for the Method, an acting style later identified with Lee Strasberg and the Actors Studio. Revolutionary theater and the politics of the left made up the greater part of Nicholas Ray's artistic experience. They were not remotely part of corporate Hollywood's.

That September morning at Warner Bros., the difference between the two cultures could not have been more evident. Ray's meeting was with Steve Trilling, Jack Warner's executive assistant. Under the impression that Ray had already agreed to direct the studio's shopworn prison story, Trilling began to describe it: a young man named Harold, a product of the slums, is referred to the prison psychiatrist, a "Dr. Linder." Linder tries to get at the root of Harold's psychoses (including a severe blinking problem) through hypnosis. The psychiatrist eventually discovers the root cause in Harold's early childhood (his father's brutality, his mother's fawning) and even stops Harold's blinking. Then, at the moment when Harold seems cured, he admits to his worst crime of all: murder. When Dr. Linder discovers that the man Harold thinks he killed has actually recovered, Harold's salvation is complete.

To Trilling's surprise, Ray explained that he had no interest in the Lindner story. He had already made two films about young people from poor backgrounds, *They Live by Night* and *Knock on Any Door*, and he did not wish to make a third. This confused Trilling. Hadn't Lew Wasserman told the studio of Ray's interest in troubled teenagers? Wasn't Lindner's story about just such a teenager? Ray clarified his position: Harold, the character in Lindner's book, was too "abnormal." Ray wanted to make a film about "normal" delinquents, the kind who lived next door.

This confused Trilling further. What kind of teenagers was Ray talking about? It was common knowledge that juvenile delinquents came from homes characterized by poverty and deprivation. All the best educators and psychologists said so. With few exceptions, criminals were from the lower class. They were the uneducated, the unemployable. Like the protagonists in every Warner Bros. melodrama from *Public Enemy* to *White Heat*, real-life criminals were those who had never reaped the benefits of the American Dream. Teenagers from middle-class and upper-class homes had no reason to turn to crime or random violence. They had concerned parents, they lived in safe neighborhoods and they went to good schools. What possible motivation could Ray give such children to make them delinquent? More importantly, what audience would believe a picture about well-heeled teenagers running amok? Why not stay with a formula the movie-going public would accept?

Ray did not understand the phenomenon well enough to explain it. He only knew what he had read in newspapers and heard from police authorities, judges, social workers and young people. America's teens were far more troubled than most of their elders were willing to admit. There was a growing sense of restlessness and alienation among them that had nothing to do with poverty or the criminal underclass. This was a new theme for the American cinema; this was on the cutting edge of social consciousness; this was the kind of film Nicholas Ray wanted to make. For forty-five minutes, Ray told Trilling "all sorts of stories" about this new type of delinquent, the well-dressed boy or girl next door who was about to explode.

A few days later, Trilling telephoned Ray. Warner Bros., he said, was interested in Ray's project and wanted him to present a story treatment. Ray agreed. The studio sent Ray a copy of Lindner's book and the yellowing scripts from the Story Department. Ray read the material, but little of it interested him. Working with a stenographer, he began to dictate his own story, which he called "The Blind Run." At four o'clock the next morning, September 18, he finished the 17-page treatment. His secretary had it typed by seven and delivered to Warner Bros. by nine. Later that same day, the studio agreed to purchase Ray's 17 pages for $5,000, the same price paid for Lindner's entire book in 1946.

2

"THE BLIND RUN"

Ray's story opened with three startling images: a teenager sets a man on fire, then watches from behind a tree as bystanders try to put out the flames; three teenage boys whip a 16-year-old girl they have stripped to the waist; two hot rods drive at high speed toward each other in a tunnel, then crash head-on (the "blind run" of the title).

In selecting the material for his story, Ray borrowed freely from recent headlines. The first two vignettes from "The Blind Run" were the actual crimes of an 18-year-old Brooklyn youth. According to a *Newsweek* article titled "Our Vicious Young Hoodlums: Is There Any Hope?" he and his companions had also murdered a man. The *Newsweek* article went on to describe a switchblade fight outside a community center in Gardena, California, and a "stomping" in Kansas City. Nine teenagers had beaten a man senseless because he did not have any cigarettes. The switchblade and stomping scenes would both find their way into the final script.

Following the opening sequence, Ray's story presented its three main characters. Jimmy, 17, is the son of a college professor. Eve, also 17, is the oldest of three daughters. Demo is actually Theodore Jerome Demos, whose other nickname is "Squint." Like Robert Lindner's Harold, Demo suffers from blinking eyes. He keeps a knife in his closet and takes it with him when he goes out.

Jimmy, Eve and Demo belong to the same teenage gang. One night they meet at a local drugstore to plan a blind run. Jimmy, the gang's leader, orders Demo and two other boys to steal a car. Eve has already volunteered her family's vehicle for the deadly contest. They agree to meet under the bleachers at the football field. Before they leave the drugstore, Eve telephones a girlfriend to provide her with an alibi for coming home late. A woman watches the teenagers closely. She is a social worker named Irene who has discovered the gang's meeting place and is trying to make contact with its members.

In the next scene, the gang has re-assembled. Two boys are fighting with switchblades, proving their *machismo*. They stop when the others show their approval. Demo arrives with the stolen car, and Jimmy decides who will race. Only Eve and Demo have not passed this test. They will drive through the same tunnel where the two cars crashed at the beginning of the story. Jimmy will accompany Eve, but Demo will make the blind run alone.

Eve and Demo race toward each other. At the last possible moment, they veer away and avoid a deadly collision. Everyone in the gang relaxes, especially Demo, whose eyelids do not flutter for the rest of the evening. Demo feels close to Eve, who has fallen in love with Jimmy. When Jimmy gets home that night, he tells his father that he has been riding around "where those kids cracked up last night." Eve arrives in time to witness a family argument. Demo's parents barely notice him.

Jimmy, Eve and Demo plan a party at Eve's for all their parents, hoping to mask their gang activities with a show of wholesomeness. Demo's father refuses to attend. This infuriates Demo, but he does not tell Jimmy or Eve. On the night of the party, Demo passes Eve's house. He thinks about going inside, but goes instead to the gang's drugstore hangout, where he meets two boys. One asks, "What's doin'? What're we gonna do?" After trying to steal a car, they end up in the park late at night. They walk to a deserted street, still looking for trouble.

Nicholas Ray was talented, well-established, but "unreliable" in the eyes of the movie moguls.

After the party, Jimmy and Eve find Demo. As they drive him home, he relates a horrifying story: he and the two boys killed a man because the man's singing annoyed them. Demo feels no guilt for the act, which he likens to killing his father. After Jimmy and Eve leave Demo, a police car stops them. Although they fail to report Demo's crime, they decide to stay away from him.

In the weeks that follow, Demo incites a number of other boys to commit crimes. This leads finally to his own arrest, and he confesses to the murder he committed the night of the party. Demo stands trial and is sentenced to death. Hoping to find a motive for Demo's actions, the police question everyone about him. The adults are baffled, the teenagers defiantly mute. Demo himself will speak only to Irene, the social worker.

Meanwhile, the teens continue on a rampage even without Demo. The newspapers are blaming Mexican gangs for the crimes committed by Demo's followers, but Demo refuses to inform on them. He does, however, predict a gang war with the Mexicans. The social worker tries to head off a rumble by enlisting the aid of parents and the local authorities. No one listens.

One night, Jimmy's gang meets at a dry reservoir. A young Mexican arrives just as someone asks, "What're we gonna do tonight?" A fight breaks out as other Mexicans appear. Jimmy dies in the rumble, and Eve, pregnant with Jimmy's child, accompanies his body in the ambulance. In the penitentiary, Demo reads about the rumble and tells Irene that the gang plans to hold a wake for him the night of his execution. Irene decides on a plan that may stop the violence, and this time the parents and police cooperate. On the night of his execution, Demo suddenly shows up at the wake. Floodlights illuminate the area, police and parents appear, and Demo tells his tragic story. As the police lead him away, some teenagers return home with their parents. Others just wander off into the night.

Meanwhile, in another drugstore in another part of town, more teens gather, ready to make the same tragic mistakes. One of them asks the familiar question, "What're we gonna do tonight?"

On September 24, Warner Bros. announced that it had signed Nicholas Ray to direct a film about juvenile delinquency. The studio called the project *Rebel Without a Cause*. There was no mention of "The Blind Run" in the press release. Apparently the studio had decided to match Robert Lindner's provocative title with Ray's explosive content. The title was ideal for the exploitation picture the studio had in mind. The decision to change the title irritated Ray ("*They* called it that," he later complained. "I called it 'The Blind Run.'"), but he had little choice. It was the first of his many concessions to the demands of the studio.

Because of his recent success, however, Ray was in a position to make at least one demand of his own. On *Johnny Guitar* he had handled the directing duties and much of the work normally done by a producer. Yet, when Republic Pictures released the film, Ray's role as associate producer was not listed among the credits. Feeling cheated and betrayed by Republic, Ray decided not to repeat that experience. Now, as part of his contract with Warner Bros. to direct *Rebel Without a Cause*, he insisted that the studio award him sole story credit for "The Blind Run." No matter how many other writers worked on Ray's story or any screenplay based on it, only Ray's name would appear in the final story credits. "Best Original Story" was one of the categories voted on for the Academy Awards. For most artists in Hollywood, winning an Oscar meant instant prestige and the chance to work with better directors, actors, writers and producers. For Ray, winning an Oscar meant the long-awaited opportunity to start his own production company, to free himself finally and completely from the tyranny of the studios. Only Jack Warner and a few others in the studio hierarchy knew about this "sole story credit" clause, and they were, at least for the moment, duty-bound to keep it secret.

Yet, as careful as Ray was to protect his interests while filming *Rebel Without a Cause*, he understood that there could be no guarantees. He may also have perceived the irony in his preferred title, "The Blind Run," for it would prove to be an accurate description of his own experience in directing the picture. Just as Jimmy, Eve and Demo drove headlong into a dark tunnel with no certainty of emerging whole at the other end, Ray would proceed without any assurance that his artistic concept would survive the production process of a major studio. He would proceed even without the certainty that the studio would agree to finish what it started.

Warner Bros. was making a blind run of its own to produce Ray's film. The studio expected to spend close to a million dollars with no certainty of breaking even at the box office. Even if the film stayed on schedule and within the budget, unforeseen circumstances could shelve it before it ever reached the theaters. Since *Rebel Without a Cause* would be about delinquency and violence, it would face the wrath of civic and church groups that opposed such films on principle. Warner Bros., like every other motion picture studio, depended on the good will of the movie-going public. It could not afford to offend its constituents too often.

3

JAMES DEAN

Shortly after the announcement of his hiring, Nicholas Ray moved into an office at Warner Bros. Elia Kazan's office was just a few doors down the hall. When Ray first came to Hollywood in 1944, he had worked as Kazan's assistant on *A Tree Grows in Brooklyn*, Kazan's first directing assignment. Now the two old friends were peers at the same studio.

Kazan's *East of Eden* had finished filming on August 13 and was in post-production. The star of that film, James Dean, had been a controversial figure at Warner Bros. since his arrival the previous April. Ray had undoubtedly heard some of the stories about Dean: that he was moody, insolent and uncooperative; that he had once kept a loaded revolver in his trailer on studio property; that he drove his motorcycle at dangerous speeds down studio streets and through sound stages; that he had bizarre and unsavory friends.

He had heard also that Dean was emotionally unstable, and that Kazan had been forced to baby-sit the young actor in side-by-side studio trailers to keep him from running away during the production. Dean's co-star, Julie Harris, whom Kazan called "an angel on the set," had worked overtime quelling Dean's frequent attacks of panic.

Like Nicholas Ray, James Dean was suspect within the industry. Actors trained in the studio system paid attention to hitting their marks and saying their lines as written. Dean scoffed at such conventions. On stage, he improvised his lines constantly, altering them from one performance to the next. In filming *East of Eden*, his approach had been much the same, to the unending chagrin of his classically trained co-star, Raymond Massey. Dean was oblivious to Hollywood as a going concern, oblivious to budgets and shooting schedules, and, according to biographer Val Holley, "completely unprepared to assume his ceremonial duties." He was also openly contemptuous of authority, including powerful men like Jack Warner. Like Nicholas Ray, Dean's radical style did not mesh with Hollywood's corporate gears.

A few days after Nicholas Ray finished his "Blind Run" treatment, he had an opportunity to form his own opinion about James Dean. Elia Kazan invited Ray to view a rough cut of *East of Eden* in the music room at Warner Bros. Leonard Rosenman, the film's composer, was improvising at the piano while Kazan screened the film. James Dean stood inconspicuously in a corner. Wearing eyeglasses, unshaven and hunched over, he did not remotely resemble a movie star. Ray's first reaction was undoubtedly puzzlement. How could this shy, awkward young man possibly be the subject of so much media attention? How could he possibly be Hollywood's newest phenomenon? The discrepancy between the man and the image seemed to intensify as Ray watched Dean portray Cal Trask so powerfully on the screen. It did not seem possible that these were both James Dean. Dean himself did not seem to believe it. He watched himself with an odd, almost adolescent fascination, as if he were admiring someone else.

Ray and Dean exchanged few words, if any, during their first meeting. Dean simply withdrew into himself. He was suspicious of anyone considered "official" at the studio, and he was shy and inarticulate around strangers. As Ray left the music room after the screening, it is unlikely that he imagined James Dean as the leading actor of his own film.

A few days later, Dean unexpectedly shuffled into Ray's office.

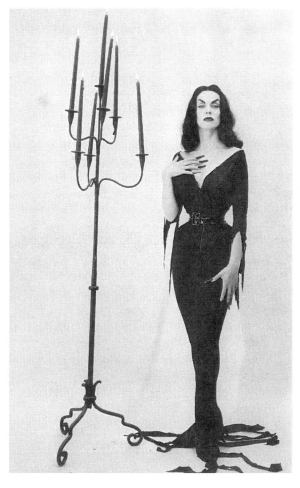

Maila Nurmi (a.k.a. Vampira), one of James Dean's "bizarre and unsavory" friends.

It was as awkward a meeting as their earlier encounter in the music room. Dean apparently said nothing at first. He just looked at Ray and studied his surroundings. Ray felt singularly ill at ease. He was not sure what, if anything, Dean wanted. Was Dean simply killing time in the corridor before seeing Kazan? Had he heard about Ray's project and become interested? Had Kazan sent him on some unrelated errand?

Ray sensed that the young actor was sizing him up. He reminded Ray of a Siamese cat, and Ray thought, "The only thing to do with a Siamese cat is to let it take its own time. It will come up to you, walk around you, smell you. If it doesn't like you, it will go away again; if it does, it will stay."

Dean stayed. In succeeding visits, he began to show a keen interest in *Rebel Without a Cause*. He questioned Ray closely about the story and the characters, and he seemed genuinely intrigued by the concept of middle-class delinquency. He even suggested that Ray speak with a young actor named Perry Lopez, who had a featured role in the studio's current hit, *Battle Cry*. Lopez was from Lexington Avenue in New

York City and was no stranger to gangs and teenage violence. "You should talk to him," Dean advised. "You may be able to get some information from him."

Dean also began to visit Bungalow 2 at the Chateau Marmont. One night, he arrived with two friends, Maila Nurmi and Jack Simmons. Nurmi was a local television personality whose stage name was Vampira. Simmons was an obscure young actor from New York. The three were charter members of a group of Hollywood oddballs and insomniacs known as the Night Watch. That night, Dean and his two companions had come to test Ray's honesty, a quality Dean valued highly. This was another part of Dean's Siamese cat routine. It involved making inquiries about Ray all over town, then confirming the answers face-to-face with Ray. The questions Dean and his companions put to Ray were puerile ("Did you [once] carry a Boxer puppy out of your [burning] house in your bare feet...?"); but Ray's straightforward answers began to win Dean's confidence. Perhaps there *was* someone "official" in the film industry that Dean could trust. Perhaps Nicholas Ray was that someone.

The two met often in the weeks that followed, either at the studio or at Ray's home. Dean also began attending Ray's Sunday socials, where he could expect to meet performers like Gene Kelly, producers like John Houseman, and writers like Clifford Odets.

Ray used these opportunities to size up James Dean. What he discovered was an intelligent and talented artist who was also vulnerable and insecure. In short, someone much like himself. As Ray later observed, "[Dean] had no hard professional shell; lack of sympathy, lack of understanding from a director or any of his staff disoriented him completely."

During one or another of their meetings, Ray concluded that James Dean should play the lead role in *Rebel Without a Cause*. He also saw clearly his own role in such a collaboration:

> To work with [Dean] meant exploring his nature, trying to understand it; without this, his powers of expression were frozen. He retreated, he sulked. He always wanted to make a film in which he could personally believe, but it was never easy for him. Between belief and action lay the obstacle of his own deep, obscure uncertainty.

In courting James Dean for *Rebel Without a Cause*, Ray also understood that he could not press the issue. If Dean suspected that Ray's friendship was a studio subterfuge, Ray would lose whatever credibility he had gained. It was hard enough winning Dean's trust; keeping it was even harder. Gradually, Ray would try to forge a creative partnership with this talented but deeply troubled young man.

4

WEISBART AND URIS

Before casting James Dean in *Rebel Without a Cause*, Ray needed a producer and a writer for his film. He began with the producer.

It was common practice at Warner Bros. to assign a producer based on his status and the importance of the picture. Ray expected the studio to assign someone with limited experience, since *Rebel* was not to be a prestige picture. Warner Bros. planned to film it without major stars, in black and white, and on a "B" picture budget. To Ray's surprise, however, he was given the choice of any producer on the lot. The list included Henry Blanke, Robert Fellows, Cedric Francis, Henry Ginsberg, Willis Goldbeck, Frank P. Rosenberg and Leland Hayward. These were reliable, predictable craftsmen with years of experience. These were men who knew the studio system, who understood the importance of the bottom line and the necessity of controls. Ray did not want any of them. From his work on *Johnny Guitar*, Ray had developed strong opinions about a producer's function. In place of a studio overlord who stayed in his office and hovered over the balance sheets, Ray wanted an active, creative partner, one who helped with script supervision, casting, budgeting, and "the general approach to an individual film." Ray wanted a producer who would also be an advocate for the film, who would fight beside Ray in his battles with front office bureaucrats. With all that in mind, Ray chose the least prestigious producer at Warner Bros., David Weisbart.

Weisbart had worked for Warner Bros. since the late 1930s, first as an apprentice in the Trailer Department (coming attractions), then as a film editor on the Errol Flynn drama, *The Edge of Darkness*. In 1948, Weisbart had capped a successful career in the cutting room with an Academy Award nomination for *Johnny Belinda*. Two years later, after editing *A Streetcar Named Desire*, he became the newest producer at Warner Bros. His first two projects were the 3-D Western *The Charge at Feather River* (1953) and the science fiction thriller *Them!* (1954).

Ray had several reasons for choosing Weisbart. First, he came highly recommended by Elia Kazan, who had worked with him on *A Streetcar Named Desire*. Weisbart's experience as a film editor would also add a creative dimension to Ray's film. Few producers had the practical cinematic knowledge that Weisbart possessed. Finally, and perhaps most importantly, Weisbart was a parent. At 39, four years younger than

Ray, he was the father of two teenagers, with a father's usual concerns. Weisbart's real-life role as parent, Ray hoped, would bring "a personal interest to the subject."

Weisbart, however, did not immediately share Ray's enthusiasm for the project. When Ray read Weisbart the outline of "The Blind Run," as Ray later recalled, "his first reaction was as if he had swallowed a hot potato." Weisbart's reluctance was understandable. At this early stage, *Rebel Without a Cause* was little more than an idea in Nicholas Ray's head. He had no story or script, only a very rough outline. Since "The Blind Run" also lacked what Ray called "the comfortable basis of an existing novel or Broadway play," it had no ready-made audience. Most importantly, its subject matter was potentially explosive, and the studio might at some point decide that it was too hot to handle. Nothing in David Weisbart's experience as a producer had prepared him for a project like this.

Choosing the right screenwriter was Ray's next task. Although Ray had occasionally supported himself as a writer, he did not define himself as one. Someone else would have to develop Ray's seventeen pages into an acceptable script, and that script would have to conform to "The Blind Run."

Ray's ideal writer was someone who, like an ideal producer, had a talent and a willingness for artistic collaboration. Such a person recognized the often uncomfortable interdependence of writer and director and was prepared to "acknowledge the creative claims of the director" whenever disagreements arose. Such a person would try to see the film through the director's eyes.

Ray's first choice was his friend, Clifford Odets, who was a respected playwright and screenwriter. Odets' work included *Golden Boy*, *Clash by Night*, and *The Country Girl*. Ray had known Odets since his days with the Group Theater. He trusted Odets' artistic instincts and admired his talent. The studio, however, had different plans. It chose one of its most bankable new writers, Leon Uris.

Uris had grown up in the Jewish neighborhoods of three cities. Born in Baltimore, he spent part of his youth in Norfolk and Philadelphia. Despite a difficult home life (his parents were poor and eventually separated), Uris developed an early love of literature. He began writing at seven. John Steinbeck was one of his idols. Although he failed high school English three times, it was not from lack of ability.

In 1942, shortly after the Japanese attack on Pearl Harbor, Uris quit school to join the Marines. After serving as a radio operator in the Guadalcanal and Tarawa campaigns, he finished his service stateside in the San Francisco area. The Marines discharged him in 1946. While working as delivery manager for the *San Francisco Call-Bulletin*, he began to write. The success of his first published article (in *Esquire* in 1950) convinced him to attempt a novel about the Marines called *Battle Cry*. A dozen publishers turned it down, but when G. P. Putnam's Sons published it in 1953, it became one of the year's best-selling novels.

Now, a year later, Leon Uris was also a successful screenwriter. His film version of *Battle Cry*, starring Van Heflin, Aldo Ray and Tab Hunter, was in wide release and doing exceptional business for Warner Bros. It was the kind of picture the studios loved: name actors, plenty of action and high drama, an epic scale and exotic locales. *Battle Cry* had made Uris instantly bankable in Hollywood, and Warner Bros. was wasting no time getting its money's worth.

Ray tried to accept the studio's choice gracefully, but Uris's approach to the material in "The Blind Run" troubled him. Uris seemed to conceive the film as a kind of juvenile delinquency epic, with a scope like *Battle Cry*. He seemed to see communities at risk rather than individuals. Perhaps Warner Bros. had the same vision. The formula had worked spectacularly well for *Battle Cry*. Why not for *Rebel* as well? But it was not what Ray wanted. No doubt, he recalled his words to Lew Wasserman: the story should be about kids and their problems.

At this early stage, however, Ray still hoped to bring Uris around to his way of thinking. He already appreciated Uris's enthusiasm for the project. At 30, Uris was still young enough to understand the fears and frustrations of teenagers, and like David Weisbart, he appeared to bring "a personal interest" to the subject. During his days as a distribution supervisor for the *Call-Bulletin*, he had acted as father confessor to a group of forty newsboys.

Clifford Odets, Ray's friend from their days with the Group Theater, lost the writing assignment for *Rebel* to Leon Uris.

Ray's background research for *Rebel Without a Cause* began in early October. Since characterization was the core of his film, he focused on that. His extensive preparation eventually included interviews with delinquency experts and child psychologists, meetings with teenage gang members and observations of gang activities. He also spoke with police authorities and the judges, social workers and psychologists at Juvenile Hall. Although Warner Bros. had its own research department, Ray wanted as much information as possible from primary sources. He was determined to make an accurate film, even though he knew that the front office cared more about action than accuracy.

Uris, too, was moving ahead with his "epic" version of *Rebel*, where character development was secondary. His story, he decided, would take place in a "typical middle class American community." All he had to do was find one. On October 4, he sent a memo to Carl Milliken, head of the Research Department, asking for a suitable model. After discussing the rough outline of the project with Finlay McDermid, head of the Story Department, Milliken suggested Colorado Springs, Colorado, a small resort city of 36,789 people. Colorado Springs was residential, progressive — and troubled. In a same-day follow-up memo to Weisbart, Milliken cited a recent incident during which a 12-year-old boy "held off a group of police-men with an automatic pistol."

Pursuing his own line of thought, Ray sought out his first delinquency expert, Dr. Douglas M. Kelley. Kelley was head of the Criminology Department at

Berkeley. He had been the Chief Examining Psychiatrist at the Nuremberg Trials and was among the nation's foremost authorities on juvenile crime. Kelley would advise Ray if the actions and motivations of his troubled teenage characters were realistic. On October 4, Ray sent Kelley a telegram asking for his assistance.

Ray and Uris also began talking with teenagers, including the clientele at Juvenile Hall. On October 6, Ray sent Uris with a letter of introduction to Sgt. Ray Perkins of the Culver City Police. Uris spent part of the day at Juvenile Hall, observing the booking process and the interaction of teenagers with police and social workers. That evening, he accompanied Sgt. Perkins in a patrol car.

The next morning, Uris reported to Ray, and Ray reported via memo to Weisbart. Uris felt that the experience at Juvenile Hall had been extremely productive, and he wanted to return. Ray quickly arranged a second observation for October 13. Uris had even more good news: Sgt. Perkins "seemed quite happy and at ease" with the picture's positive approach. This was quite different from Perkins' experience with writer-director Richard Brooks, who had not received police cooperation for his film, *Blackboard Jungle*. Brooks had alienated police officials by withholding controversial script material. By being forthright about the content of *Rebel Without a Cause*, Uris insured further cooperation from the authorities.

Barely a week into his research, Ray's list of technical advisors was growing, and his appointment book was filling up. Dr. Kelley had accepted Ray's offer and planned to meet with him soon. Ray (with Uris) also planned to confer with Big Brothers of America. In the same memo of October 7, Ray announced a next-afternoon meeting with Judge William B. McKesson of Juvenile Court and lunch on October 11 with child analyst Myrtle Mandiberg, a protégée of Anna Freud. Mandiberg worked exclusively with disturbed children from middle and upper-class families.

Ray was pleased with his progress, but one important element was still missing. The psychiatrists, judges, police and social workers all presented a view from the outside. Even interviewing the troubled teenagers at Juvenile Hall was second-hand experience. How did the teens act among themselves when no adults were around? How did they speak and gesture and behave? What codes, if any, did they follow? Ray believed the answers might lie with his twenty-five-year-old nephew, Sumner Williams. Ray informed Weisbart in the October 7 memo that he planned to have Williams, an actor, booked with other delinquents in Long Beach or some similar middle-class community. Williams would then be able to study their behavior and report back. Ray was confident that his sister's son, an ex–GI, could hold his own among the hoodlums.

Ray also seemed pleased with Uris's early progress on the story. In the memo to Weisbart, he noted that Uris was making progress in developing not only the characters, but also the story line. Perhaps Uris was beginning to modify his view, to swing the film back toward Ray's character study.

Uris hoped to spend ten days as an "apprentice social worker" at Juvenile Hall, observing procedures, interviewing young criminals and working closely with both Judge McKesson and Dr. Coudly, the court's chief psychiatrist. Ray planned to accompany Uris on many of his visits. Ray's memo concluded, "[T]he excitement gathers and I think we will be able to keep it that way."

There was little excitement gathering in the Warner Bros. front office, however. Studio executives were not yet sold on *Rebel Without a Cause*. They were not yet sold on James Dean, either. Cautiously, they extended his contract for only another six months.

5

STORY INTO SCRIPT

On October 13, 1954, Uris began to create a story line for *Rebel Without a Cause*. His notes included information on the film's imaginary middle-class community. Much to Ray's displeasure, Uris called the town "Rayfield."

Uris's Rayfield was to be near a large industrialized city. Most of its citizens either worked in town or commuted. Although Rayfield was outwardly prosperous and calm, it suddenly faced problems it had never seen before, including delinquency. Uris continued to show more interest in the location and scope of the film than in its characters. In his five pages of background notes, he went into lengthy detail on the fictional Rayfield. He gave it a population (22,650), an elevation (54 feet), and a complete history.

As Uris worked on his version of *Rebel Without a Cause*, Ray gave more attention to his own interpretation of "The Blind Run." After re-naming Demo "the Professor," he created three possible scenarios for the main characters. In Ray's first scenario, Jim and Eve become the Professor's substitute parents; the Professor sees their love for each other as a rejection of him, and he kills them. In the second, Jim does not die in the gang fight, but is accepted back into "normal" society. In the third, the three teenagers run away after being convicted of murder. The police capture Jimmy and Eve just before they play out a Romeo and Juliet fantasy "to the death."

By October 18, not quite three weeks into his creative partnership with Leon Uris, Ray's early optimism had begun to sour. In a memo to David Weisbart, Ray admitted a growing impatience with the pace of Uris's work. Uris had done enough research, Ray complained, and now it was time to start writing the story. The conflicting views that Ray once hoped would converge were moving off in their own directions.

Ray's behavioral research was nearly concluded. So far, he and Uris had interviewed three psychiatrists, a Juvenile Court judge, three policemen, three probation officers and a university professor. In the memo, he reminded Weisbart of an upcoming meeting on November 5 with Dr. Kelley, the criminologist from Berkeley, and one on October 20, only two days away, with an Officer Barth of the West Los Angeles Police Department. Aware of his recent difficulties with Leon Uris, Ray chose not to invite him to that meeting.

Ray reminded Weisbart how important these consultations had been and would continue to be in moving the *Rebel* project forward. Despite some early skepticism, he explained, all the experts that they had consulted had embraced the project and offered their fullest cooperation.

The studio, however, might not reach the same conclusion as the police and psychologists. If church groups or educators objected, or if some tragic headline turned public opinion against teen violence as a proper subject for motion pictures, would Warner Bros. defend Ray's film or back away from it? Ray was certain that *Rebel* would prevail against its critics, just as it had made believers of the police and the delinquency experts. If only the studio would listen. Unable to share these intense feelings with Uris, Ray once again confided in Weisbart, hoping that his producer would convey Ray's message forcefully, yet diplomatically, to the front office.

Perhaps to turn his attention from his problems with Uris and the studio, Ray began thinking again about actors. He reminded Weisbart in the October 18 memo not to forget their upcoming interviews with three young actors: James Dean, Perry Lopez and Pat Crowley. Lopez was the New York actor whom Dean had brought to Ray's attention as a gang expert. Crowley was a young contract player whom Ray was considering for the role of "Eve" ("Amy" in Uris's story). She had appeared in *Forever Female* (1953), a Martin and Lewis comedy called *Money from Home* (1953), and *Red Garters* (1954).

Gradually, a sense of trust had grown between Ray and James Dean. Soon, Ray might confidently offer him the lead role in *Rebel Without a Cause*. But would Dean accept it? If *East of Eden* made Dean a major star when it opened in March, would Dean's career be hindered by Ray's obscure "B" movie? Given a choice of roles from the studio's list of prestige pictures, would Dean still want to play Jimmy in *Rebel*? Dean had his own future to consider, and he was already making plans. He had been visiting the office of George Stevens, hoping to win the role of Jett Rink, the rebellious cowhand in Stevens' upcoming production of *Giant*. Compared to *Giant*, the studio's most important project, Ray's film was a sideshow.

If Dean needed further proof of *Rebel*'s insignificance at Warner Bros., he need only have examined Ray's expense account for the picture. Since starting his background work in late September, Ray had spent a grand total of $57.82: $22.32 for "magazines, books, periodicals, pocketbooks and out of town newspapers"; $17.00 for lunch with child analyst Myrtle Mandiberg; $12.00 for lunch with Officer Pinkson from Juvenile Hall and other minor expenses. If the men with the money did not take Ray's film seriously, how could James Dean? Given a choice, Dean would obviously choose *Giant*. Only a major delay in the start of that picture, and a monumental sales pitch from Ray, would get James Dean into *Rebel Without a Cause*.

On October 20, Leon Uris began the first draft of his story treatment. He titled it "Juvenile Story." Three days later, he submitted the first twenty-four pages of a revised treatment to the studio. A week later, he completed the final outline and delivered it to the Story Department with the title *Rebel Without a Cause*.

Like Ray's "The Blind Run," Uris's story opened with a series of violent vignettes, including a grocery store robbery. The fatal blind run follows. The main character, Jimmy Gibson, watches it from a distance. Jimmy wants to join a gang because he lacks a satisfying relationship with his parents, who are hopelessly materialistic. After the blind run, he returns home to a gathering of the in-laws. He retreats to his room to practice music, which his father considers effeminate. His mother encourages him, but she is overprotective.

Later, Jimmy goes to Fatty's Cafe and tries to join Biff's gang. He meets a girl named Amy and an angel-faced, slightly built thirteen-year-old boy called the Professor. The Professor has joined the gang to escape his father's brutality. Amy protects him from the older boys.

Almost as soon as Jimmy arrives, Biff bullies him into a fight with switchblades. During the fight, the Professor screams at Biff to "rip him open." Amy stops the fight and Biff poses the real test, a blind run. The Professor provides two stolen cars. Biff veers away first, and Jimmy joins the gang.

Later, Jimmy and Amy discuss Biff's unhappy home life and the Professor's hatred of his father. Amy fears that the Professor's frequent threats to kill his father may be real. Jimmy returns home deeply disturbed, but his own father shows little interest in his problems. Jimmy paces all night in his bedroom. The next morning, his father lectures him on good citizenship while his mother coddles him. When Jimmy tries to escape through his music, his father complains about the noise. Jimmy runs out of the house.

The situation is not much better for Amy. Her mother does not keep their house clean, and Amy has to be both daughter and housekeeper for her father, who barely notices her. She, too, runs from her house and finds Jimmy at Fatty's Cafe. When her parents leave later that evening for a football game, she brings Jimmy home and seduces him.

A few weeks later, Jimmy's parents finally notice the change in him. He appears always neat and well-groomed, and they suspect that he has a girlfriend. One evening, when the gang meets at Fatty's to plan a raid on another gang's territory, Jimmy, Amy and the Professor refuse to go along. They have formed their own "family," with Jimmy and Amy as parents, and the Professor as their son. In Lover's Lane that night, Jimmy and Amy dream about their future while the Professor sleeps in the back seat. Jimmy covers the sleeping Professor with his jacket.

Later, at home, Jimmy's father becomes more irritated by his son's strange new behavior, especially his emotional withdrawal. In a sudden rage, he smashes Jimmy's record collection. Jimmy storms out of the house. At Fatty's, Amy and the Professor wait for Jimmy. The Professor has stolen his father's gold cigarette case and wants to present it to Jimmy as a gift. They wonder why Jimmy is so late. Meanwhile, Jimmy

Leon Uris, Ray's first writer for *Rebel Without a Cause*, had a vision of the film that was seriously inconsistent with Ray's.

directs his own rage at the proprietor of a liquor store. He assaults the man and smashes the liquor bottles, just as his father had smashed his records.

When Jimmy finally arrives at Fatty's, Amy and the Professor have left. Biff tells Jimmy that the two gangs will have their showdown that night at the high school stadium. Biff and the gang still fault Jimmy for refusing to join them at the rumble. When Jimmy finds Amy in a park, he tells her about the gang's plans and suggests that they go to the police. Jimmy has seen his own potential for violence at the liquor store, and he fears where it will lead him. Amy warns him not to quit the gang now. They will beat him up if he tries. She leaves him there to think it over.

While the gang assembles at Fatty's for the rumble, Jimmy paces in his bedroom. He decides finally that he cannot bear to lose Amy, even if it means staying in the gang. He arrives at Fatty's just as the kids are piling into their automobiles.

Jimmy fights well at the rumble, but the Professor becomes hysterical and runs away screaming hatred for his father. Jimmy and Amy go looking for him, but when they find him it is too late: he has killed his father and set his house on fire. Suddenly, Jimmy understands what has been happening to all of them. He urges the Professor not to run from the police. The Professor is sick, but the doctors can help him. Amy offers her support.

Before going to the police, the three teenagers stop at Jimmy's house. The news about the Professor shocks Jimmy's parents, but they seem finally to understand their part in what has happened. They recognize that Jimmy's decision is honorable, and that it deserves respect instead of criticism. Yet, Jimmy spurns them. The Professor needs Jimmy the way Jimmy once needed his parents; but now Jimmy doesn't need them anymore. He slams the door in their faces as he leaves....

When Ray read Uris's final outline, he knew that their artistic partnership had failed. Although the picture's shooting script would retain and even build upon some of Uris's story details (Jimmy, Amy and the Professor becoming a "family"; Jimmy covering the sleeping Professor with a jacket), Uris's vision of *Rebel Without a Cause* still seemed irreconcilable with Ray's. As Ray observed later, "It was like an eye test at the optician's—could he read the characters in my mind as he might a chart on the wall?" The answer, clearly, was that Uris could not.

Ray now had the "ungrateful task" of informing Uris that the picture no longer required his services. The studio would agree, grudgingly, and assign him another writer, but that would delay the film's production. The studio did not like delays.

6

LINDNER AND SHULMAN

On Monday, November 1, 1954, Robert M. Lindner was in Los Angeles giving the first of two talks on juvenile delinquency. The author of *Rebel Without a Cause: The Hypnoanalysis of a Criminal Psychopath* was a guest of the Hacker Foundation for Psychiatric Research and Education. He titled his lectures, "The Mutiny of Adolescence" and "Must We Conform?" Lindner was also the guest of honor at a cocktail party at the Beverly Hills Hotel hosted by the Foundation.

Nicholas Ray attended the party because he wanted to meet the author of *Rebel Without a Cause* before moving ahead with his film. Lindner was an acknowledged expert on delinquency, and Ray wanted to compare his own views on teenagers with Lindner's.

They had a polite but uncomfortable conversation. Lindner knew that Ray and the studio had rejected the content of his book and kept only the title. He was not angry about the decision, but to Ray he seemed "genuinely bewildered" by it. He also rejected Ray's idea for the film. No naturalistic treatment of the subject could possibly succeed, he argued. His psychoanalytical approach was the only correct way to present the delinquency problem on the screen. "You must do it this way," he insisted. "You must make a developmental film."

Lindner argued that the conflict between protest and conformity was the primary cause of delinquency. It was the individual's need "to preserve himself in the face of overwhelming conformism" that produced rebellion. That was the substance of his two lectures. To Ray, Lindner's enthusiasm for this idea seemed obsessive. He sensed that Lindner was "grappling with a delayed rebellion of his own." Lindner urged Ray to reconsider Lindner's story of Harold, the disturbed young criminal cured through hypnosis, but Ray declined. Lindner then offered his services as technical advisor for the picture he'd just asked Ray to abandon. Ray declined again.

Ray left the cocktail party with mixed emotions. He admired Lindner's sense of mission as fully as he felt justified by his own. Yet, Ray later admitted, he still had "some pressing doubts." Would the studio continue to support his story about affluent delinquents, or would his failure with Leon Uris make the front office think again about Robert M. Lindner?

Lindner had already begun to apply some pressure toward that end. In an earlier telephone call to Finlay McDermid, he had objected to the use of "*Rebel With-out a Cause*" as the title for Ray's film as long as "The Blind Run" was the basis of its story line. If Ray did not adapt Lindner's book faithfully, Lindner had threatened, he might take legal action against Warner Bros.

The day after Ray's talk with Lindner, Leon Uris moved out of his office. His next projects would be a novel called *The Angry Hills*, the screenplay for *Gunfight at the O.K. Corral* and another epic novel, *Exodus*.

On November 10, a little more than a week after Uris had left, *Rebel Without a Cause* had a new screenwriter. Finlay McDermid of the Story Department informed R. J. Obringer of the Legal Department that as of Thursday, November 11, 1954, Ir-ving Shulman would begin work on *Rebel Without a Cause*. Shulman's salary, on a week-to-week basis, would be $650 per. If the studio approved the story outline which Shulman was expected to produce, he would earn $750 in his final week.

Once again, the studio had made Ray's creative choice for him, and once again Ray felt helpless to protest. Irving Shulman was a successful novelist (*The Amboy Dukes*) and a talented screenwriter; but these attributes were no guarantee that he would understand Ray's concept of the film any better than Leon Uris. However, like Uris, Shulman seemed enthusiastic about the project. He also had a positive track record: in 1947, he had offered to re-write Peter Viertel's script of *Rebel Without a Cause*. Warner Bros. had denied him the opportunity then, but this time he might well succeed. Shulman had also been a teacher, and his many experiences with young people would be an asset.

Ray saw something else in Shulman that he hoped to exploit for the good of the production: an interest in racing cars. Racing was one of James Dean's passions. Ray understood that *Rebel*'s success would depend in large part on how well Dean played Jimmy. Ray understood also that Dean could not function well unless he operated within "a special kind of climate," one of "reassurance, tolerance, [and] under-standing." One way to nurture this climate was to involve Dean in every phase of the film's development and to surround him with sympathetic, supportive artists. Perhaps if Shulman and Dean could become friends through their mutual interest in racing, Dean might feel more comfortable working on Ray's film.

Three days after Shulman's hiring, Ray invited Shulman to meet Dean at his next Sunday afternoon social at the Marmont. Unfortunately, the meeting did not go well. After a few minutes of idle conversation and automotive talk, Dean began to feel uncomfortable and, once again, withdrew into himself.

That same night, Nicholas Ray watched James Dean on television in a taped per-formance of Sherwood Anderson's "I'm a Fool." The story was about a young farm boy (Dean) who assumes a false identity to impress a young woman. The cast included two juveniles. One was Gloria Castillo, who also had a role in the new Robert Mitchum thriller, *Night of the Hunter*. The other was sixteen-year-old Natalie Wood, who played the gullible young woman. Although Dean had met Wood when he vis-ited the set of *The Silver Chalice* the previous summer, "I'm a Fool" was the first time they had acted together.

7

CHANGES

Shulman's work on a new script began immediately. Unlike Uris, however, research did not interest him. He did not conduct interviews or make late-night visits to Juvenile Hall. He did, however, seem eager to work with Ray on the story, and he seemed to approach the project without preconceptions. Soon, he and Ray were having serious discussions about plot, theme and character development.

One discussion involved "the Professor." In both "The Blind Run" and Uris's story, Demo/the Professor had been the child of indifferent parents. Ray and Shulman decided to create "a new background" for the character, whom they now called "Plato." Ray saw Plato as "hesitant, craving affection, filled with violent inner struggles." He came from a wealthy but fragmented family, lived "in a large house with his neglectful, pleasure-seeking mother, and had contact with his father only from a check that arrived with a typewritten note pinned on it —*for support of son.*"

Ray and Shulman also planned to make Plato more "overtly psychotic." He would continue to be Jim's loyal friend and Jim and Judy's surrogate child, but with a greater propensity for violence. He would become the film's emotional lightning rod. Ray understood that the studio and the censors might object to a truly disturbed teenager in the film, but he was willing to take the risk.

Ray had other suggestions for *Rebel Without a Cause* that would alter its tone and structure. He considered *Romeo and Juliet* "the best play ever written about 'juvenile delinquents.'" Now, with Shulman's help, he wanted to reshape *Rebel* to convey "a Romeo and Juliet feeling."

Ray and Shulman were also reshaping the role of Jimmy. In the Uris version, Jimmy needed only acknowledgment and understanding to reconcile him with the family he finally spurns. In Shulman's story, the character now known as "Jim" had to become the decisive adult his father was not. He had "to be a man, quick."

By November 15, Shulman was at work on a first story treatment for *Rebel Without a Cause*, basing it on his discussions with Ray. Like Leon Uris, he titled it "Juvenile Story."

Shulman's story takes place in the fictional town of Barlow. One night around ten o'clock, Buzzy Walker is racing other kids along Dixon Street. He has a minor accident with another teenager named Jim. They almost fight, but they agree to meet instead at a drive-in restaurant called Wimpy's.

Jim drives back to his comfortable middle-class home. His mother scolds him for missing dinner. Although his hapless father tries to intercede, the scolding continues. She complains that Jim is falling behind in his school work and dresses inappropriately. Jim goes to his room while his mother continues to criticize him. Finally, his father comes upstairs to have a heart-to-heart talk, but Jim won't tell his father what's on his mind. Quietly, Jim leaves the house and drives to Wimpy's, where he expects to settle with Buzzy.

At Wimpy's, "a slender girl, about sixteen, with good regular features and a mouth too strongly accented by lipstick" uses her cowboy belt to teach one of the boys a lesson in manners. Her name is Amy. Buzzy and the others watch with amusement. Amy then dances to the radio "with her eyes half-closed, in complete abandonment to the music...."

When Wimpy, the owner, tries to quiet the kids, they heckle him. Jim arrives and fights with Buzzy. Jim appears to be losing when a boy named Plato hands him a tire iron. Another boy pulls it away. The fight ends without a clear winner. Amy's friend, Helen, says that she recognizes Jim from one of her classes. Buzzy says that he and Jim are "even," and the gang welcomes him with the usual rite of passage: Amy's full, hard kiss on the mouth.

Several days later, Amy is practicing the piano at home. She shocks her mother with talk of the "kicks" that piano lessons and school can't provide, then quickly apologizes. Amy's father, a handsome, athletic-looking man, arrives. He kisses Amy on the cheek, admires her, and says that school isn't important "if you're young and beautiful." After dinner, Amy tells her parents that she is going to Helen's to study. Instead, she and Helen wander the streets. Two men in a car try to pick them up. Helen observes, "Some adults'll try to make a delinquent out of anyone. Then they blame us for getting tempted."

They meet Jim outside a sporting goods store. He hasn't been to school since that night at Wimpy's. Amy tells him that the gang isn't angry, and he walks them to the drive-in. At Wimpy's, the gang wants action. Buzzy asks, "What're we gonna do?" They consider breaking school windows and stomping a "square" downtown, then decide just to talk about their parents. Plato offends Buzzy by claiming that some parents are mentally ill. The others take Buzzy's side. A boy named Jerry says to Plato, "Why we keep you around I don't know. You're too chicken to help us clip hubcaps yet you're always wantin' us to take you places." Jim stands up for Plato and suggests that the gang take out its frustrations on some adults instead. When Amy describes her encounter with the two men, Buzzy suggests that she pick up "some grown-up wolf" downtown and lure him to the river, where the gang can stomp him. Jim hesitates to join them until Jerry calls him a "chicken." He agrees to go along only if someone keeps an eye on Amy downtown.

As Jim waits near the river with Buzzy and Plato, he imagines himself a knight, Sir James, who will save the Fair Damszel Amy from the Knights of Darkness. Amy arrives with a man, and Jim and Buzzy kick and beat him. After the stomping, Plato claims that he, too, kicked the man. He wants Buzzy to tell the others.

Later, Jim, Amy and Plato are eating hamburgers at a luncheonette. Plato feels good about the stomping, but Jim wishes it had never happened. Amy tries to console him. She knows that neither Jim nor Plato is a "chicken." Plato says, "Too bad we've gotta keep proving that to each other." He thanks Jim for backing him at Wimpy's, and they discuss Plato's parents. His mother is out of town; his father, a Navy commander stationed in Guam, never sees him. Jim wants to know why Plato is "so burned" about them. Plato says, "I try to figure out why getting back at them is so important. It must be ... otherwise why should it bother us?"

Plato leaves Jim and Amy alone together. They argue about the dangerous things she does. Jim wants them both to stay out of trouble. He suggests they go someplace to "celebrate" their new relationship. Plato has been outside, watching them. He walks home in a buoyant mood, imagining himself an explorer, "intrepid [and] fearless," who rescues Jim and Amy from a desert island. Ahead on the dark sidewalk he sees a drunk. Plato tries to help him, but suddenly the man lunges at him and demands money. Plato grabs a rock and wraps it in his handkerchief. He strikes the drunk on the head, killing him. He tosses the rock away, puts the bloody handkerchief back in his pocket and walks on as if nothing has happened.

At Forest High the next day, the students are talking about the "dead bum." Without admitting his guilt, Plato tries to justify the crime: "Suppose he would have died just from being a drunk? So what?" The conversation turns to the man the kids stomped near the river. Buzzy worries about the police, but he accepts Plato's argument that the drunk's murder will draw attention away from the stomping. As the bell rings for class, Plato tells Amy that Jim is "tops in my deck." Plato wants to know if she minds him hanging around. Amy reassures him, "You're with us."

Later, at Amy's house, Jim's and Amy's parents meet for the first time. Some kids drive by and shout Amy's name. This upsets her father so much that he almost strikes her. The recent murder also disturbs him, and he decides to "lay down the law" for Amy. "I want to know who my daughter's traveling with," he says. "These aren't the best of times." Jim and Amy go into the kitchen to argue. He complains because the kids "think they own you" and because Amy lied to her parents about how long she's known Jim. Amy asks, "Why should we argue as if they're important?"

Plato peers through the living room window. He greets Jim and Amy as they step onto the porch and invites them to his house. Amy decides to have a big party at Plato's and invite all the kids. Plato isn't sure it's a good idea, but Amy insists, and the party soon gets out of control. A food fight erupts in the kitchen. In the living room, the kids smash a crystal chandelier. The housekeeper tells Plato, whom she calls "William," that his friends are destroying the house. Some kids are making long distance telephone calls. Plato cuts the phone wires with shears. Then, he goes to his mother's bedroom and begins ripping it apart while Buzzy and a girl are necking on a couch. Plato seems to take a perverse thrill in the destruction. However, he decides that Amy has been drinking too much and asks her to stop....

Shulman did not complete the treatment, stopping after seventy-seven pages. He still needed to write an ending and to insert a dramatic new sequence that he and Ray had just discussed: a "chickie run."

One of Shulman's strengths lay in "inventing or remembering incidents." One such incident was from a newspaper story about teenagers racing stolen cars at Pacific

Palisades. Two boys had to drive fast toward the edge of a cliff and jump before the cars crashed into the ocean. Whoever jumped first was a "chicken." On the occasion cited in the newspaper, one of the racers failed to jump in time and crashed to a fiery death. Ray immediately approved this "chickie run" for *Rebel Without a Cause*. It would replace the blind run through the tunnel and provide the picture with its most dramatic moment.

Meanwhile, Robert Lindner's threat of legal action still hung over the production. On November 17, at home in Baltimore, Lindner wrote a letter to David Weisbart, with whom he had briefly spoken in Los Angeles. The tone of Lindner's letter was cordial, but the message had not changed. Lindner seemed genuinely dismayed that he could not convince Ray or Weisbart to make the film his way. In a final appeal to Weisbart's "social integrity," Lindner repeated once more his offer to act as a consultant.

On November 19, the studio's Legal Department considered its response to Lindner's threat. In a memo to R. J. Obringer, head of Warner Bros.' Legal Department, Finlay McDermid outlined the problem: Lindner would object to the use of his title unless Ray's film followed his book's content. The use of the title alone, Lindner argued, would harm his professional reputation as both a psychiatrist and an author. According to McDermid, Lindner had presented the studio with only two options: change the title or remove Lindner's name from the picture's credits.

David Weisbart, staying out of the legal maelstrom that Lindner's letter had created, continued his own quiet research. The same day that McDermid sent his memo to Obringer, Carl Milliken sent Weisbart a report about youth disturbances in two California communities the previous Easter. The communities, Newport and Balboa, were middle class and progressive. They were not the usual places for teenagers to rampage in the streets. Yet, it *had* happened. The report proved that Ray had been right. Middle-class delinquency *was* a real issue, and audiences would believe it on the screen.

Shulman was also busy. On November 20, he delivered the first seventy-seven pages of his treatment to the Story Department. Regardless of Lindner's threats, *Rebel Without a Cause* was moving ahead. By November 24, the day before Thanksgiving, the Legal Department had devised a solution to the Lindner problem. R. J. Obringer explained the details to McDermid. Their contract with Lindner *did* permit the use of his title, whether or not they filmed the content of the book. They could not, however, use Lindner's name in the screen credits, nor in any publicity associated with the film. If Warner Bros. associated Dr. Lindner's name "with a work of which he is not the author," then Lindner had grounds to sue the studio.

Elsewhere in the city, the holiday spirit flourished. Keenan Wynn and his wife, Sharley, continued a tradition by inviting several Hollywood bachelors to Thanksgiving dinner. That year's guests included Arthur Loew, Jr. (grandson of Marcus Loew, theater chain owner and founder of MGM), and actors Rod Steiger and Ralph Meeker. A fourth guest, Jim Backus, was not a bachelor. The Wynns had invited him because his wife, Henny, was out of town. Although he, too, was an actor, Backus was better known as a radio performer and as the voice of the popular cartoon character, Mr. Magoo. Backus had been acting in movies since 1942. His films included *Father Was a Fullback* (1949) with 11-year-old Natalie Wood, *His Kind of Woman*

(1951) with Robert Mitchum, *Deadline U.S.A.* (1952) with Humphrey Bogart and *Pat and Mike* with Spencer Tracy and Katharine Hepburn. Backus usually played comic sidekicks or buffoons, but now he was looking for more serious roles.

The Wynns extended their hospitality to still another actor: James Dean. Moody by nature, he appeared even more withdrawn and sullen than usual that Thanksgiving afternoon. His behavior was understandable: his former girlfriend, Italian actress Pier Angeli, had married pop singer Vic Damone the day before. A heartbroken Dean had sat on his motorcycle across the street from the church and raced his engine in protest.

At the Wynns', Dean limited his socializing to motorcycle talk with his host. Listening to their conversation, Backus reached the false conclusion that the shy young man in the conservative blue suit and oversized horn-rimmed glasses was a mechanic. Dean never said a word when the conversation turned to acting. Backus finally took Wynn aside and asked why he would invite a shy young mechanic to have dinner with a group of ham actors.

After the holiday, Irving Shulman picked up the pace of his writing. By December 1, he was at work on a Story Progression, or outline, for the screenplay. He divided the story progression into thirty-seven major scenes. The outline incorporated his most recent changes in *Rebel*, including the chickie run and a new opening scene: a class trip to a planetarium. The planetarium scene had originated with Ray and Weisbart.

As Ray explained it:

> The students go to an astronomy class at the Planetarium. Confronted with a giant replica of the sky, pinpointed planets and constellations glittering on it, they listen to a dry cosmic lecture. The voice drones on, of universality and space and the immense cycles of time....

On December 2, Ray made margin notes on Shulman's treatment and wrote six pages of observations about Jim and his family situation. He also rewrote one of Jim's lines to incorporate the new planetarium scene: "We had field study in the observatory," says Jim. "I got lost in the phony stars."

The planetarium scene, unfortunately, created a serious rift between Ray and Shulman. Shulman argued that the planetarium was merely a location. Ray, however, saw

Jim Backus, a popular radio and film actor, was even better known as the voice of the cartoon character, Mr. Magoo.

the show as a metaphor. The planetarium scenario reflected perfectly the teenagers' own worldly dilemma. Like planet Earth in its lonely, unobserved corner of the universe, they existed at the dark periphery of their parents' lives. They felt trivial and anonymous even within the greater society. These feelings of insignificance and alienation among middle-class teenagers was leading them down the path to delinquency, and Ray was determined to show it.

Soon after he and Weisbart conceived the first planetarium scene, Ray imagined a second:

> At the climax of the story, when Plato believes that Jim, his only friend, has deserted him, I thought he should return to the deserted planetarium at night, seeking shelter under its great dome and artificial sky. It was the kind of unexpected dramatic reference I felt the story should contain; there was for me a suggestion of classical tragedy about it.

After discussing the new scene with Dean and Leonard Rosenman (Ray wanted Rosenman to compose the film's music), Ray explained it to Shulman, who still saw no special significance in the setting. Once again, Ray and his writer seemed to be moving in opposite directions.

8

STEWART STERN

During the first week of December, James Dean made an afternoon visit to the home of Arthur Loew, Jr., whom he had met at Keenan Wynn's house. Loew expected another guest that afternoon, his cousin Stewart Stern, who had come from New York to spend the holidays. Stern, 32, was a talented young writer with one screenplay (Fred Zinnemann's *Teresa*) and numerous television scripts to his credit. Recently, he had been writing for the *Philco TV Playhouse*. His latest teleplay, "Thunder of Silence," starring Paul Newman, had received excellent reviews. After the holidays, Stern planned to return to New York to write more teleplays. His plans would soon change.

Stern, a veteran of the Battle of the Bulge, had begun writing plays while recuperating from severe frostbite and trench foot in a military hospital. After the war, he worked in a variety of theatrical jobs as an actor, playwright, assistant casting director and stage manager. In 1946, he came to Hollywood on the advice of Adolph Zukor, Chairman of the Board at Paramount Pictures. He worked for a time as a dialogue director and acting teacher at Eagle-Lion, one of the "Poverty Row" studios. After losing his job at Eagle-Lion, Stern met Fred Zinnemann. He worked on a script for Zinnemann's unproduced film, *Sabra*, then re-wrote Alfred Hayes' screen story for *Teresa* and did the screenplay. After a stint as a junior writer at MGM, Stern returned to New York, working with the New Dramatists Committee as a director of scripts. For $42.00 a week, he helped young playwrights by directing actors in performing their scenes. It was invaluable experience for all concerned, and Stern had made the most of it.

Stern had never met James Dean. When Stern arrived at the home of Arthur Loew, Jr., that December afternoon, Dean was sitting in a swivel chair in the living room. As usual, he was keeping to himself. He gave Stern a terse greeting and then ignored him. When Stern sat in the swivel chair across from him, Dean swiveled the other way in his, turning his back. Stern did the same. After about ten minutes of silence, Stern heard a loud mooing sound from across the room. Stern mooed back convincingly. After a few variations on cows, they moved on to imitations of sheep, chickens, horses, and pigs. This odd encounter created an instant friendship between the two men.

That same day, Dean invited Stern and Arthur Loew, Jr. to a preview of *East of Eden* in Encino, a suburb of Los Angeles. Warner Bros. had screened sneak previews at the Egyptian Theater in Hollywood and several suburban Los Angeles theaters. The sneak preview was an important part of the movie-making process. It allowed the studio to show the film in selected venues before its release to the critics and the general public. If the preview audience laughed in the wrong places, grew restless, or booed, the studio had time to make necessary changes. If no quick fix worked, the studio could shelve the picture. A studio gambled with its prestige each time a picture opened. The more important the picture, the more humiliating and costly the defeat if it failed.

Despite the rumors of his greatness generated by the Publicity Department at Warner Bros., few moviegoers had actually seen James Dean act. Like Jim Backus, even those who had met Dean had no way of assessing his considerable talent. Thus, taking small, unsuspecting groups of friends to the *East of Eden* previews became a game for Dean. He arranged similar ambushes for his friends Lew Bracker and Joe Hyams. Bracker was Dean's insurance agent, Hyams a popular Hollywood columnist.

Soon after the previews, Gene Kelly hosted an evening of charades at his home. The guests included Nicholas Ray and Stewart Stern. Someone introduced them. Ray told Stern that both James Dean and Leonard Rosenman had brought his name to Ray's attention. Stern claimed to be "mystified" by this, but he was undoubtedly flattered. The conversation quickly turned to Stern's work on Fred Zinnemann's *Teresa*. Ray expressed his admiration for the film, especially Stern's ability to bring out the beauty and sensitivity of the characters. All along, Ray had seen *Rebel Without a Cause* as just such a character study. Perhaps, after two failures, Ray might finally find a true collaboration with Stern. Although he did not discuss *Rebel* with Stern that evening, Ray asked Stern to meet him at the studio "to discuss something."

A few days after Kelly's party, Stern complied. Ray introduced Stern to David Weisbart and asked Stern if he would read and evaluate Shulman's script, just as he had done with *Teresa* before writing a screenplay of his own. Stern contacted his agency, which negotiated a salary of $1000 per week. Stern then took the Shulman script home to study, "along with a folder of newspaper items Nick had been saving about juvenile delinquency among the children of the urban middle class." After reading Shulman's script, Stern understood why Ray was not happy with it:

> It felt to me ... a kind of period study. It felt like his book *The Amboydukes* [sic], felt like Chicago, felt like his childhood more than the current situation. It didn't seem to have the texture of the mid–1950's.

Stern met Ray for lunch twice during the following weeks. They discussed, among other things, the teenage knife fight that Ray had read about in *Newsweek*. Stern presented his evaluation of Shulman's work and they agreed that he would begin his own research after the holidays. He was prepared to "start from scratch" on a new screenplay and to begin a (hopefully) successful collaboration with Ray.

9

DEAD END

Irving Shulman was as eager as Nicholas Ray to end their own painful collaboration. He felt uncomfortable working with Ray, and he disliked being summoned to Ray's Sunday afternoon socials, preferring to spend the time with his family. As he labored over the final version of his script, he was already thinking of a new project: a novelization of *Rebel Without a Cause*. As soon as his script was completed, he could ask Warner Bros. for permission to write the novel.

On December 4, Ray put his idea for the first planetarium scene on paper: the planetarium lecturer, using a pointing device, indicates the various constellations. The students pay little attention. Buzz (Ray's name for Buzzy) and his gang wonder about the new kid sitting behind them. When the lecturer asks questions, only Plato has the correct answers. Jimmy, the new kid, congratulates him.

That same day, Shulman delivered his seven-page Story Progression to the studio, along with the first twenty-four pages of the script and his own version of the planetarium scene. He also gave Amy a new name: Judy.

In Shulman's text, Buzzy's group also ignores the planetarium lecture. They are planning a chickie run at River Bluffs between Buzzy and another boy. Jim, a new kid at school, wants to join Buzzy's gang. Someone tells him about the chickie run, which Jim may witness if he contributes a dollar toward the stakes. In the parking lot, Jim meets Plato and asks directions to River Bluffs. Jim gives Plato a ride there.

At River Bluffs, Buzzy and his opponent discuss the rules of the race. Whoever jumps first is a "chicken." The last to jump wins the stake money. Buzzy will race against a young married man whose pregnant wife watches nervously from the sidelines. The "Young Husband," as Shulman describes him, races because he needs the money. Buzzy races only for the thrill. Judy, Buzzy's girl, observes Jim closely when he first arrives. She is "a vivacious extrovert" who "flaunts her sexuality."

The boy next to Jim holds the stake money as the race begins. Buzzy jumps close to the edge, but the "Young Husband" goes over the cliff in his car. His wife screams. Jim tells the stake holder to give her the money. She drops it on the ground as the crowd scatters. Jim picks up the money as Buzzy and some of the kids drive away, wondering what went wrong. Maybe the "Young Husband" went over on purpose.

Jim drives fast, catches up with Buzzy, and hands him the stake money. Buzzy takes the gesture as an insult and hits him. Jim says that he will meet Buzzy somewhere to fight, and Buzzy suggests Wimpy's Drive-In. As Judy drives away with Buzzy, she smiles "tauntingly" at Jim. Plato frowns; he does not approve of Judy's interest in Jim.

When Jim arrives home, he gets a lecture from his mother. Jim wants his father to stand up to her, but his father lacks the courage. Jim goes to his room as his parents discuss him. He wonders if he has enough courage to face Buzzy. The boy who went over the bluff didn't "chicken." Finally, Jim leaves through the window.

At Wimpy's, Jim and Buzzy fight, but no one wins. The kids decide to leave before the police arrive. Jim takes Judy and Plato in his car. When Plato arrives home, he finds his mother packing for a trip. She will not take him with her. Jim drops Judy at her house. She leaves her cigarettes with him so her parents won't discover them. She tells Jim that she wants to go "necking" with him sometime. As he drives away, Judy feels suddenly confused about her true feelings.

Judy's parents have fallen asleep in front of the television. She goes to her room, takes off her makeup, "and is revealed as [a] youngster — now she looks shy, her age." She sits in her nightgown and robe in front of her dresser mirror and dreams of being in love with a Lochinvar who wears a mask. Judy's parents appear at her door. She needs to talk to her father, but he goes to bed. Later, lying in bed but still awake, Judy sees her shining knight again. She and "another woman" fight for his affection.

The next day at school, Jim watches Judy play the piano. After school, she and her friend Helen go downtown instead of going home. Jim passes them in his car. Judy is upset when he does not stop for them. Two older men try to pick them up, but the girls brush them off.

Plato's mother leaves on her trip. The housekeeper, who sympathizes with Plato's loneliness, makes his dinner. He tells her about his new friend, Jim. Meanwhile, at a drug store counter, Jim eats a hamburger as Judy and Helen enter. Jim gives her back her cigarettes, which surprises and pleases her. They decide to go to Wimpy's because, as Judy says, "What's the sense of going home if your quote — family — unquote's still awake?"

At Wimpy's, the gang makes a commotion. A squad car arrives and Wimpy tells the police that he doesn't want Buzzy and his friends around anymore. The kids plan revenge against an adult. Later, at the riverbank, they decide to have Judy lure a man close to the planetarium, where the gang will stomp him. After Jim foils the plan, he and Judy remain there. Plato later reappears and is happy when Jim and Judy seem to accept him. They talk about the planets and stars until Plato decides to give them some privacy. Jim tells Judy that he can only be serious about her if she wants more than a "casual relationship."

On his way home, Plato daydreams. He sees himself as a soldier of fortune. In the park, he encounters a drunk, whom he kills and then goes on daydreaming. At school the next morning, all the kids are talking about the murder. They also tease Jim and Judy about their romance. Plato, showing his disapproval, "eyes Judy narrowly."

When Judy invites Jim and his family to meet her parents, Plato lurks outside. The evening does not go well, and the adults finally suggest that Jim and Judy go to the movies. Plato invites them to his house. This annoys Judy, because she wants to be alone with Jim. Her rejection hurts Plato, but he recovers. At Plato's house, they sit and talk. Plato thinks that he has finally found a "family" with Jim and Judy. He seeks Jim's advice as he would from his own father. Jim asks Judy to make sandwiches while the two boys plan a camping trip. Judy wants Jim to stop encouraging Plato's fantasy. She feels bored and suggests a party with all the kids.

The party soon gets out of control. The kids vandalize the house, but Plato does not seem to care. Jim tries to get everyone to go home, but Judy wants the chaotic evening to continue. Plato becomes violent when one of the boys puts on his father's Navy uniform. He thinks that Jim is the only other person worthy to wear it. Juvenile Officers arrive to break up the party. They immediately recognize Judy and Buzzy, who have been in trouble before. Although Jim disapproves of Judy's bad reputation, he takes sole blame for the party. Plato, however, blames Judy. He argues with Jim about her after the others leave. Jim takes Judy's side. He cannot spend the night at Plato's, he explains; he must take her home instead. Judy flashes a look of hostility "and triumph" as she and Jim leave. Plato goes upstairs and rips apart his mother's bedroom. He wants to kill Judy for taking Jim away.

At school the next day, Plato acts as if nothing has happened; but Judy is wary. She and Helen discuss the wild party and decide to keep a low profile. Inside her locker, Judy finds a strange compact. When Helen opens it, it explodes in her face. Later, in the principal's office, Judy, Jim, and Jim's and Helen's parents try to find out what happened. Helen is in the hospital. Judy's parents have been called, but they have still not arrived. Helen's parents blame Judy. Jim tries to defend her, but his father argues that she is no good. He makes Jim leave Judy at school, even though she fears Plato. Jim promises to protect her.

That evening, Judy waits at school for her parents. Plato approaches and seems friendly. He says he wants to confess his part in stomping the man at the planetarium. She begs him to keep quiet, for the sake of Jim and the others.

Plato asks Judy to come with him to the planetarium so she can give him advice. Reluctantly, she agrees. He follows her out to an observation deck and tells her why he is going to kill her: she has been "ungrateful" for not wanting to share Jim with anyone else. Coldly, he orders her to "prepare for death." Meanwhile, Judy's parents arrive at Jim's house. They haven't been able to find her anywhere. Jim begins a search that leads him to the planetarium....

Shulman's outline left the ending still open. Once again, the planetarium location seemed to create a special problem for him. He planned a violent end for Plato; but if Plato were to die, should it be at the planetarium or Plato's own home?

On December 11, Shulman delivered another sixteen pages of the script and two revised pages to the Story Department. On the 13th, he began work on a new treatment that would update his work of November 15 and the Story Progression of December 4. The first twenty-three pages of that treatment incorporated some interesting changes: "Jim" was now "Jim Stark"; the "Young Husband" was now "Chuck"; a more violent Plato had acquired a dubious new talent, as a maker of zip guns.

Shulman added another fantasy sequence: Jim daydreams that he drives off a cliff during a chickie run; but instead of crashing, he rockets toward the stars, where he sees Judy as a beautiful constellation. In another scene, Jim goes to a bar, where he unknowingly "treats" a call girl to drinks, and then must pay by surrendering his wristwatch. Shulman replaced Jim's "Sir James" fantasy at the riverbank with a new fantasy for Plato, who imagines saving Jim and Judy from various dangers.

After the stomping, when Jim and Judy go to the planetarium, they see one of the presentations inside. The lecturer tells the audience that their problems are insignificant when compared with "the immensity and timelessness of the universe." To this, Jim replies, "What does *he* know about it?"

Plato arrives. He tells Jim and Judy that Buzzy is angry with them for deserting him and Plato at the stomp scene. Judy hurts Plato's feelings when she tells him bluntly that she wants to be alone with Jim. Plato then refuses Jim's offer of a ride home. Walking through the park, and deep in a fantasy (in which he saves Jim from Amazons), he murders a woman with his zip gun. The next day at school, Plato argues that the murder "takes the heat off anything and everything anyone else's done against society." Besides, he says, the woman's violent death has made her briefly famous....

By December 14, Shulman had finished his revised treatment. Jim and Judy have been quarreling about getting their parents to meet. She likes being with him instead of the gang, but she dislikes trying to socialize with parents. That evening at Judy's house, no one seems to be able to carry on a conversation. When the adults finally agree to a game of bridge, Jim and Judy leave and discover Plato lurking outside. Although his presence annoys Judy, she goes along when Plato invites them to come home with him.

Plato's house contains a small arsenal, filled with gun racks and weapons. Almost immediately, Judy and Plato begin exchanging angry words. When Plato makes insinuations about Judy's checkered past, she storms out. She goes to Wimpy's, where one of the waitresses is talking about the zip gun murder. Judy realizes that Plato must be the killer and hurries back to his house. She parks her car carelessly, and this attracts the attention of two policemen in a patrol car. When the officers approach Plato's front door, he thinks that Judy has called them. He shoots one policeman and takes Jim and Judy hostage. They escape, and Jim tries to get Plato to give himself up. Instead, Plato falls on the grenade he was about to throw, and the house blows up with him.

Shulman's final scene took the action away from the planetarium, away from the ending that Ray had expected him to write. Ray was adamant that Plato should die at the planetarium location after a confrontation with the police, but Shulman still "tenaciously disagreed."

Ray observed later:

> This was a crucial point for me because it symbolised the more violent statement, the more sweepingly developed conflict that I was searching for and that Shulman seemed unable to accept. It was a gesture of anger and desperation that matched the kind of thing I had heard at Juvenile Hall.

The continuing dispute over the planetarium scene convinced Ray that, like Uris, Shulman had taken an "essentially different" view of the film. Despite Shulman's valuable contributions to the story line, "we were once again at a dead end."

10

A CRITIQUE

On December 16, Ray's Shulman problem temporarily took a back seat to some potentially good news: Hedda Hopper's column announced that James Dean would indeed play Jim Stark in *Rebel Without a Cause*. Elizabeth Taylor, the female lead in *Giant*, was pregnant and the production of *Giant* was delayed until at least February, when her baby was due. Dean, who had already signed to play Jett Rink, would not have to report until April. It would be just enough time to squeeze him into *Rebel Without a Cause*. Hopper's announcement, however, was only wishful thinking. Dean's availability for the role did not guarantee that the studio would sign him, and Dean himself had not yet decided to make the film.

That same morning, Ray and Weisbart met with story executive Walter MacEwen. MacEwen had read Shulman's updated treatment and the first forty pages of his screenplay. His job was to analyze the potential film not only as art, but as product. After listening to MacEwen's comments, Ray communicated them to Shulman in a memo.

MacEwen had reacted favorably to most of the script. However, he had criticized the story for lacking "sufficient sense of the normal youth activities." The chickie run was a good example. It was strictly a gang event, yet half the school seemed to be there. The studio did not want audiences to believe that every onlooker belonged to the gang. Such a large number of delinquents in one school was an intolerable idea. It eroded the wholesome image that most communities expected of the nation's schools.

Ray had a solution for that problem. In his memo to Shulman, he suggested that the members of Buzzy's gang be isolated in one area during the first scene at the planetarium to distinguish them from other onlookers who later show up at the race. Ray also suggested a recess period scene (during which Judy would sing) and another scene on the school lawn to emphasize the gang as a separate group.

MacEwen had also complained that Jim moved "too precipitously" from bad to good at the end of the picture. Audiences might have trouble accepting such a sudden change in behavior. Ray's memo to Shulman suggested developing Jim's conflicting impulses as a more central feature of his character. He suggested further that Jim's refusal to participate in the planetarium beating was one good example of moving in that direction, "hoping that he will not go off the deep end but knowing that it is possible."

Another of MacEwen's complaints had been the effect of Chuck's death — or the lack of it — on the teenagers their next day at school. To ignore the consequences of such a horrible event would be unrealistic. It would also make the teenagers appear callous. Ray was aware of the omission. He had left the reference out, he explained, "until we could do it without involving Judy so emotionally."

The story's fantastic elements (Plato as a soldier of fortune, Jim blasting off to the Constellation Judy) had sounded contrived to MacEwen. He had suggested a stronger motivational link between the daydream and the person having it. Plato's dreams should all be destructive, Jim's and Judy's positive. Ray agreed, and suggested to Shulman that the fantasies "might help our change of pace with humor."

Plato's murder of the woman, MacEwen had argued, also occurred without enough foreshadowing in the plot. The zip gun itself, MacEwen had felt, should appear earlier in the story. Ray passed along another recommendation: that Plato's violence should contain a sense of tragic inevitability. The audience must sense "that Plato had to do something like this TONIGHT." None of the other teenagers, MacEwen had suggested, should anticipate Plato's violent outburst at the climax of the film.

MacEwen had offered one final thought: that a narrator or "representative of authority" should "connect the acts of violence, school vandalism, or truancy into a pattern which will have significance for everybody." On this last point, MacEwen was conscious of front office policy as well as the concerns of the Story Department. The Production Code, which determined the "proper subjects" for American films, forbade unpunished criminal activity on the screen, especially by juveniles. If *Rebel Without a Cause* was to be a "message" picture, that had to be the primary message.

On December 18, Shulman completed a new forty-page outline, plus fifteen pages of his revised script. The revisions did not include any change in the film's climax. Shulman still wanted Plato's death to occur at his own house. Until now, Ray's disagreement with Shulman over the planetarium scene had been only a paper war fought with scripts and inter-office memoranda. As pre-production approached, their creative argument would escalate. Pre-production required spending money to cast actors, assemble props, assign a production crew and choose locations. With pre-production in mind, Ray tried to put his differences with Shulman aside and concentrate on something else.

He began arranging for a planetarium.

11

LOS ANGELES AND NEW YORK

The Griffith Park Observatory, overlooking Griffith Park and the City of Los Angeles, was a local landmark and a popular tourist attraction. The movie studios and local advertising agencies made frequent use of the building and its surroundings. One of James Dean's first jobs in Hollywood had been a Pepsi-Cola commercial filmed in Griffith Park.

On December 18, the same day that Ray and Weisbart met with MacEwen, Weisbart wrote a memo to Eric Stacey, whom the studio had assigned as Unit Manager for *Rebel Without a Cause*. Part of Stacey's job was to secure locations for filming outside the studio, determine special conditions or restrictions for their use and arrange for blocks of time. Weisbart informed Stacey that Ray's company would need to film inside the planetarium lecture area, in the exhibit area and all around the building's exterior. Weisbart sent a copy of the memo to William L. Guthrie, the studio's Location Department Manager.

Five days later, Kenneth Cox of the Location Department reported to Guthrie about his recent conversation with Col. Charles H. McCormack, Head of the Los Angeles Parks and Recreation Department. Cox told Guthrie that McCormack would allow using the Griffith Observatory for a location, and that he would cooperate "in every way possible." The planetarium's schedule of shows and lectures would limit the interior shooting, but no time restrictions would apply outside the building. Mondays, the observatory was closed to the public and would always be available. Tuesdays, "with proper notice," Ray could film without restrictions. Morning work inside the building might be scheduled for later in the week.

With the script meeting behind him and the observatory/planetarium location established, Ray gave more thought to casting the picture. He planned to fly to New York with William T. Orr, the studio's executive in charge of talent, to interview actors for possible roles in *Rebel Without a Cause*.

On December 13, the week before his meeting with MacEwen, Ray had sent Orr a memo with detailed descriptions of the picture's major characters. These descriptions would be useful when the two men went East. Ray reaffirmed for Orr that the delinquents in *Rebel Without a Cause* were not to be products of the slums, but middle-class children "with relatively identical" backgrounds.

As Ray flew to New York, he considered his impasse with Shulman. He considered also MacEwen's evaluation of the script, which indicated the need for more work. If he decided to drop Shulman now and entrust the writing to Stewart Stern, he would incur more delays. James Dean, even if he were willing to play Jim Stark, could not wait forever. If Ray could not start *Rebel* within the next two or three months, he would lose Dean to *Giant*.

Rebel itself was apparently in jeopardy. Ray had heard rumors that Warner Bros. was looking for an excuse to back out of the film. Studio executives had been badgering him for a start date he could not give them. After almost three months of work, Ray still had no satisfactory script and no cast. Even David Weisbart and Steve Trilling, who supported the film vigorously, could not sustain a sense of enthusiasm with the front office much longer.

Even without a finished script, *Rebel* was creating controversy. Some studio executives condemned Plato's family situation: a neglectful, pleasure-seeking mother and a father whose only contact with his son was a monthly child support check. Hoping to overcome such objections with "equally strong reality," Ray had cited his own domestic situation. He had two sons whose only contact with their father was a check and an occasional visit. Ray planned to make one of those rare visits in New York that Christmas season. His 16-year-old son, Tony, lived there with Ray's first wife, Jean Evans.

James Dean was also in New York for the holidays. He preferred it to Los Angeles and kept an apartment on 68th Street. Ray expected to spend much of his time with Dean, hoping to lure him to the role of Jim. Since Ray was satisfied with only the first fifteen pages of Shulman's script, that was all he would present to Dean as an enticement.

On arriving in New York, Ray visited the Actors Studio, home of "the Method." Many of the best young actors studied there, and many had roles in current Broadway shows. By the end of their first working day, Ray and William T. Orr had interviewed forty-four of them.

One of those Ray considered for the role of Judy was Kathy Nolan. She was 21 years old, 5'3" tall, weighed 100 pounds, had hazel eyes and auburn-blonde hair. She was currently playing Wendy in *Peter Pan*. Brian Hutton and Scott Marlowe tried out for the role of Buzzy. For the role of Plato, Ray and Orr looked at Edwin Bruce, Ivan Cury, and Arte Johnson (of future *Laugh-In* fame). Johnson, 23, was performing at a club in the city, and Ray wanted to catch his act before leaving. Patti Bosworth tested for the role of Judy's friend, Helen. Although a number of the actors did not fit any particular role, Ray hoped to give them a second look at the end of January.

Ray and Orr rejected some outright. Betty Logue did not have "enough experience or excitement"; Gene Persson seemed too typically a Californian; Lowell Harris was just "not the right type for this film"; and June Evert and Nancy Devlin (Kathy Nolan's sister), were dismissed as being too "girlish."

Ray and Orr also rejected some future Hollywood mainstays. At 25, John Cassavetes looked "too old," while Lee Remick, 19, was turned away because Ray thought she would not photograph well.

They accepted Tom Brannum conditionally. He looked good as Buzzy, but his height (6' 2") could rule him out. He would tower over James Dean, who was only 5' 8". Carroll Baker, one of the brightest rising stars at the Actors Studio, seemed perfect as Judy. She had just completed a role in *A Hatful of Rain* and would be available. To pique her interest, Ray decided to send her a *Rebel* script.

When Ray was not at the Actors Studio, he was with James Dean. They had dinner each night, and Ray attended a few Christmas parties with Dean and his friends. Ray even introduced his son, Tony, to Dean, yet another ploy to attract Dean to *Rebel*.

Ray spent much of his time with Dean just talking. Dean was still wary of being exploited by the studio, still unsure of his abilities despite the *East of Eden* previews. The fact that the Publicity Department had announced him for *Rebel*, and that Hedda Hopper had reported it, meant nothing to him. He would make the film only if *he* wanted to. As a final incentive, Ray made him an unprecedented offer: Dean could create his own Jim Stark. Working closely with Ray and the film's screenwriter, he could virtually direct himself. As Ray said good-bye, he and Dean shook hands. Dean told him, "I want to do your film, but don't let *them* know it."

Three days after Christmas, Nicholas Ray flew back to Los Angeles. Although he was confident that Dean would honor their unwritten agreement, he knew that he could no longer work with Irving Shulman. How would the studio react if he simply fired Shulman and hired Stewart Stern? What would happen if he threw out Shulman's script and started over? With Stern in mind, Ray might have recalled a mental note he had made during his earlier difficulties: "Dave [Weisbart] and I should be considering the new young writers as possibilities. Someone who will stay right there and work with us through the rest of the show."

Nineteen fifty four was ending. Nicholas Ray, beset with troubles, could not easily contemplate a new beginning for *Rebel Without a Cause* in 1955. He had failed to agree with either of the two writers the studio had assigned him. He had no script. The studio moralists were gathering against him. Perhaps, as he thought about his failures with Uris and Shulman during that long flight home, he wondered if his third choice would be the charm.

Carroll Baker of the Actors Studio was Nicholas Ray's first choice to play Judy in *Rebel Without a Cause*.

PART II

Pre-Production

12

A PRIVATE HELL

On January 6, 1955, Warner Bros. announced that Stewart Stern would begin work on the script for *Rebel Without a Cause*. The studio backdated Stern's contract to December 30.

Stern's evaluation of Shulman's script confirmed Ray's own feelings. Rather than include Shulman further, Ray and Stern decided to bypass him, salvaging what they could from his story line and script while brainstorming for new ideas. They began a series of all-night work sessions, trying to reach agreement on their concepts of the characters. The sessions gave Ray a long-overdue opportunity to unburden his soul.

Stern later recalled:

> Nick was in agony, a kind of private hell, at that time. A creative hell. He had a concept and a vision of what he wanted to say, but he had not found a way to say it through the writers he had had. He was almost inarticulate about what he wanted and why he was not satisfied. Through [the] all-night sessions, talking mostly about ourselves, I began to get a picture of what that agony consisted of. Nick, like most artists, is part child. His child talked to my child. His bewildered adult talked to my bewildered adult, and out of the horns of our private dilemmas, I began to get a picture of what we both wanted to say through a story about children.

If Irving Shulman perceived any threat from Stern's arrival, he did not officially express it. He had completed most of his work and could feel satisfied with his accomplishments. Even if Stern

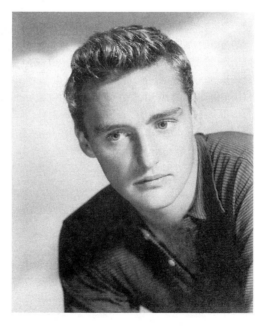

Dennis Hopper had only a single acting credit (in TV's *Medic*) before winning the role of Goon in *Rebel Without a Cause.*

53

received credit for the final screenplay, Shulman expected to receive at least partial credit for the story on which it would be based. No one had told him about the clause in Ray's contract that would deny him that credit.

As if to reinforce the notion that Shulman was still the writer of record, David Weisbart sent him a reassuring memo on January 7, the day after Stern's official arrival at the studio. The studio, observed Weisbart, was "fortunate" to have Shulman writing *Rebel*'s script.

Meanwhile, Stern's work on an alternate script was moving ahead. Like Leon Uris, he believed in first-hand experience. Using Ray's previous contacts at Juvenile Hall, Stern interviewed teens and court officials, posing as a social worker from Chicago. He sat through booking interviews and observed the interplay of teenagers and their parents: angry, sullen children; disbelieving, outraged or indifferent adults. He saw in the booking interviews a perfect dramatic framework for his script's first major sequence. After two weeks of observation, he secluded himself in a small apartment and began to write. Stern's contract ran for twelve weeks; but Ray, pressed for time, expected a final draft within five.

On January 13, the studio announced the signing of an 18-year-old actor to a term contract. Simultaneously, it announced his casting in *Rebel Without a Cause*. His name was Dennis Hopper. Hopper's only film experience had been the January 3 episode of television's *Medic* series, in which he played an undiagnosed diabetic saved by doctor Richard Boone. The studio's Publicity Department quickly assembled a file on Hopper. Jonah (Joe) Halperin, whom the studio had assigned to collect and distribute spot news about *Rebel* for the newspapers, wrote a brief biography: born in Dodge City, Kansas, Hopper had lived for many years in San Diego before moving to Kansas City "to work the wheat harvest on his grandparents' farm." While living in Kansas City, he entered the Golden Gloves boxing competition, winning in the middleweight class.

After graduating from high school in June 1954, he spent the summer at the La Jolla Playhouse. His work caught the attention of actress Dorothy McGuire, who urged him to pursue an acting career. Hopper soon found a Hollywood agent, auditioned for the role in *Medic*, and won it by besting thirty-one other actors. Shortly after the program aired, three studios offered him contracts. He chose Warner Bros.

On January 17, 1955, James Dean returned from an extended Christmas vacation in New York. He had two reasons for coming back to Hollywood: his promised meetings with Nicholas Ray and rehearsals for a *Schlitz Playhouse of Stars* television program. The episode, titled "The Unlighted Road," was to air in May. It would be Dean's last venture into television.

The night that Dean arrived in Los Angeles, he had dinner with Nicholas Ray and Susan Strasberg, daughter of the Actors Studio director. The next day, Ray and Dean began ten days of production meetings in Ray's bungalow at the Chateau Marmont. As they had agreed in New York, Dean would have complete creative control over his own character. Because so much of the film rested with that character, Dean would almost certainly shape the story as well.

13

Screenplay by Stewart Stern

On January 22, Stern delivered the first forty-two pages of his script to the studio, including five revised pages. He had not had time to write a treatment, but he did not see that as a disadvantage.

Stern later recalled:

> I felt that it would be a waste of creative energy. On some projects I feel very insecure unless I have a very detailed step by step prediction of everything that is going to happen in the screenplay, which means copious and detailed research and then very meticulous structuring... In those days I felt that it (the treatment) was a terrible duplication of effort and that it bled out a lot of creative impulses.

Stern's story begins on Christmas Eve. Some teenagers (Buzz Gunderson and his gang) accost a shopper, beat him and leave him moaning on the sidewalk. Later, two policemen escort a drunken Jim Stark into Juvenile Hall. Plato, a boy of 15, sits on a bench beside his Negro nurse. Judy, "blonde and sixteen," enters next. Three small Mexican children also sit in the waiting area.

Stern's "stomping" scene almost certainly developed from the incident that Ray had read about in *Newsweek*. Stern would have seen it while studying Ray's research files. The scene at Juvenile Hall came directly from Stern's visits there.

While a social worker talks with the Mexican children, a policeman named Ray interviews Judy. She was wandering the streets when the police picked her up. Ray asks if she knows anything about the beating of the shopper on Twelfth Street. She doesn't. Reluctantly, she gives him her phone number so her parents can pick her up. Jim, meanwhile, amuses himself at an officer's expense. He tries to give his jacket to a shivering Plato, but Plato refuses. Jim's parents arrive from "the club" to pick him up. A "DCU (Delinquency Control Unit) man" calls Plato and his nurse into an office. Plato has destroyed all the Christmas presents his mother left for him before going out of town. Before that, he killed some puppies at the house next door.

At Ray's insistence, Stern had written two daydream sequences. In the DCU man's office, Plato drifts into the first fantasy, where he imagines himself inside a crayon drawing, singing to himself about being alone.

Plato's daydream continues. A crayon car arrives with his father, who wears a naval officer's uniform. The father hugs Plato. Plato's mother appears, smiling. Plato and his father walk down the crayon road and go fishing. They sit on the bank of a blue crayon lake under the yellow stars of a crayon sky. Plato shivers. His father offers him his uniform jacket. The father has Jim Stark's face.

Plato emerges from his daydream. The DCU man tells him he must stay at Juvenile Hall until his mother returns from Chicago. Meanwhile, Jim talks to another DCU man. When Jim's father and mother argue about his behavior, he escapes into his own daydream. He imagines himself at a shooting gallery with a .22 rifle in his hands. As he shoots at the moving metal ducks, three large balloons appear. Each has a bull's eye in the center. Jim shoots at the first one, which has his mother's face. As the air goes out of it, he tries to talk to her. His father's face appears on the second balloon. He shoots that one, too. Then he shoots the third, with his grandmother's face on it.

He picks up the three deflated balloons and runs to a service station. Each time he tries to re-inflate them, they burst. He returns to the shooting gallery, and this time his own face is on a balloon. Jim cries out to be punished, a shot rings out and "a look of relief passes over his face."

The DCU man warns Jim to keep out of further trouble and releases him to his parents' custody. As Jim and his parents leave, they hear the distant sound of a children's choir. The sound rises as Jim moves further from the camera. The scene fades out.

Fade in on the next morning, the street outside Judy's house. Some children, including Judy's 6-year-old brother, Beau, have set a community Christmas tree ablaze. She calls to Beau from the sidewalk. Jim comes out of a house across the street, sees Judy and remembers her from the precinct station. She rejects his attempts to be friendly, catches up with Beau, and walks off toward school. The scene dissolves to a self-serve gas station, where Buzz and his gang wait. Buzz has dyed his hair "a brilliant peroxide blond."

The other teenagers include Helen, Sweet William, Chick and Chili-Picker. Judy and Beau arrive and get in the car as Buzz fills the gas tank and Chick puts air in the tires. Jim arrives in his car and asks the way to school. They give him a series of wrong directions. When the attendant arrives to collect for the gas, Buzz tells him to put it on his bill and roars off. The scene dissolves to the bicycle rack at school. Plato arrives on a scooter. Jim parks his car as the gang arrives. Judy drops Beau at "University Elementary," just across from "University High." Plato goes to his locker, and Jim sees Judy again. She and her girlfriends are "sneaking a smoke" in the corridor. As Jim approaches, they march past him, arms folded, whistling "We Are the Girls of the Institute" and laughing. The class bell rings.

Plato also watches Jim approach. He drifts into another daydream, singing the same song as before. We hear Plato, but his lips do not move, and there are no dream images. Plato tries to introduce himself, but Jim does not remember him. Plato slams his fist against the wall in frustration after Jim walks past. Jim sees a planetarium field trip notice on a bulletin board and exits.

At the planetarium theater, the lecturer presents a program about the end of the world. The problems of humanity, he says, are insignificant when compared with cosmic events. Man, existing alone, won't be missed. During the show, Jim sits near the gang. Plato sits near Jim. He warns Jim about Buzz and Judy; they do not make friends easily. After Buzz pretends that he is Cancer, the Crab, Jim moos at Taurus, the Bull. This irritates the gang. After the "end of the world" takes place inside the planetarium dome, Plato begins to cry. He complains to Jim about the lecturer: "What does *he* know about man alone?" As the students leave, an "old lady schoolteacher" tries to get their attention, but fails.

In the parking lot, Buzz's gang waits for Jim to come outside. Plato runs back to warn him. He finds him in the Display Lobby leaning over the pendulum pit. They introduce themselves, Plato warns Jim about Buzz's gang, and then they leave for the parking lot, where Buzz and his gang are waiting.

The gang has slashed a tire on Jim's car. After Jim and Buzz exchange a few harsh words, Buzz puts a cigarette into Jim's mouth and lights it. It has "SQUARE" printed on it in ink. Jim puts on his glasses and reads it. The gang laughs and Buzz gives him another cigarette. This one has "CHICKEN" written on it. Jim walks very close to Buzz and Judy. Suddenly, he asks Judy, "Why are you so unhappy?" The remark startles Judy. Buzz grabs Jim suddenly by the hair, jerks his head up and slaps him across the face. Jim's eyes stay fixed on Judy, like a challenge. He has angered her by exposing her real feelings, but impressed her by recognizing them. Buzz slaps Jim until Jim finally breaks free. He and Buzz fight briefly with their fists as the others form a circle around them.

Chili-Picker throws a switchblade at Jim's feet, and he picks it up as Buzz pulls out his own blade. They open them at the same time and stalk each other. The crowd shouts "Ole!" when Buzz nicks Jim with the knife. Jim is still "getting the worst of it" when Plato suddenly pushes through the crowd with a tire chain. Chili-Picker warns the group as the planetarium Lecturer and Guide approach.

Buzz folds up his knife, but the fight is not over: Buzz challenges Jim to meet him at Wimpy's, the local drive-in. As Buzz leaves, he smiles at Jim and says, "You're cold, Jack. You're dead."

The gang piles into Buzz's car and drives away. Judy glances back at Jim. The Lecturer sees blood on Jim's shirt and asks about his wounds. Jim replies, "I scratched my mosquito bites." He and Plato get into his car, flat tire and all, and drive away...

Stern's freedom in developing his script was twice-burdened. Because he had entered late in the creative process, and because he had had so little time to prepare, he was unable to start "from scratch." Although much of the final script would be his, he would have to mold his concept of the film to fill out a pre-existing structure.

He also felt burdened by Ray's daydream scenes. Ray wanted the fantasy level to reveal the workings of the teenagers' troubled minds. Stern believed that such fantasy scenes were an "artistic presumption." He felt strongly that "the inner lives of the characters must be revealed through behavior and dialogue, not by imposing fantasy images on an audience."

Ray argued to keep the daydream sequences. He expected to film *Rebel* in the new CinemaScope process, using a split-screen effect with fantasy and reality playing side-by-side. This was Ray's first experience with the new format, and he felt a certain anxiety about how he would fill up the screen.

14

START NOTICE

On January 27, 1955, Finlay McDermid sent a memo to Roy Obringer in the Legal Department: Irving Shulman had completed his work on *Rebel Without a Cause*. The studio would pay him $750 for his last week of work, as stated in his contract.

January 27 was also the start date of Shulman's contract to novelize his version of the screenplay. As he read the contract, Shulman found something unexpected: his novel was based upon a story by Nicholas Ray titled "The Blind Run." Having never heard of Ray's story, he immediately turned the contract over to his attorney.

Meanwhile, James Dean was having lunch for the first time at Romanoff's Restaurant on Rodeo Drive. Humphrey Bogart, Margaret O'Brien and Nicholas Ray sat at the table. Ray and Bogart were good friends, having met while filming *In a Lonely Place*. Margaret O'Brien, like Natalie Wood and several other young actresses, was campaigning for the role of Judy in *Rebel Without a Cause*.

That night, Dean flew to New York. He planned to spend time at the Actors Studio and attend classes at Katherine Dunham's dance school. There, he hoped to see his friend, Eartha Kitt, the only person who called him "Jamie."

A photographer named Dennis Stock returned East with Dean. Dean had met him at one of Nicholas Ray's Sunday socials, and they had become friends. Stock planned to photograph Dean in New York and in Fairmount, Indiana, Dean's hometown, where Dean was to attend the annual "Sweetheart Ball."

The columnists had announced that James Dean would star in *Rebel Without a Cause*. Dean's New York agent, Jane Deacy, had helped convince the studio to sign him, and Dean had his own verbal agreement with Nicholas Ray. Yet, Dean had no contractual obligation to appear until he received a 45 day "start notice" from Warner Bros. This notice gave Dean 45 days to prepare for his role and clear his calendar. If the project fell through before the expiration date, the studio could reassign him. If he failed to report to the film at the end of the period, the studio could suspend him from working at Warner Bros. or any other studio. On January 31, Roy Obringer of the Legal Department sent a memo to Steve Trilling: Dean's start date would be March 15th. Dean would work for ten weeks "at the contract price," and *pro rata* thereafter until the picture was finished. The contract allowed the studio one week of "free time," either the week before Dean's start date (for "preparation work") or

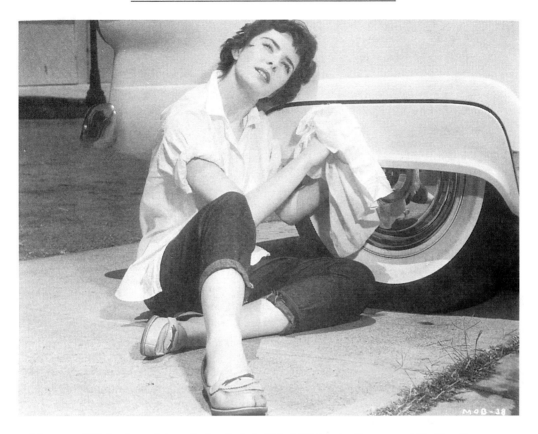

Margaret O'Brien hoped that playing Judy in *Rebel Without a Cause* would bridge the gap between adolescent and adult roles.

the week after filming ended (for publicity purposes). During this period of "free time," Dean's services would be offered *gratis*. Dean's official salary for the picture was $12,500, $2,500 more than he received for *East of Eden* and $12,490 more than his 1950 Pepsi-Cola commercial.

On the day that Dean received his start notice, the studio announced that Jayne Mansfield, "of the 40 inch bust," would test for a part in *Rebel Without a Cause*. According to Harrison Carroll of the *Los Angeles Herald & Express*, she would "most likely wind up with a Warner contract." Mansfield was 21 years old. In her attempt to become a genuine movie star, she had entered and won several beauty contests, played cameo roles on a few television programs, and performed publicity work for the Jane Russell picture, *Underwater*.

Mansfield had little acting experience. She did not look anything like a high school student. Yet, Warner Bros. was considering her for a role in Ray's film. *Rebel*, after all, was only an exploitation film. A buxom blonde with no acting ability was an asset of sorts in such a project. The message from the front office was clear: *Rebel Without a Cause* was not being taken seriously.

By January 31, Stewart Stern had completed the first seventy-three pages of his revised script. The script had substantial changes. In Stern's earlier draft, Judy expressed hatred for both her parents. Now she would direct it only at her father. The new script also suggested that the police had picked up Judy for prostitution. The DCU man who interviewed her was still named Ray.

Stern, with Weisbart's support, had won at least part of his argument with Ray over the fantasy sequences, removing Plato's crayon-world daydream and Jim's imaginary shooting gallery from the precinct station scene. He had also developed the exchange between Jim and his parents. In this new draft, Jim not only participates in the heated discussion, but keeps a running, internalized commentary on it.

Stern also removed Plato's daydream song from the school corridor scene. He retained the knife fight from the first draft, adding a conversation between Jim and Plato. After the fight ends, Plato uses his handkerchief to daub the blood from Jim's wounds. He puts it back in his pocket as Jim buttons his shirt. As they watch the setting sun, Plato asks Jim if the world will end at night. Jim answers, "No, it'll be at dawn."

The doomsday dialogue between Jim and Plato was significant to Stern, who saw it as preparation for a similar conversation he planned for the film's climax. In that scene, Jim and Plato return to the observatory. Plato dies at the base of the dome, where for him the world really does end at dawn. Stern understood the need to reinforce the cosmic implications that Ray wanted in the story. The script could suggest the messages through action, but it also had to state them directly, through dialogue.

The return to the observatory triggered another idea: maintaining Aristotle's unities of time and place. This was one of the many points Stern had argued in his late-night meetings with Ray. The observatory and its planetarium, Stern believed, would provide a "formal classic" setting for this "tragedy of misunderstanding." This was consistent with the "doomsday" theme that Stern had incorporated into the planetarium show. Plato dies, but on an altar of sacrifice. Stern also decided that the story, apart from the prologue, should take place in a single day. Ray disagreed at first, concerned that the audience might find the picture artificial if so many dramatic events took place in just twenty-four hours. Stern argued that life changed with amazing swiftness for teenagers. He wanted to give the audience "the same sense of urgency" that the teenagers in the film were experiencing.

Stern added more new material to the next scene. Jim has arrived home. He thinks he sees his mother at the top of the stairs, but it is his father, wearing an apron over his business suit. Jim's mother appears. His father apologizes for some offense, then turns to Jim and says, "I tell you, you can't win."

Stern also built on the tension between mother and son that started back at the precinct station: "How was school?" she asks when he returns home from the observatory. His bland response triggers an angry reaction. "You don't need to say anything," she snaps. "I don't need any favors." Later, alone in his room, Jim struggles with his feelings. Like Shulman's character, Stern's Jim Stark feels ignored and uprooted.

The next scene, at Judy's house, parallels the one at Jim's. Here, however, the father is the source of friction. When Judy tries to kiss him, he becomes angry. Her use of lipstick also offends him. When she presses him about his inexplicable coldness toward her, he slaps her.

Following the slapping scene, Stern's script cuts to Jim's house and a new dream sequence. Jim falls asleep in his room and sees a rose tree growing out of the pattern in the carpet. Judy's face appears in one of the blossoms. She says she wants to be with him and asks if his wounds hurt. *She* would never hurt him. In his hands are two stone tablets. They are blank except for a single commandment: "HONOR THY FATHER! YOU CAN'T WIN!" Jim hears his hapless father's familiar advice about women: "Stay out of their way, son, and you won't get hurt." Jim wants Judy to say it isn't so. He hears his mother's voice, and it is *her* face now in the blossom. She laughs and points at Jim, who is now wearing an apron.

Stern's scene, at Ray's request, had evolved from one of Stern's own short stories. However, the idea of a dream sequence in *Rebel* still seemed ridiculous and unworkable to Stern. He would keep arguing with Ray to remove it.

Stern inherited the next scene from Irving Shulman. Jim leaves the house and arrives at Wimpy's. Plato is at a phone booth as a car full of kids pulls up. Their names are Martha, Ginger, Moose and Goon. Buzz has not yet arrived. The car radio blasts and the horn sounds stuck. Goon yells out the waitress's name, Brando-like, over the din: "Stella! Hey, Stel-l-l-a-a!" Moose turns the radio even higher. Buzz arrives looking for Jim as Wimpy, "a middle-aged man with a pot belly," tries to get them all to leave.

Stern kept most of Shulman's dialogue. As in Shulman's version, Stern's teenagers are desperate for "action." And when Jim arrives at Wimpy's, Buzz quickly challenges him to a chickie run on "the bluff." The ideas for the bluff and the chickie run also belonged to Irving Shulman. Stern understood the dramatic importance of Shulman's scene and its connection with Ray's cosmic theme. These teenagers, rather than accept their fate passively and in silence, would confront it head-on.

The location shifts to a high bluff outside of town. As Jim and Buzz inspect the pair of stolen cars that they will race to the edge, Goon passes among the crowd collecting a dollar a head for the "chicken pot." Stern's version of Shulman's scene added a humorous commentary on middle-class teenagers as Goon tries to collect from one of the bystanders: the boy, who has just received his allowance, wants change of a ten.

Stern's pre-race sequence included a scene between Jim and Buzz. As they stand alone at the edge of the bluff, Buzz announces, "I like you. You know?" Jim replies, "What are we doing this for?" Buzz says, "We got to do *something*. Don't we?" It is a poignant moment that will take on a bitter irony when Buzz dies and no one but Jim knows that they could have been friends.

The race follows Shulman's external model, except that it is Buzz, not the boy named Chuck, who goes over the edge to his death (his sleeve catches on the door handle). Stern also developed the aftermath of the race. Judy has been holding the stake money. As the kids flee, she remains at the edge with Jim and Plato. Plato calls to her and she follows them to Jim's car. Plato gets behind the wheel, and Jim hands him the ignition key. Judy looks at Jim as if in a trance, then screams "Chicken!" and waves the stake money angrily in his face. Jim grabs the money from Judy's fist and flings it from the car. Plato starts the engine, but it stalls. Jim, screaming back at Judy, begins to cry. She is already crying. "You have to hurt?" he pleads. "Why do you have to hurt?" Plato restarts the car and they drive away, still in tears...

Stern's version internalized the race. It introduced elements that he felt Shulman's scene lacked, such as the sad irony of the friendship "between two outstanding leaders" that might have been had Buzz not gone over the cliff. Stern used the scene as well to develop the growing relationships among Jim, Judy and Plato. These would be critical to the film's success.

Stern's use of a "flare path" formed by the onlookers' automobile headlights also added a sense of ritual to the run. He and Ray had discussed the ritualistic behavior of gangs and the often tragic consequences of that behavior. Stern's chickie run sequence and its aftermath, he hoped, would demonstrate the tragic folly of gang ritual.

15

CASTING

In early February, Nicholas Ray found his second consultant on teenage gangs: Frank Mazzola. Mazzola belonged to the Athenians, a "club" at Hollywood High School. "He was head of a gang," Ray later observed, "but he lived in a better house than either my producer or myself."

Mazzola was familiar with every aspect of gang behavior, including language, dress and rituals. On February 5, he met with Ray and David Weisbart for two hours to discuss delinquency and review a list of gang expressions. As Ray talked with Mazzola, he considered him for a role in *Rebel*. Although Mazzola had little more acting experience than Jayne Mansfield, he had a look and an attitude that belonged in Ray's picture.

With James Dean in New York and Stewart Stern at work on the script, Ray began to think about the rest of his cast. On February 7, Hedda Hopper's column reported that he was considering a number of actresses for the role of Judy. Aside from Pat Crowley and Margaret O'Brien, however (Carroll Baker had turned down the role), the Publicity Department claimed that Ray was giving serious consideration to only one other actress: Debbie Reynolds. At 23, Reynolds was perhaps too old for the part, but she was versatile and a top box office attraction, especially since her success in the Gene Kelly musical, *Singin' in the Rain*.

Natalie Wood had expressed a keen interest in the role, but Ray saw her more as a type than an actress. He would consider her as Judy's friend, Helen, but not as Judy. Ray's judgment was guided by his attitude toward all child performers after they grew up. He believed that Helen Hayes was the only child star ever to become a great actress. In underestimating Natalie Wood's talent, he also underestimated her shrewdness and tenacity. Wood had been raised in the intensely competitive Hollywood environment and knew well how it operated.

She was also grown-up beyond her years. While projecting the image of the demure, well-bred young lady on screen, she frequently tested the limits of her wholesomeness off screen. Steffi Sidney, who played Mil in *Rebel Without a Cause*, recalled that Wood had been testing those limits as early as age fourteen. One such occasion was a USC party held not far from the Chateau Marmont:

...Everybody was drinking zombies, and Natalie was so loaded she couldn't stand up. I asked one of the guys if he realized she was jail bait—in those days they were very strict about age out here—so he went to find whoever she was with to take her home. By then, Natalie had passed out on a bed near the bar.

Meanwhile, Stern continued to develop the script. By February 8, he had written a grisly scene that was almost certain to arouse the censors' wrath. In it, Buzz's wrecked car burns on the highway at the base of the bluff. An old man and his middle-aged daughter have been watching Buzz's body burn inside the flaming wreck, but now she leads him away. She covers her mouth with a handkerchief. "Crazy, crazy kids," she says, over the noise of a police radio. Ray Framek of the Juvenile Division, the officer who interviewed Judy at the precinct station, is the voice on the police radio, relaying the grim details of Buzz's death to a police dispatcher.

Meanwhile, Jim, Judy and Plato have evaded police roadblocks. Jim drives Judy home, then parks in his own driveway. He and Plato feel numb from the tragedy on the bluff and cannot break the tension that envelops them. Stern's new scene, one of his favorites in the script, allowed for the release of that awful tension through laughter. First, Plato laughs, then Jim. Still reeling from Buzz's death, they begin joking about Plato's mother, who is in Hawaii. When Plato finally begs Jim to stop laughing, Jim answers, "I'm not laughing. I'm crying!"

Plato asks Jim to come home with him. Jim declines, but they agree to meet in the morning. When Jim enters his house, he finds his father and grandmother playing Scrabble. They barely notice him. Jim tries to get the phone number of a "Judy Grannis" from Information. He finally gets through, but Judy's father hangs up on him. Jim wanders outside with a bottle of milk and a "fistful" of bread. Judy puts her radio near her window. She turns the volume up in time to hear a dedication song "from Buzz, who wants to play it for Jim."

Jim has his radio tuned to the same station. He and Judy both hear and understand the message: the gang blames Jim for "killing" Buzz. Meanwhile, Chili-Picker and Goon arrive at Plato's house. They demand to know where Jim is. Plato's nurse chases them away, and Plato goes to his mother's bedroom to get a gun.

In the alley between their houses, Jim and Judy meet. Judy feels cold, and Jim tries to warm her hands. "Everybody's cold," she explains, and they discuss their mutual fears and their loneliness. Judy apologizes for treating Jim badly that morning: "You shouldn't

Natalie Wood's shrewdness, tenacity and delinquent behavior helped to win her the role of Judy.

believe what I say when I'm with the kids. I just act crazy. Nobody says what they mean or anything."

Their conversation turns to matters of sexual intimacy: "Have you ever had…?" Judy begins. She admits that she has, but now she wants to actually fall in love with someone. Plato arrives to warn Jim about the gang. He tells him about "a big mansion near the planetarium" where they can hide. They decide to bring blankets and liquor. Fearing the gang's arrival, Plato tries to speed up the preparations. Jim, still confused and upset, tells Plato, "Don't rush me. I'm walking underwater." They leave for the mansion.

The mansion scene was the result of Ray's recent visit to the J. Paul Getty property at Crenshaw and Wilshire Boulevard in Los Angeles. The building had provided the location for Billy Wilder's *Sunset Boulevard* in 1950. In Ray's initial thinking, it was simply the place where the three teens would meet after the alley scene and before the climax at the observatory; but as Stern later recalled:

> …Then he had a notion that they would play games there and that there could be a wonderful kind of crazy Walpurgus Night celebration, that maybe Jimmy would pretend that he was a real estate man. So that seemed very exciting to me.

Stern had no objections to this kind of "fantasy" sequence. He saw *Rebel* as a kind of *Peter Pan* story, where the teenagers escaped their unresponsive parents to form their own make-believe family. Although Stern's and Ray's reasons for creating such a sequence differed, Stern believed they were compatible:

> He wanted a rest — a flute interlude in the middle of the tympanis before the whole thing crashed down — a chance for Judy, Jim and Plato to be together in the edgy, somewhat hysterical aftermath of the death of Buzz. Their own homes didn't support them — they had to make their own. I used Peter Pan and the lost boys and Wendy as my image — Peter as the "pretend father," Wendy as the "pretend mother" in the underground house while the pirates hunted for them above. It seemed a perfect place for the love affair between Jim and Judy, the emotional "betrayal" of Plato that sent him over the edge with abandonment and jealousy.

Stern wrote out the entire mansion sequence on a yellow pad in David Weisbart's outer office one afternoon on his lunch hour, fleshing out Ray's "Walpurgus Night" idea with details of his own.

After Jim and Judy have fled to the deserted mansion, Chili-Picker, Moose and Goon arrive at Jim's house. They nail a dead chicken to his front door, briefly terrorize his parents, and drive off in search of him.

At the mansion, Plato pretends to be the real estate agent showing the property to "newlyweds" Jim and Judy. They discover an empty swimming pool on the grounds. Pretending that he is a psychiatrist with a heavy foreign accent, Plato analyzes Jim on the diving board. Later, Plato explains that he once had to go to a "head shrinker." Then his mother decided it was too expensive, "so she went to Hawaii instead." When Plato appears to fall asleep, they cover him with a blanket. Jim lights a candle and they go off to explore the empty mansion. But Plato is not asleep. He thinks that Jim and Judy are abandoning him, just like his real parents. He sees the liquor, reaches for it and takes a drink. The empty pool echoes the sounds of his weeping.

In a library room at the mansion, Jim and Judy are falling in love. They kiss passionately, and Jim blows out the candle. Meanwhile, the three gang members have spotted Jim's car outside the mansion. The police, in turn, have been tailing them. As the gang enters the mansion, the police call for back-up units.

Plato has finally fallen asleep. As he wakes up, Chili-Picker stands over him, holding a switchblade. Goon and Moose laugh, and Chili-Picker says, "Good morning." Plato runs to the empty swimming pool. They surround him, but he breaks away and hides under a piano inside the mansion. He hears Jim and Judy talking behind the door to the library. He accuses them of deserting him, reveals their hiding place to the gang, then runs outside, where he shoots at the police with the gun he took from his mother's room. One officer holds Jim and the others while the second chases Plato toward the observatory. Plato breaks in by diving through the glass door.

Two more patrol cars arrive. Ray Framek and Jim's parents sit in one of them. Plato's nurse arrives on foot. Jim begs Ray Framek to let him get Plato out before he gets hurt. Framek allows Jim to go in alone. Plato hides inside the darkened planetarium theater, under the dome. When Jim enters, he finds Plato frightened and contemplating his own death. He asks Jim once again if the end of the world will come at night, and Jim says, prophetically this time, "No, at dawn." Jim offers to trade his jacket for Plato's gun, but Plato has already drifted into a final fantasy. "No," he says, "I need it. It's my new gun that my Daddy gave me."

When Plato finally agrees to surrender the gun for just a moment, Jim secretly removes the bullets and returns the gun to Plato. He convinces Plato to follow him outside. They emerge at the first light of dawn. The police cars frighten Plato, and he bolts for the roof. An officer fires a shot as Jim follows Plato to the base of the dome. Jim convinces Plato finally to give up the gun, but as Plato is about to toss it down, a policeman shoots and kills him. Plato "drops like a stone and plummets down the dome to Jim's feet." When Ray Framek reaches the roof, he sees Jim sobbing and rocking Plato's body back and forth. Ray wants Jim to move away from Plato. Jim refuses, and when Ray tells Jim that his father has arrived, Jim cries, "Tell him to go to hell." When his father touches him, Jim screams, "Get your damn hands off me!" and strikes him repeatedly in the face before collapsing into his arms. Judy, crying in the midst of the crowd, sees her own father approach. He puts his arm around her. Plato's nurse cries out, "Lord, Lord, Lord. Why you give us a day without children[?]" Jim zips up Plato's jacket and observes, "He was always cold."

16

MR. WARNER

Soon after Stern submitted his script to the studio, Jack Warner received a copy. If Warner liked Stern's version of *Rebel Without a Cause*, he might have second thoughts about Jayne Mansfield, the exploitation angle, and the picture's small budget. If he disliked it, Nicholas Ray might soon be knocking on the doors of other studios.

Warner had mixed feelings about Stern's work. He liked the title sequence, but he did not understand where the sound of the children's choir was coming from when Jim and his parents leave the precinct station. He wondered about Buzz's peroxide hair, found some "unnecessary footage" at Wimpy's, and crossed out the woman's use of a handkerchief as she watches Buzz burn inside his car. He did, however, enjoy the love scene in the alley.

Warner did not react well to the themes that Ray and Stern believed were significant. He failed to understand the point of the mansion sequence and questioned its purpose in the film, especially the mock psychiatric scene at the pool. He also questioned the mock real estate scene and the cruising scene with Chili-Picker, Moose, and Goon, wondering if such scenes were "SOP" (standard operating procedure) for pictures about teenage rebels. He even wondered why the pool "echoes [Plato's] weeping" after Jim and Judy seem to abandon him. Since he could see no purpose for the mansion scene, Warner also questioned the need for a mansion location. He had not discussed that yet with Ray, but renting another location (the first being the Griffith Observatory) would cost the studio money.

Warner also considered the wrath of the censors. He marked several passages that referred to Plato's gun and circled a few "offensive" words. Jim's lines, "Tell him to go to hell" and "Get your damn hands off me," would have to be cut.

Among Warner's more cryptic remarks was his evaluation of a line in the script where Plato's nurse says, "Lord, Lord, Lord. Why you give us a day without children?" Warner circled the words NEGRO WOMAN in the script and wrote, "message white woman," meaning that he wanted a white woman to say those lines. Warner's lifelong racial intolerance, which he made little attempt to conceal, may explain the statement. According to one source, Warner once removed a scene of two black people kissing from one of his features, then had the piece of film destroyed.

His reason: "It's like watching two animals." On another occasion, Warner backed out of a project he had originally supported (a film of James Gould Cozzens' novel, *Guard of Honor*) when he discovered that the main character was black.

At noon on February 10, Ray met with Frank Mazzola. They spent the afternoon "setting up fight plans." That evening, they attended a club meeting and observed an actual fight. For the next ten days, Mazzola met regularly with Ray and Stewart Stern either at the studio or at the Chateau Marmont.

Ray was willing to take chances to get accurate information on gang behavior, and his nighttime encounters with gangs were not without dangers. He often wore a hidden microphone to record their voices. If they discovered the device, they might tag Ray as a police informant *posing* as a movie director. On one occasion, rowdy gang members even trashed Ray's bungalow.

On February 11, the studio announced Malcolm Bert as the Art Director for *Rebel Without a Cause*. The choice of Bert, who had designed the sets for *A Star Is Born* and *East of Eden*, suggested that Ray's project was finally gaining some respect in the Warner Bros. front office. Perhaps Jack Warner did admire the picture's concept after all.

At the same time, Stern was writing a "Revised Estimating Script" for *Rebel*. The script had numbered scenes. The studio would use this script to estimate budget and scheduling to determine the physical and financial limits of the production: the approximate running time, the number of locations and scenes, how many "extras" the picture would require, and so on. Once adjusted and polished, it would become the final shooting script.

On February 14, Valentine's Day, James Dean and Dennis Stock arrived in Fairmount, Indiana, after spending two weeks in New York. Dean had been raised in Fairmount by Ortense and Marcus Winslow, his aunt and uncle. For the next few days, Stock photographed the local hero's return to his hometown. Dean sat in the Winslows' kitchen, played his bongo drums among the livestock, walked the familiar streets, and attended the "Sweetheart Ball" at his old high school. While he enjoyed the hometown attention, Dean's own attention stayed fixed on the New York premiere of *East of Eden*, only three weeks away. His future in films rested with the critics and the movie

Jack L. Warner (shown here with Rosanna Podesta) was not altogether happy with Stewart Stern's script.

public. If he felt any foreboding about the premiere, he did not reveal it publicly in Fairmount. Soon, he would return to New York.

Despite Jack Warner's misgivings about the mansion sequence, the studio's Location Department was still trying to rent a mansion for *Rebel Without a Cause*. On February 16, W. F. Fitzgerald of that department sent a memo to William L. Guthrie regarding a "mid Victorian" structure on the MGM lot. It had most recently appeared in *The Bad and the Beautiful*. Fitzgerald would visit MGM, observe the structure, and report back with a rental estimate and a time frame. The Location Department was still considering the abandoned Getty mansion at the corner of Crenshaw and Wilshire. Getty, who lived in England, had not yet given the studio permission to use the property.

Fitzgerald continued his search the next day. In the morning, he visited 20th Century-Fox, which had a Colonial house. A small swimming pool "not tied up with this set" was also available. Later, he visited the Columbia Pictures ranch, Universal Studios, RKO, Paramount and United Artists. None of those places, he reported, had a suitable structure.

Meanwhile, Nicholas Ray's research took him to San Francisco, where he encountered an unusual gang hangout and attended a meeting. The large house was in an exclusive section of the city. Ray saw two new Cadillacs parked in the driveway. The owners, who were the parents of one of the gang members, were vacationing in Miami Beach.

According to the studio's publicity release, the gang members arrived inconspicuously in twos and threes, dressed in blue jeans and black motorcycle jackets. That night they planned to attack another gang. At the end of the meeting, the boys joined hands, said a short prayer, then stuffed their pockets with various weapons and went out to beat "holy hell" out of their rivals.

17

FREE-FOR-ALL

Shortly after returning to Los Angeles, Ray conducted open auditions for *Rebel* at the studio. Whatever doubts Warner Bros. might have about the picture, there was no lack of enthusiasm among the hundreds of young actors who came to try out. Most would be happy to get minor roles as hoodlums in Buzz's gang, but some faces stood out from the crowd.

One of those faces was Sal Mineo's. Ray pulled him out of a line of "tough guy" types because he looked like Ray's own son, Tony, "only prettier." At 16, Mineo already had Broadway experience (*The Rose Tattoo*, *The King and I*), but he had made only one film, *Six Rivers to Cross*. He, too, belonged to a gang (in the Bronx, New York), and he had the appropriate credentials: at the age of eight, he had been expelled from a parochial school as a troublemaker.

Ray asked Mineo what work he had done recently, then called over Corey Allen, whom he was considering for the role of Buzz. Ray improvised a scene between the two and decided to consider Mineo for the role of Plato.

Corey Allen, 21, was a native of Ohio and a recent graduate of UCLA, where he had majored in drama. Ray had seen him in *The Pick Up Girl*, a local stage play. Allen had played minor film roles in *The Mad Magician* and *Night of the Hunter*, and he had extensive experience in local theater. He resembled a young Marlon Brando.

Although Ray was looking for "toughness" in this mass audition, he was also looking for spirit and an attitude. He devised a somewhat unorthodox method of testing those qualities. At the Warner Bros. studio, near a side entrance on Hollywood Way, a series of platforms and risers occupied the space between two parking lots. Ray asked the several hundred actors to run to the top of the structure and back down again. Next, he staged a "king of the mountain" free-for-all on the risers. According to a studio press release, Ray's mock fight became so violent that "several of the youths suffered cuts and abrasions." The cameraman supposedly muttered that even stuntmen wouldn't take such chances.

The survivors of that "mass improvisation" participated in still another. Ray instructed Frank Mazzola to play a "bad guy" who would try to take a ball away from one of the other boys. They would fight over the ball, and the rest of the boys would pile on. When it was all over, Corey Allen and Frank Mazzola found themselves at

Sal Mineo (shown here with cap in a scene from *Six Bridges to Cross*) stood out among the tough-guy types at Nicholas Ray's open audition.

the bottom of the pile. They had not necessarily won the contest, but they had impressed Ray.

Ray's quiet, persistent search for "Judy" continued amid the mayhem. He asked each applicant pointed and personal questions, such as, "How do you get along with your mother?" He was looking for rebelliousness, even delinquent behavior in these young actresses. Such qualities would be assets in portraying Judy. Margaret O'Brien, an early favorite for the part, apparently lost her chance when she admitted liking teachers and other adults. Natalie Wood, however, made a conscious attempt to look and behave like a "bad" girl. As she left her interview with Ray, he watched her meet a young man "with a fresh scar on his face." Ray decided to give Wood a second look. Perhaps his blanket assessment of child stars had been premature.

Wood matched her persistence with audacious behavior. One evening not long after Ray's meeting with her, he received a call from Dennis Hopper. Hopper told Ray that he, Wood, and her friend, Faye Nuell, were at a police station. They had been in an automobile accident, and they had also been drinking. Wood had suffered a possible concussion. Ray told Hopper to contact Wood's parents, but Hopper said that she did not want to see them. She wanted Ray to come instead. Ray telephoned his own physician, called Wood's parents, and drove to the police station. When he arrived, he found Wood lying on a stretcher. She still refused to see her parents, but she agreed to talk to Ray. As he approached, she grabbed his arm and pointed to the precinct doctor. Then she pulled him close and whispered, "You see that son of a bitch? Well, he called me a juvenile delinquent. Now do I get the part?"

As a result of his recent mass auditions, Nicholas Ray now had a "short list" of the actors and actresses he would test individually. Solly Baiano of the Casting Department made a schedule for the following Monday, February 21. The same day, Warner Bros. finally received permission to use the J. Paul Getty mansion at Crenshaw and Wilshire. Mr. Getty's secretary informed W. F. Fitzgerald that the studio was to pay $200 per day, with a $500 minimum. The studio was to list the scenes Ray would film at the location and sign a letter of responsibility to cover any possible damage.

At the studio, Ray planned a series of sound and photographic tests. The results would determine most of *Rebel's* cast. Ernest Haller, a cinematographer with forty years of experience and an Academy Award (*Gone with the Wind*), would film the tests in black-and-white CinemaScope. The actors would perform various scenes and Ray would view the results later in a screening room.

The first day's tests began at nine in the morning and ran almost until noon. With James Dean still in New York, Dennis Hopper took his place as Jim. John Carlyle and Peter Miller also tested for the role. The studio routinely tried other actors for a role already assigned, if only to sample their range. If, for any reason, Dean could not assume the role of Jim, the tested actors would provide a quick replacement pool. That morning, Chris Randell, John Saxon and Corey Allen tested as Buzz. Nancy

Billy Gray, popular teen star of television's *Father Knows Best,* was the front runner for the role of Plato.

Baker, Lorrie Stein, Susan Whitney, Gloria Castillo and Natalie Wood tested as Judy. Later that morning, Ray also tested Pat Crowley (Ray's early favorite) and Kathryn Grant. Grant, 21, had appeared in *Arrowhead* (1953), *Rear Window* (1954) and *Forever Female* (1954). Within two years, she would give up her acting career to become Mrs. Bing Crosby.

Those not tested for any specific role, the "general group" that made up the gang, included Frank Mazzola and his brother Tony, Tom Bernard, Jack Grinnage and Nick Adams. Adams was 22 years old. In 1950, he had hitchhiked to Los Angeles from his home in Nanticoke, Pennsylvania. He met James Dean that year when they both found work in a Pepsi-Cola commercial. Unsuccessful at finding acting jobs, Adams then enlisted in the Coast Guard. While in the service, he won a small role in the film *Mister Roberts.*

Jack Grinnage, also 22, was a veteran of Korea, where he had served with the

First Marine Division. After his discharge, Grinnage majored in dramatics at Los Angeles City College. He appeared in two pictures, *Lady Godiva of Coventry* and *Interrupted Melody*. Tom Bernard had appeared in a television series, *The Ruggles*, which ran from 1949 to 1952.

The tests continued the next day, February 22. Billy Gray, 17, the popular television star from *Father Knows Best*, tried for the role of Plato. Hopper, Carlyle, Saxon, Natalie Wood and Nick Adams all tested again. Jayne Mansfield tested as Judy. Convinced that Mansfield's test was "an aberration of the casting department," Ray refused to take it seriously. Later, he insisted that he had tested Mansfield in front of an unloaded camera.

On February 23, the tests concluded. Jayne Mansfield tested again as Judy, along with Natalie Wood and Kathryn Grant. John Saxon tested a third time as Buzz, and Hopper and Carlyle tried once more as Jim. Tony Mazzola, Frank's brother, also tested. Ray was considering both of them for small roles. Frank continued as a gang consultant.

That same day, Dr. Douglas M. Kelley, the film's other gang consultant, sent Ray a letter and a "rough round of preliminary notes" on Stewart Stern's first draft. Kelley reacted favorably and made only minor objections: the Juvenile Officers' interviewing procedures were somewhat unrealistic, and some of the officers' terminology sounded false. Kelley also believed that Jim convinced Plato too easily to come out of the planetarium at the end, although he admitted that more realistic psychiatry "might slow down the action."

18

LOCATIONS

Now that Ray had secured locations for *Rebel*'s observatory and mansion scenes, he began to search greater Los Angeles for other exteriors. He took with him David Weisbart, set designer Mal(colm) Bert, and W. F. Fitzgerald from the Location Department. Shooting at the studio and on its back lot would be more cost-effective, but Ray believed that the picture would have a better look if he filmed on location.

On February 25, Don Page, one of two Assistant Directors assigned to *Rebel* (the other was Robert Farfan), sent a memo to the film's Unit Manager, Eric Stacey. Ray, Weisbart, Bert and Fitzgerald had found a number of good locations, and they asked Stacey to secure as many as possible.

The locations included the Serve-Yourself Gas Station at Slauson and Overhill (where Jim asks the gang for directions) and Clock's, a drive-in restaurant at Sepulveda and Venice boulevards (doubling as Wimpy's). For Jim's and Judy's back yards, they selected the property at 6122 Citrus Avenue, about ten miles from the studio. Jim would live at 3180 Oakshire, Ventura Boulevard Hills, near the studio. The exterior for Juvenile Hall would be the Hollywood Police Station or the Georgia Street Jail. Ray would film the chickie run at the Warner Bros. Ranch in Calabasas, about twenty miles northwest of Los Angeles.

On February 26, Ray forwarded Dr. Kelley's preliminary notes to David Weisbart. Ray reported that Kelley had approved of the story and had been "moved" by it. Ray included further suggestions made by Kelley during a recent phone conversation. Kelley's suggestions included building up the grandmother's role and giving her "bits of business," such as turning her back whenever her daughter-in-law speaks to her. Like Jack Warner, Kelley also suggested eliminating the mock psychiatric scene from the mansion sequence.

That same day, Stern completed the 126-page Revised Estimating Script for *Rebel*. Once again, he made important changes. In the precinct station sequence, he removed Jim's "silent" lines and gave Ray Framek a more active role in the argument about Jim's drinking. At the height of that argument, Jim now shouts, "You're tearing me apart!" at his parents, and he and Ray Framek exit to a corridor. Jim tells Ray to "get lost," then throws a punch which Ray easily blocks. Ray drops Jim to the floor and quickly gains his respect. After a heart-to-heart talk, Jim promises Ray that if the "pot starts boiling again," he will seek Ray's advice.

Stern also made name and character changes in the Revised Estimating Script. "Chili-Picker" became "Crunch," "Mil" was a new female gang member, and "Cookie" replaced "Sweet William." Stern also added a tender moment between Judy and her father just before the slapping scene. Judy stands in the back yard looking up at the moon as her father appears and starts to sing a children's song, "Man in the Moon." She can't believe that he knows it. He, too, learned it in school.

Stern continued to struggle with Ray's request for a fantasy scene. Although he had eliminated the rose tree dream, he had not yet replaced it. The words "Scene 113A — JIM'S DREAM —" were all that remained. To fill the void, Stern decided to expand Jim's conversation with his father before the chickie run. Jim seeks his father's advice, but he finds the usual weakness and indecision.

Stern also eliminated much of the teen banter when the gang meets at Wimpy's before the chickie run. Stern added a brief conversation between Judy and Plato. She sits in the front seat of Buzz's car, and Plato is in a phone booth. Since they are talking about Jim, Judy must be careful not to let Buzz, who is nearby, overhear them.

Stern changed the chickie run scene by eliminating Judy's screaming and crying at the end. The new ending to the sequence, though less dramatic, was more poignant. Judy stands at the edge of the bluff, looking down at Buzz in his burning car. Jim moves toward Judy and silently offers his hand. After a moment, she takes it and he leads her away from the edge.

Stern kept the scene on the highway where Buzz's car burns, but, perhaps because of Jack Warner's objections, removed the two onlookers. Jim and Plato still laugh to break the tension after Buzz's death, but Stern shortened the scene. Plato asks Jim to come home with him; Jim declines. Stern also replaced the "Scrabble" scene, in which Jim's father and grandmother ignore him. Instead, Jim and his parents have a confrontation in the parents' bedroom. Jim sits on the bed next to his father, then starts pacing the room. Jim explains that he was involved in Buzz's death, his mother lashes out at him and his hapless father tries to mediate. When Jim finishes explaining, his mother exclaims, "Good lord!" Jim wants to go to the police, but his parents are both against the idea. Jim thinks that admitting his role in the chickie run is the only way he can beat "going around with my head in a sling."

Jim also thinks of Buzz's parents, and suggests a visit to their house. "Maybe there's something we can do," he says. His father agrees, but he is still against Jim's telling the police what happened. They hear the sound of a police siren in the distance and Jim runs out. Jim's father looks at his wife and says, "We missed, Katherine. We missed on him. Let him try to make it right."

Outside the precinct station, Jim runs into Crunch and Moose on his way to see Ray Framek. Crunch asks, "This place appeal to you or something?" Crunch decides that Jim is about to "fuzz" on them. "We're going to bring him down," he tells Moose. Inside, Jim finds a "BALD [social] WORKER" who tells him that Ray has left the station.

After Crunch, Moose and Goon visit Jim's house, Jim's and Judy's fathers meet in the alley. Both are looking for their missing children. Stern introduced a split-screen montage in which the various adults contact Ray Framek on the telephone.

He also changed part of the mansion sequence: when Crunch, Moose, and Goon pursue Plato at the mansion, Plato no longer reveals Jim's location. Instead, he yells at Jim, "Get away from me!" and runs outside. When Plato confronts one of the officers, he drifts dangerously into another fantasy. As the officer approaches, Plato imagines him to be his naval officer father, the man who abandoned him.

In this new draft, the police do not detain Jim and the others. Instead, Jim follows Plato and the pursuing officer into the woods that separate the mansion from the observatory. In an exchange of gunfire, an officer shoots Jim, but Jim continues. Judy catches up and insists that they go back. She says that Plato is beyond their help. Jim disagrees and leaves her behind. At the observatory, Jim follows Plato inside. Ray Framek follows with his gun drawn. He takes cover behind the pendulum pit and tries to talk Jim out of the shadows. Jim refuses to desert Plato. When Ray tells Jim that the police will "take care" of Plato, Jim answers, "Yeah, and he'll take care of them, too." Jim reminds Ray that Plato has become Jim's responsibility. Plato is scared, he says, and what Plato doesn't need "is a lot of heroes like you shooting him up."

As in the earlier draft, Ray lets Jim go in after Plato, and the police shoot Plato on the dome just as he is about to give Jim his gun. Jim observes sadly that Plato "was always cold." Stern's final shot was a "HIGH GENERAL SHOT" of the observatory. As the ambulance drives away, the lecturer from the earlier scene arrives for another day at work.

19

MR. WARNER RETURNS

Jack Warner had read the latest version of Stern's script. He made his observations, as before, on the cover and in the margins: James Dean headed his list to play Jim Stark, but Tab Hunter might also be acceptable if the price was right. Hunter was already a major star at the studio. He had won his starring role in the studio's *Battle Cry* after besting Dean in a screen test. Warner also suggested Lois Smith as Judy. Smith, 25, a graduate of the Actors Studio, had played Ann, the nervous bar maid in *East of Eden*.

Warner still did not entirely approve of Stern's script. He repeated his earlier complaints and added some new ones. Stern had included the stomping of the Christmas shopper as part of the title sequence. Warner objected to this because it would be difficult to see the action "behind and thru [the] titles." He also feared that the censors would object to a fifteen-year-old boy, Plato, as a delinquent. Warner wanted to know why Judy's father slaps her. He wanted to know how Stern would replace the deleted dream scene. Its absence left a gap in the story. He still found the mock real estate scene inappropriate, asking again if it was routine. The teenagers' carefree behavior seemed "too cute" at this stage of the film. The only scene he seemed to like was Jim's and Judy's romantic moment at the mansion. He wrote "Good sex" in the margin.

His questions about the rest of the mansion sequence stressed economy of means: couldn't Ray use a studio sound stage for the mansion interiors? Nicholas Ray, the rebel artist, wanted realism; Warner Bros., the going concern, wanted to minimize expensive location shooting.

As part of his critique, Warner offered suggestions for improving Stern's script. In the scene where Plato imagines that the police officer is his father, Warner suggested a dissolve from the policeman's uniform to the father's naval uniform. He also suggested eliminating Jim's gunshot wound. How could Jim continue his strenuous activity with a bullet in him? Stern had described Jim as "bolt[ing]" and "running hard" for the observatory entrance after being shot. Warner also objected to Jim's remark that Plato didn't need "heroes" like Ray "shooting him up." That would not sit well with police authorities. The constant repetition of characters' names in the dialogue also annoyed him. Eliminate these references now, Warner argued, so they would not have to be cut or "painted out" later.

Finally, he objected to the reappearance of the planetarium lecturer at the end of the picture, and he found "dangerous symbolism" in Stern's description of the lecturer's arrival: Stern's lecturer holds his briefcase under his arm and quietly disappears inside the building, "where the world ends, safely, every day at two."

By March 1, Ray had evaluated the sound and photographic tests. He was not pleased with the results. In a memo to David Weisbart, he complained that although the black-and-white CinemaScope was "effective and exciting," it fell short of "the maximum." The studio, however, still wanted to film *Rebel* in black and white. Ray suggested discussing the issue further with Eric Stacey, who would pass Ray's suggestion to the front office.

One of the scenes Ray tested in black and white was the mock psychiatric scene. Ray had already discussed it with Stern and Dr. Kelley. After seeing it on film, Ray agreed to eliminate it. Another test scene took place in the alley between Jim's and Judy's houses. It presented one of the film's most tender moments, but it still contained some potentially controversial dialogue, such as Judy's admission that she has had sexual experience. Ray wanted to retain most of the scene and do the minimum re-writing to keep the censors from excising it.

In the memo to Weisbart, Ray argued that the brief exchange was a way for Judy to "cleanse herself" of her past while she prepares for her relationship with Jim. When Judy offers Jim a reason to back out, Ray explained, "she is trying to hurt before she gets hurt." Then, when Jim accepts her, she becomes "as pure and innocent as Juliet."

The censors would probably not appreciate the analogy, nor the dramatic subtleties of the exchange. They would see only two teenagers' admissions of sexual activity. Steve Trilling added one of his own objections to the love scene that Warner had labeled "Good Sex." Trilling saw the possibility of "vulgarity" in the scene. While Ray agreed in principle, he suggested that the audience's need to see Jim and Judy "have their moment together" was more important than whether the audience believed the teens were about to become intimate.

20

MAJORS AND MINORS

Despite Ray's frustrating battles with the front office, he was still making progress with his actors. One in particular. In his March 1 memo to Weisbart, he explained that of all the actresses he had tested for the role of Judy, only Natalie Wood had stood out. Ray added that, although all the girls tested had played "Judy" scenes, he had only given four or five serious thought. The others were testing only for parts that would "fill out the ensemble." Ray suggested to Weisbart that Warner Bros. "might develop a star of its own" with Wood. He volunteered to coach her "on voice, wardrobe, hair, etc."

While Ray championed Natalie Wood, another young studio actress kept getting write-in votes. According to the Publicity Department, Ray had received more than 400 hundred letters from Lori Nelson fan clubs around the country. Nelson had appeared in such films as *Bend of the River* (1952), *All I Desire* (1953), and *Destry* (1954). Ray answered the letters, standing by his choice of Wood.

Despite his positive reaction to Sal Mineo during the open auditions, Ray had still not decided who would play Plato. Ray did not even discuss Mineo in the Weisbart memo. He still saw Billy Gray of *Father Knows Best* and Jeff Silver as "the best candidates." Dennis Hopper might even get the part if he later tested successfully with James Dean (Dean had been out of town during the auditions). Corey Allen, Nick Adams, Jack Grinnage, Tony and Frank Mazzola, Ben Gary, Doyle Baker, Butch Cavell, Jerry Olken, Ken Miller, Bruce Barton and Peter Miller all remained under consideration for gang roles.

Ray's list of young actresses included Steffi Sidney (the daughter of columnist Sidney Skolsky), Norma Jean Nelson, Nancy Baker, Mylee Anderson and Georgette Mitchell. He planned to use most of them as waitresses at Wimpy's Drive-In. Jayne Mansfield would also play a waitress, if she got any part at all. For the role of Judy's friend, Helen, Ray was considering Beverly Long, who had nearly missed the auditions. Her friend, Jack Grinnage, had telephoned her at the last minute. Long, 21, was no stranger to close calls. According to a Warner Bros. publicity release, she and her mother had been in the Philippines the day the Japanese attacked Pearl Harbor. Three days later, as they were driving to get on a ship to the United States, their car broke down. An Army private picked them up and delivered them to the dock just as the ship's crew was hauling up the gangway. On the voyage home, the ship narrowly avoided a torpedo.

Long was a graduate of Los Angeles State College, where she had majored in drama. Her first important part came in the play, *Susan Slept Here*. She had been a regular on Charles Ruggles' television show for two years.

Gloria Castillo's name had also been mentioned in Ray's inter-office discussions with Weisbart. Ray had great respect for her ability after seeing her performance in *Night of the Hunter*. He predicted future success for her in character roles, but he added, "I don't think her figure allows for much beyond character at this time."

Castillo, like Natalie Wood and Sal Mineo, was under 18. While it made perfect sense to cast teenagers as teenagers, the Warner Bros. front office had other considerations. In a memo to Solly Baiano, Eric Stacey had insisted that no actors assigned to *Rebel Without a Cause* were to be under 18 years of age. Stacey reminded Baiano that minors could not work at night except under special conditions, and then only until 10:00 P.M. Since about 80 percent of *Rebel Without a Cause* would take place at night, the use of minors would cause serious scheduling problems. To make sure that everyone heeded the directive, Stacey sent copies to seven other concerned parties, including Ray and Weisbart.

Ray's attention turned to the actors who would play *Rebel*'s adults. For the role of Jim's father, he was considering eighteen different actors. They included Walter Matthau, Rod Cameron, Raymond Burr, Hume Cronyn, Royal Dano and John Dehner. The list did not include Jim Backus. For the role of Jim's mother, Ray's list included half a dozen excellent actresses, including Mae Clark, Sylvia Sidney, Peggy Converse, Ann Doran and Marsha Hunt. Also among the hopefuls was Natalie Schaefer, who would play Jim Backus's wife ten years later on the popular television comedy, *Gilligan's Island*.

Ray was considering more than twenty candidates for the role of Judy's father. They included Everett Sloane, Warner Anderson, Leif Erickson, Edward Binns, Richard Denning, Carleton Young and William Hopper. Hugh Beaumont, the future father of *Leave It to Beaver*, closed out the list. The candidates for Judy's mother included Jeanette Nolan, Ann Dvorak, Ruth Hussey, Maureen Stapleton, Martha Scott, Evelyn Keyes, Jim Backus's wife Henny, Rochelle Hudson and (again) Marsha Hunt. Ray had not ruled out Barbara Billingsley, the future television mother of Beaver Cleaver. He was looking at the same actresses for the role of Plato's "pleasure-seeking" mother.

Ray continued casting for another role that would not survive much longer in Stern's script: Wimpy, the owner of the drive-in. The candidates included some of the best character actors in Hollywood: Ed Begley, Elisha Cook, Jr., Jesse White and Walter Sande. The role of Ray Framek, the Juvenile Officer, remained unfilled. The candidates included a number of "police" types, including Lyle Bettger, James Daly and Edward Platt. Ray also considered Chuck Connors, the future Lucas McCain of *The Rifleman*, George Reeves, television's hopelessly typecast *Superman* and Russell Johnson, who would later surface on *Gilligan's Island*.

21

THE EXCITEMENT GATHERS

By early March, the gossip columnists were showing an interest in *Rebel Without a Cause*. Louella Parsons reported that the studio had tested Edward G. Robinson, Jr., for a role in the film, probably as a courtesy to his famous father, who was filming *Illegal* on another sound stage. Parsons also reported a typically absurd Hollywood rumor: Nicholas Ray and Jayne Mansfield had been dating and were possibly "becoming steady."

More likely, Ray spent his time searching for a cinematographer. The Director of Photography, as he was called officially, often meant as much to a film's success as its director or screenwriter. Ray had been hoping for Franz Planer, whose fluid camera style (*Letter to an Unknown Woman*, *One Touch of Venus*) Ray admired. Planer had also filmed a recent *General Electric Theater* presentation of "High Green Wall," which Ray had directed. When Ray learned that Weisbart had failed to sign Planer (who had just been signed by 20th Century Fox), he sent a testy memo on March 3. Weisbart's equally testy reply argued that he (and the studio) had done "everything possible" to get Planer for *Rebel Without a Cause*. Weisbart explained that he had failed only because he could not give Planer a definite starting date for Ray's film.

In a follow-up memo, Ray suggested Lee Garmes if they could not get Planer. Garmes had worked mostly with black-and-white (*Nightmare Alley*, *Detective Story*), but he also understood color. He had photographed (uncredited) the first third of *Gone with the Wind*. Garmes and Nicholas Ray had worked together before on *The Lusty Men* and *Roseanna McCoy*.

The same day, the studio heard once again from Irving Shulman through his attorney, Louis Naiditch. Naiditch confirmed Shulman's position that he had never heard of Nicholas Ray's story, "The Blind Run," and therefore could not base his novelization on it. Naiditch asked that all such references be stricken from the contract. Four days later, R. J. Obringer of the Legal Department sent copies of the revised contract to Naiditch.

Meanwhile, James Dean was preparing to leave New York before the gala premiere of *East of Eden*, only four days away. Even Jane Deacy's last-minute appeal had not convinced him to stay. Dean hated the pretense and formality of such occasions, and he did not want to be present if the audience disliked his performance. He had never taken criticism well. Before flying back to Los Angeles, Dean granted his first in-depth interview, to Howard Thompson of *The New York Times*.

At the studio, Stewart Stern continued to fine-tune his script. He added new dialogue to the precinct scene and altered some existing lines. Jim now greets his family with a mocking, "Merry Christmas." Judy says of her father, "He hates me." Instead of calling her "a sexual delinquent," he now calls her "a dirty tramp." Stern also added a breakfast scene on the morning of Jim's first day at school. While Jim's mother and grandmother bicker, his father encourages him to "Knock 'em dead" and warns him about choosing the wrong friends: "Don't let them choose you."

Stern had moved two scenes: the gang gives Jim wrong directions on his way to the observatory instead of on the way to school; some of Judy's dialogue at the service station shifts to a school corridor. There, she huddles with Buzz, who has had a close call with the police. "I'm glad they let you out," she says.

Stern added another new scene at school. Jim, still asking directions, talks to a hall monitor who seems more interested in basketball tryouts. Finally, he tells Jim to see Mr. Bassett in Room 203. Stern left the planetarium scene intact, but in the next scene, where Jim and Plato try to evade the gang, Plato points to an old deserted mansion nearby. Stern had not yet replaced the "rose tree" fantasy. Jim simply lies in bed trying to decide about the chickie run. In Jim's return to the precinct station, Stern replaced the "Bald Worker" with a less sympathetic desk sergeant who is trying to book a young hoodlum named Wojtowicz. In the alley scene, Jim tells Judy about the deserted mansion without Plato present. Stern used the opportunity to develop the teenagers' need for mutual trust. At the end of the scene, Judy borrows Jim's line from an earlier draft to describe her state of mind: "I feel like I'm walking underwater."

Before the split-screen montage of the parents telephoning police, Stern inserted a scene in which Plato arrives at Jim's house after Jim and Judy have gone. He runs, literally, into Jim's father. When Plato realizes where Jim and Judy have gone, he makes a hasty exit. With Plato's need to warn Jim, Stern now had a new opening for the mansion sequence. Jim and Judy climb in through a window, followed closely by an out-of-breath Plato, who informs them that the gang is out to kill Jim: "Crunch and Goon and everybody."

Stern had also developed the love scene in the mansion's library. In his earlier draft, Judy was not yet sure about Jim. Now that Judy has learned in the alley scene to trust Jim, she is free to give herself without hesitation. "I love somebody," she explains in a moment of romantic epiphany. "All this time I've been looking for someone to love me, and now I love somebody."

In the violent scene that follows this quiet interlude, Plato shoots Crunch and then runs outside.

Stern's next major change involved the climax at the observatory. In the new draft, Jim's father, not Ray Framek, tries to stop Jim from entering. He cannot understand why Jim would risk his own life for Plato. Judy arrives as Jim's father tells him, "I love you." Ray Framek suddenly arrives. He won't let Jim go in after Plato. To win back his son's respect, Jim's father stops Ray from pursuing Jim into the planetarium. Ray tells the father, "You're out of your mind," to which the father responds, "Not any more." The brief exchange between father and son has also affected Judy, who admits that she has never heard a father say "I love you."

After the police shoot Plato, Jim collapses into his father's arms. His father swears to him that he will not fail him again. Stern's final change eliminated the reappearance of the planetarium lecturer. This time, Jim and Judy, followed by their families, "thread their way through the crowd."

22

COLD FEET

On March 7, Dennis Stock's photographic essay of James Dean, "Moody New Star," appeared in *Life* magazine. The provocative black-and-white photos presented Dean as complex and unconventional. Dean would intrigue the public just as Marlon Brando had five years earlier. His image as the newest Hollywood rebel guaranteed extraordinary attention for the opening of *East of Eden*.

Dean had already returned to Los Angeles. At 7:00 P.M. on March 8, he met with Nicholas Ray and Frank Mazzola to discuss "different types of delinquent personalities." Later that evening, they took Dean to various gang hangouts. The tour ended at two the next morning.

That same day, March 9, 1955, *East of Eden* opened at the Astor Theater on Broadway and 43rd Street. Elia Kazan, Jack Warner and John Steinbeck attended the celebrity gala. Raymond Massey and Richard Davalos, who played Dean's father and brother in the picture, smiled for the fans and the cameras. Marilyn Monroe, Marlene Dietrich and Eva Marie Saint served as "honorary usherettes."

The next morning, the critics responded. Although Bosley Crowther of *The New York Times* panned James Dean's performance as "a mass of histrionic gingerbread," the other New York critics praised Dean and the picture. The long line outside the Astor Theater meant that Warner Bros. could expect healthy box office returns and a ready audience for Dean's next feature. He was now officially bankable.

The success of *East of Eden* should have put Dean more at ease about his future in films. His sudden success, however, made him even more uncertain about making *Rebel Without a Cause*. Despite Ray's attempts to create a climate of trust between them, Dean now began to wonder if Ray was capable enough to direct him.

Ray later recalled:

> Agents and well-wishers were eager to advise him. It would be foolish, they told him, to appear in any film not based on a best-seller, not adapted by a $3000-a-week writer, not directed by Elia Kazan, George Stevens, John Huston or William Wyler. He was not a person to take this kind of advice very seriously; but, intensely self-aware as he was, he could not fail to be troubled by "success." If there were aspects of it he enjoyed, it also added to his doubts.

Since the studio had given Dean a start date for *Rebel*, failure to report could mean suspension. As the accolades and the advice poured in, Dean secluded himself in a room at the Sunset Plaza Hotel on Sunset Boulevard and refused to answer the telephone.

On March 10, Ray, Weisbart and Stern met with Dr. Kelley to discuss "the psychological motivations of all of the characters in the picture." After the meeting, the Publicity Department quoted Kelley that *Rebel Without a Cause* would be the first film to dispel the notion that "rampaging youth" came only from lower-class homes and "specific racial areas." That evening, James Dean appeared in a live television interview following the *Lux Video Theatre* presentation of "The Life of Emile Zola."

On March 11, only two days after the *East of Eden* premiere, the newspapers confirmed the rumors that Dean might not accept the lead in *Rebel Without a Cause*. The headline of Kwendis Rochlen's column in the *Los Angeles Mirror-News* read: "Dean Is Deliberating." Rochlen reported, "Jimmy feels he can't be too careful about his choice of a picture to follow his great debut in *East of Eden*. Warner Bros. has assigned him to do *Rebel Without a Cause*, a story of juvenile delinquency, but Dean is doing a little rebelling of his own." Dean's West Coast agent, Dick Clayton, tried to put the best spin on Dean's actions. "When the studio first announced [Dean's role], they didn't even have a finished script," Clayton explained. Supposedly, Dean was still reading the Stern script he had received on his return to Los Angeles.

Yet, as Dean "deliberated" about *Rebel* for the benefit of the press and studio officials, his pre-production activity on the film continued. That night he met with Ray, Stern and Frank Mazzola from seven o'clock until three the next morning. They discussed the script and the "dress, manner and dialogue of delinquents."

Earlier in the day, the studio had announced that Moss Mabry would design the costumes for *Rebel*. He was also designing the costumes for *Giant*. Mabry planned to spend several days at a number of Los Angeles high schools to observe students' clothing styles.

Despite the growing confusion over the future of James Dean and *Rebel Without a Cause*, Stewart Stern rushed to meet a final deadline on the script. On March 12, he was working on the "Man in the Moon" scene that takes place in Judy's back yard. Judy's father sings the song to her as they look at the night sky.

Stern, remembering the song from his own school days, wrote to Bernie Werthman, his music teacher and choral director at the Fieldston School in New York, for assistance. Was "Man in the Moon" the true title? Were the lyrics correct? Was the song in the public domain? If not, who owned the rights? Stern requested an immediate answer, since *Rebel* started filming in about two weeks.

On March 13, *The New York Times* published Howard Thompson's interview with James Dean. Sounding confident and relaxed, Dean belittled the influence of his high school drama teacher, Adeline Nall, but praised actor James Whitmore, whose advice (in 1953) had sent him to the Actors Studio. The role of Cal in *East of Eden* was easy for him, he said, "because I think I understood the part." Dean admitted that he preferred New York to Hollywood. However, he looked forward to working on *Giant* with George Stevens, whom he described as "the greatest of them all." Nowhere in the interview did Dean refer to Nicholas Ray or *Rebel Without a Cause*.

Although the studio and the gossip columnists were kept guessing, Dean's doubts about Ray and *Rebel* had actually peaked while he was in New York. Not long before leaving for the West Coast, Dean had awakened Stewart Stern in Los Angeles with a telephone call at four o'clock in the morning. Dean admitted to Stern that he was afraid to make *Rebel*, afraid that Ray would not direct him well. He did not trust Ray the way he had trusted Kazan. Stern reminded him that the studio could suspend him if he did not report. Dean said he would do the picture if Stern asked him. Stern replied, "If you did that and were miserable in it or if the picture turned out badly, then it would be on my head, and I couldn't take that responsibility."

Warner Bros. had taken Dean's threat seriously. Ray, no doubt reluctantly, had offered the names of three other actors for the role of Jim Stark: Tab Hunter, John Kerr, and Robert Wagner. Hunter's name had already shown up on Jack Warner's list. Kerr had bested Dean for the lead in the Broadway play, *Tea and Sympathy*. Wagner, a contract player at 20th Century-Fox, had recently starred in *Prince Valiant* and *Broken Lance*.

On March 14, Ray and Weisbart met with Don Pursuit, director of the "Delinquency Control Unit" (DCU) at the University of Southern California. Pursuit's organization had loaned them data on the causes of delinquency in the greater Los Angeles area. Hedda Hopper, meanwhile, reported that Leonard Rosenman, "young musician friend of James Dean," would write the music to *Rebel Without a Cause*. The unasked question was: would Rosenman agree to write *Rebel's* music score if James Dean refused to do the film?

For Stewart Stern, the answer to the larger question came with Dean's unannounced visit to Stern's office only days before the March 15 start date. Dean said nothing about their early morning phone conversation. Instead, he pretended that he saw Picasso's *Guernica* on the bare wall behind Stern's desk. Stern played along. Dean's relaxed manner convinced him that Dean had finally prepared himself for *Rebel*.

23

REHEARSALS

The day after Dean visited Stern, part of *Rebel*'s cast assembled unofficially at Ray's Chateau Marmont bungalow to read the script aloud. Script readings, common in the theater, rarely occurred in motion pictures. Tight schedules did not often permit the luxury of ensemble rehearsals. Along with James Dean and Natalie Wood, some of Ray's latest casting choices arrived for work. Jim Backus had won the role of Jim's father. Nick Adams and Frank Mazzola had roles as gang members. Even Jack Simmons, Dean's friend from the Night Watch, had won a small role.

Stewart Stern, David Weisbart and photographer Dennis Stock were also at the readings. Ray had assigned Stock as the film's "Dialogue Coach," but his real function was to act as a human "security blanket" for Dean.

Ray hoped that the readings would be a first step in developing a sense of camaraderie among the actors. Although he knew that Dean would keep his emotional distance during the production, Ray wanted the "gang" to think and act as one. He encouraged them to go to the beach together and "hang out" in coffee shops. He also encouraged them to study delinquent behavior. He planned to offer "classes" in delinquency during pre-production and to introduce many of the cast to real gang members. Recalling his own experiences with the gangs, he warned his young players about the real delinquents they would meet: don't "get smart" or try to "play games" with them. They were dangerous people.

Ray and Dean had already spent several days studying Stern's script. As promised, Ray was allowing Dean to shape not only his own performance, but the script as well. Dean had found one scene, the confrontation in the Starks' bedroom, especially difficult to play. One evening in Ray's bungalow, he and Ray tried to improvise a solution. Ray sat in a chair in his living room opposite a blank television screen so he could watch Dean behind him. Dean entered with a milk bottle in his hand, as in Stern's script. He rolled it across his forehead and cheek as if to cool a fever. Then he lay down on the couch and stared first at Ray in the chair and then at the staircase across the room.

As Dean improvised, he felt comfortable with the scene for the first time. The staircase would be the perfect location for the family argument, as well as the perfect metaphor for the Stark family's dilemma. The mother would stand at the top, the father at the bottom, with Jim symbolically in the middle. Dean felt so sure about the revised scene that Ray decided to move it from the Starks' upstairs bedroom to *this* living room. He instructed Art Director Mal Bert to replicate the entire room, including the staircase, on a sound stage. He also asked Stern to re-write the scene to accommodate the changes.

On March 15, *Rebel Without a Cause* received an official production number: 821. The same day, Marjorie Hoshelle (Mrs. Jeff Chandler) visited Ray at the studio. Hoshelle, like a growing number of middle-aged actresses, wanted to play James Dean's mother. After Hoshelle's meeting with Ray, the Publicity Department reported it to Louella Parsons. That evening, Frank Mazzola took Dean to another "club" meeting that lasted five hours.

Ray and Weisbart, still looking for realistic locations, spent March 17 touring greater Los Angeles. The next day, Ray communicated his needs to Don Page, who sent a memo to Eric Stacey. Ray was considering the Pacific Coast Highway, north of Carl's Drive-In, for part of the chickie run sequence. He had also scouted several locations in Baldwin Hills that might represent Jim's and Judy's back yards, the alley between them, and the surrounding neighborhood. The gas station scene and the Christmas tree burning would also take place at the Baldwin Hills location. The exterior of Jim's house was at 5975 Citrus Avenue. The scene in which a police car trails Crunch, Goon and Moose was a block away. The Hollywood Police Station was the exterior for the precinct station, and the corner of Franklin and Sierra Bonita was the setting for Ray's opening "stomping" sequence. It would be a night location. The studio needed special permission to film there, since the city was doing construction work in the area.

Ray was still looking for a suitable high school location. His options included Santa Monica High School, Santa Monica City College and Hollywood High School. Ray's company would film the school scenes during the Easter vacation.

On March 17, W. F. Fitzgerald reported to William F. Guthrie that arrangements were complete for exterior daytime use of the Griffith Observatory. March 28 was the first day the company could film there. The studio was to pay $150 per day, plus an additional $100 to photograph people, plus $5 for every vehicle used in the sequences. Ray's production unit was to arrange for police and fire protection during filming. The Board of Directors of the Parks and Recreation Department had not yet decided on fees for interior shooting. The next day, Ray received permission to film at the Observatory through May 4. The company had permission to film night scenes beginning May 2. Night shooting would continue well into early morning.

On March 19, however, Ray's timetable to secure locations received a setback. W. F. Fitzgerald sent a memo to William F. Guthrie explaining that another location would have to be secured for the Stark family's residence. The owner of the house, a physician, had decided that it would be bad for his business if the studio filmed there.

Stewart Stern, meanwhile, had completed his "4th revised script" for *Rebel*. Jim now appears at the stomping scene and discovers a windup monkey in the street. The Bald Worker who interviews Plato has become "Gene." Jim no longer expresses his rage by crying. Instead, Ray Framek lets him punch and kick the desk in Ray's office. The gas station scene returns to its original place in the script. Buzz no longer has peroxide hair. Judy's line, "I'm glad they let you out," now has a specific reference: the Christmas Eve stomping.

Stern also trimmed the monitor scene at school and added more lines to the brief exchange between Jim and Plato in the corridor. At the observatory, Buzz punctures Jim's tire with a switchblade as Jim and Plato watch from a balcony. When Buzz offers the cigarette with the word "CHICKEN" printed on it, Jim asks, "Does that mean me?" The gang laughs. Jim takes off his glasses and looks at Buzz "disapprovingly." Then he says, "You shouldn't call me that." Jim turns to Judy and asks, "Are you always at ringside?...You always travel in such rank company?"

When the switchblade fight begins, Plato, not Crunch, tosses Jim a switchblade. Buzz pulls his own switchblade and challenges Jim. "No killing," he explains with a smile. "Just sticking." When Jim makes no attempt to defend himself, Buzz taunts him with a derisive nickname: Toreador. Still, Jim makes only a half-hearted attempt. Buzz, frustrated by Jim's lack of bravado, calls him a "crud chicken" and slaps him across the face. Finally, Jim lashes out, missing, but earning some respect.

Plato suddenly rushes in with a tire chain and someone pulls him down. Buzz kicks Plato while he's on the ground. This enrages Jim, who fights back and earns an "Ole!" or two from the crowd. The fight ends with the arrival of the planetarium Guide. Jim and Buzz face each other. Buzz is clearly not satisfied with the outcome and suggests a chickie run at the Millertown bluff.

When the planetarium Guide arrives to break up the group, the teens bait him. Judy asks, "What's the matter with the nice man?" Stern eliminated the "end of the world" exchange between Jim and Plato. Also, now that Jim and Buzz have made the arrangements for the chickie run, the Wimpy's sequence served no purpose. Only the brief conversation between Judy and Plato survived. Slightly altered, that conversation would take place on the bluff just before the race. Judy asks Plato if he's Jim's only friend, Plato answers, "Me?" and Judy offers Plato a hamburger.

Stern also complied with Ray's request for a revised family argument scene. It now took place in the Stark living room. Jim comes home and finds his father pretending to be asleep in front of the television. Jim can't decide if he should leave or stay and talk with his father. He turns off the television and lies down on the couch across from his father's chair, his head hanging upside-down off the couch. The father again opens his eyes briefly, sees Jim and pretends again to be asleep. Jim's mother appears suddenly at the top of the stairs "in bathrobe and nightgown" and cries out to Jim as the father pretends to wake up, "You're home! You're home!"

In the previous version of Stern's script, Jim called Judy from Wimpy's after trying to find Ray Framek at the precinct station. Now he calls from a sidewalk booth. Stern changed a line in the cruising scene with Crunch, Moose and Goon. Crunch's advice to Moose ("Keep a cool stool") was now, "Shut your mouth before your guts run out." At the mansion, Plato cries out, "Save me!" when he hears Jim and Judy behind the library door. He shoots Crunch and runs outside.

Steve Trilling, Jack Warner's assistant, took a turn critiquing the script. He objected to the use of the word "punk" on page 26. In 1955 teen slang, "punk" could also mean "homosexual." Homosexuality was a forbidden topic for the movies. He also suggested that Stern replace the picture of Burt Lancaster in Plato's locker with a picture of Alan Ladd. Ladd made films for Warner Bros., but Lancaster didn't.

Trilling suggested a new song, "Two Sleepy People," to replace "We Are the Girls of the Institute" in the school corridor. He also thought there was too much dialogue just before the switchblade fight. "The action tells everything," he argued. The gang's baiting of the Guide, Trilling observed, was a "Blackboard Jungle routine." The movie, *Blackboard Jungle*, opened in a week.

Like Walter MacEwen, Trilling had several objections to the chickie run scene. He thought that a much smaller group should watch the race. Stern's script, according to Trilling, had "sixty or so kids present." Trilling suggested crashing the cars into a wooded area beyond the highway instead of Buzz's car landing on the highway below the bluff. The censor might not object to that. Buzz's car would burst into flame when it struck "the projecting part of the cliff." Then, "like a rocket," it would fly across the highway and land on the other side.

Trilling argued that the scene outside the precinct station and the scene where the gang ambushes Plato conveyed the same information. He suggested that Jim call Judy from Wimpy's, even though that location no longer had a function in the story. Trilling wrote "process— Star Is Born" in his notes. He no doubt remembered a process shot of a drive-in restaurant among the out-takes from *A Star Is Born*. Judy Garland, dressed as a car hop, made a phone call in front of that process screen. The same screen might be used in *Rebel* as a background for Jim's call.

Like Jack Warner, Trilling objected to the mansion sequence, claiming it to be both "self-conscious" and overlong. He also objected to the teenagers drinking liquor there. Finally, he thought that Plato's death at the hands of the police should seem more accidental than deliberate. A deliberate shooting would make them appear cold-blooded or trigger-happy.

On March 21, Harrison Carroll reported that James Dean, Nicholas Ray and Natalie Wood had eaten lunch at the popular Luau Restaurant on Rodeo Drive in Beverly Hills. Wood was already beginning to attract media attention. The Publicity Department issued a typical release: Dennis Hopper and Natalie Wood were involved in "the youngest romance on the [Warner Bros.] lot these days."

Unknown to Dennis Hopper and the Hollywood gossips, sixteen-year-old Natalie Wood had also begun a romance with forty-three-year-old Nicholas Ray. Hopper discovered what many in the cast already knew when he made an unannounced visit to Bungalow 2 at the Chateau Marmont. When no one answered the door, Hopper entered and found Ray and Wood together in bed. The discovery infuriated Hopper and soured his working relationship with Ray during the entire production. It also cast doubt on Ray's reasons for selecting Wood as Judy. Had she earned the part through talent, or by charming her way into the director's bed?

While Ray was having his affair with Wood, he was also using his home as a rehearsal hall. One afternoon he invited Sal Mineo to meet James Dean there. Ray was still considering Mineo as Plato, but Mineo was under-age. If the studio approved Natalie Wood as Judy, there would already be one minor in the cast. A second minor would overburden an already tight shooting schedule. Before Ray took on that responsibility, he had to find out if Dean and Mineo could work well together. They shared too many important scenes to leave acting chemistry to chance.

Ray had them read a key scene, then let them talk a while. Mineo told Dean that he was from the Bronx, and soon they were discussing New York City, one of Dean's favorite places. They moved successfully to the subject of cars and returned to the scene they had rehearsed. Ray suggested that they improvise the dialogue. Mineo picked up the technique quickly, and the scene went well. By the end of the rehearsal, Ray knew that Mineo could be his Plato.

24

BLACKBOARD JUNGLE

On Monday, March 21, MGM's *Blackboard Jungle* opened in a charged atmosphere that bordered on moral hysteria. The same civic, educational and religious leaders who had protested Evan Hunter's sensational novel a year earlier now attacked the film on the same grounds: it glorified hoodlums, insulted the teaching profession, and it suggested that anarchy was the norm among America's teenagers. The day the film opened in New York City, a teacher was stabbed and thrown off a roof.

Bosley Crowther of *The New York Times* echoed most critics in his review of the film:

> It is a full-throated, all-out testimonial to the lurid headlines that appear from time to time, reporting acts of terrorism and violence by uncontrolled urban youths. It gives a blood-curdling, nightmarish picture of monstrous disorder in a public school. And it leaves one wondering wildly whether such out-of-hand horrors can be.
>
> …From scenes that show the painful inability of the teacher to control his class, let alone interest his pupils and get something into their heads, to incidents of straight assault and battery, culminating with an attack upon the teacher with a knife, the emphasis is wholly upon impudence, rebellion and violence.

Crowther also echoed the sentiments of the nation's censors and unofficial moral watchdogs when he added:

> More than a question of entertainment is involved, however, in this film, since it treats of a contemporary subject that is social dynamite. And it is on the question of its faithfulness to over-all conditions that we suspect it may be challenged not only as responsible reporting, but also as a desirable stimulant to spread before the young.

The success or failure of *Blackboard Jungle* had obvious repercussions for Warner Bros. Front office executives would watch the film's progress carefully over the next days and weeks. They would weigh adverse community reaction against the box-office figures. If *Blackboard Jungle* became a liability to MGM, Warner Bros. might decide not to make the same mistake with *Rebel Without a Cause*.

Meanwhile, Ray and Weisbart continued to scout locations, looking for a high

Blackboard Jungle created a storm of controversy that *Rebel Without a Cause* could not weather. Pictured: Glenn Ford and Sidney Poitier.

school. Although they had not yet decided on a place, they did have a name: Dawson High. Carl Milliken and the Research Department had made sure that no current area high school bore that name. Weisbart informed Mal Bert via memo on March 21, and the Art Department began making the appropriate signs.

Assistant Director Don Page reported to Eric Stacey that Ray and his staff had looked at both interior and exterior locations at the Griffith Observatory and had chosen camera positions for the first day's shooting. Interiors posed no problem, except for a cramped shot where the lecturer shows Jim the control switches for the planetarium program. After inspecting the location, Ray decided to stage the start of the knife fight at the front of the building and then move it to the roof rather than the parking lot. He needed special permission for that. He also planned to use the roof and the planetarium dome for the film's climax, which was to take place at night. Plato would use a Jacob's ladder to climb the dome.

In the afternoon, Ray and company returned to some of the selected locations in Baldwin Hills. They brought along cinematographer Ernest Haller, gaffer Victor Johnson and head grip Kenneth Taylor. The gaffer was the production's chief electrician. His job was to provide portable electricity on location and to set up the necessary lighting wherever Ray's company was filming. He worked under the direction of the cinematographer. The head grip assembled whatever structures the company needed, either at the studio or on location: scaffolds for the cameras, tracks for moving shots, lighting platforms and stages.

On his last visit to Baldwin Hills, Haller had thought the house chosen as Judy's was too white and would not photograph properly. Now, however, he decided that they would not have to paint it. Vic Johnson would install two generators on nearby sites to supply adequate electricity for lights and cameras. The studio would need permission to use the back yard next to Jim's back yard. The studio required radio phones at all locations.

On March 22, Fitzgerald reported to Guthrie that Santa Monica High School, formerly Santa Monica City College, would double as Dawson High. The studio would not pay fees for the use of the building and grounds. Instead, it would donate $150 to the Student Body Association. Some of the students would act as extras. Two students would serve as attendants and receive $15 per day. Meanwhile, Fitzgerald continued the search for Jim's house. He had looked from north of Sunset Boulevard down to Franklin and from Garner Junction over to Fairfax. He had taken photographs of five possible sites. More than the usual sense of urgency prevailed, since Ray wanted the interior for the Stark family argument to be a replica of his living room at the Chateau Marmont. The exterior that they used needed to conform to the dimensions of the interior set. The carpenters could not build that interior until Fitzgerald secured the matching exterior.

The search also continued for a chickie run location. Ray learned that he could not use the Pacific Coast Highway location he had scouted earlier. A cliff on Hollingsworth Drive in Griffith Park might work as a substitute. Meanwhile, casting continued. Solly Baiano made a schedule of tests for the next day. The company would use Stage 1.

As *Blackboard Jungle* made headlines, the movie industry's chief censor took a hard look at *Rebel Without a Cause*. Geoffrey M. Shurlock, the head of the Motion Picture Association of America, had already met twice with Steve Trilling and Finlay McDermid. Now he sent his report to Jack Warner. Shurlock was the third administrator in the history of the Motion Picture Production Code, which had taken effect in 1934. He had succeeded Will Hays, the original "czar of all the rushes," and Joseph I. Breen. The Production Code dictated what subjects could appear on a motion picture screen. The taboos included nudity, homosexuality, rape, incest, blasphemy (and other offensive language), brutality, lewdness and obscenity, and drug addiction.

The Code had resulted from a series of scandals, both on and off screen, during the 1920s. These had brought condemnation on the industry from a wide range of civic and religious organizations. Although adherence to the Code remained voluntary, the Code's seal of approval had become a kind of industry standard. The studios recognized that without a Production Code seal, their films might be subject to boycott.

One especially zealous supporter of boycotting was the Legion of Decency, which forbade Roman Catholics from watching "condemned" movies under pain of Mortal Sin. Only recently had a studio dared to release a film without the seal. Otto Preminger's *The Moon Is Blue* (1953), an otherwise innocuous comedy, had dared to use the word "virgin." The Motion Picture Association had refused to pass it, and Preminger had refused to delete the word. He would soon challenge the Code again with *The Man with the Golden Arm*, a film about drug addiction. Most films, however, still adhered to the Code, and most of the major studios, including Warner Bros., still feared the censor's wrath.

Shurlock's first report on *Rebel Without a Cause*, as expected, attacked its alleged emphasis on sex and violence. The violence would have to be toned down for the picture to avoid "release difficulties, both here and abroad," and the teen sexuality would "have to come out entirely."

Shurlock listed nineteen specific objections, with page references:

Page 2: The stomping of the Christmas shopper should be done "without detailed brutality being shown."

Page 3: Jim's "derisive gesture" to the policeman in the precinct station "should not be nose thumbing."

Page 5: Ray Framek, the Juvenile Officer, asks Judy, "Have you talked to strangers before?" This created the appearance that she was being booked for prostitution. Stern would have to change the line.

Page 41: When Buzz goads Jim into a switchblade fight, he says there will be "no killing." The expression suggested that on some occasions these teenagers *did* fight to the death with knives. Shurlock also wanted the fight kept to "the absolute minimum" of violence and shock value.

Pages 50 and 51: The slapping scene suggested an incestuous relationship between Judy and her father.

Page 54: Jim's talk with his father about the chickie run ends when Jim's father tells him that he dresses "like a bum." Jim answers, "Like a man, Dad." Jim's line glorified the teens' violent ritual, Shurlock argued, by equating it with a test of manhood.

Page 59: There must be nothing objectionable about Judy's "body movements" just before the chickie run.

Page 66: The cars used in the chickie run should not be stolen, since this emphasized the teens' criminal behavior.

Page 67: Like Steve Trilling, Shurlock wondered what happened after the cars went over the cliff and crashed. He wanted no suggestion that the lives of "innocent passengers on the road below" were endangered.

Page 80: Jim's mother says, "Good lord," when he tells her of Buzz's death. Shurlock wanted the words removed because they were not used "entirely reverently."

Page 85: Crunch threatens to bring Jim "down." The audience must know that the gang only planned to beat him up, not to kill him.

Pages 87 and 88: The word "punk" implied homosexuality. The audience must not see Plato's attachment to Jim as homosexual.

Page 94: Jim invites Judy to go with him to the deserted mansion. Shurlock objected to the dialogue as a clear indication that Jim and Judy planned to have an "illicit affair."

Page 103: Shurlock found the expression "Keep a cool stool" (which Stern had already changed) objectionable.

Page 104: Shurlock wanted no "liquor and drinking" at the mansion because it was "offensive in the case of teenagers."

Page 105: Plato remembers strange noises from his parents' bedroom when he was a child: "I thought they were fighting, but they weren't." Shurlock found the sexual inference objectionable. In the same scene, Judy wants to explore the mansion. There should be a reason "other than the implied desire for sexual intimacy" for this exploration.

Page 108: Jim and Judy are in the library. Shurlock did not want the audience to think that the two had just "indulged themselves sexually."

Page 110: Stern must remove Plato's liquor bottle and Crunch's switchblade. Shurlock argued that the brandishing of tire chains "would be sufficient to give the feeling of menace."

Page 118: Shurlock wanted Jim's line, "Get your damn hands off me," removed.

In conclusion, Shurlock advised Warner, "You understand, of course, that our final judgment will be based upon the finished picture."

On March 23, screen tests for *Rebel Without a Cause* began on Stage 1 at the studio. Ray tested three Platos: Sal Mineo, Gregory Marshall and Richard Beymer. Although Mineo had made a favorable impression in the Chateau Marmont test with Dean, Ray still felt obliged to look at other actors. Dean and Natalie Wood played Jim and Judy for Mineo's test at 9:00 A.M. Marshall tested alone at 11:00, and Beymer did the same at 1:00 P.M. Beymer, 16, was a former child star from local television.

Nicholas Ray, Natalie Wood, James Dean and Marsha Hunt during photographic tests on Stage 1.

He had made his motion picture debut in 1953 in Vittorio DeSica's *Indiscretion of an American Wife*. He appeared next in *So Big*, based on the Edna Ferber novel.

On the same sound stage, Ernest Haller was making wardrobe tests in black-and-white CinemaScope. The actors were present only to model their clothing, but James Dean could not resist the temptation to do some emoting. In between putting on and taking off jackets, he did a Marlon Brando impersonation, shouting "Stell-l-l-a-a!" at the top of his voice. The Publicity Department dutifully reported it. It was no accident that Dean had chosen Brando's famous cry from *A Streetcar Named Desire*. Elia Kazan had filmed *Streetcar* on Stage 1, and the circular staircase used in the film was still standing.

On hand for the photographic tests were most of the finalists for the film's gang roles: Corey Allen, Dennis Hopper, Frank Mazzola, Jack Grinnage, Nick Adams, Tom Bernard, Ken Miller, Jerry Olken, Bruce Roberts and Jack Simmons. Steffi Sidney, who would play Mil, and Beverly Long, who would play Helen, were also present. Frank Mazzola, still working as a gang consultant, spent most of the day working with Dean on wardrobe.

Elsewhere, W. F. Fitzgerald reported that the exterior of a home owned by Mr. Hugo Hass at 1542 N. Orange Grove Drive would represent Jim's home in the picture. Mr. Hass would receive $125 a day for the use of his property.

On March 24, Steve Trilling added to his commentary on Stern's script. He wanted to remove the Christmas carolers from the first page of the stomping sequence. He also argued that Stern was "opening up a bag of peas" when he placed a drunken Jim at the scene of the crime. The police would certainly hold Jim for questioning, yet Ray Framek does not even mention the incident to Jim's parents. Also, Trilling did not understand why Jim's family keeps moving. Even Jim's heart-to-heart talk with Ray Framek, he argued, did not reveal much of Jim's delinquent past. Trilling also objected to Ray's use of the word "Juvey" for Juvenile Hall. Even if it was authentic police jargon, most of the audience wouldn't know what it meant. Trilling defended two lines of dialogue that Stern had apparently decided to cut. In one, Jim says of his weakling father, "If only he had the guts to knock Mom cold once." In the other, Judy says, "Dig the square wardrobe," when she meets Jim on his first morning of school.

Meanwhile, Eric Stacey had a problem that involved crashing and burning two stolen cars in the chickie run. The Air Pollution Control Board of the City of Los Angeles had developed strict requirements for any burning within its jurisdiction. The studio was to get special permission for the car burning or change the story "to fit the circumstances." Stacey informed Ray and Weisbart and sent copies to Don Page and W. F. Fitzgerald.

While Ray and Weisbart attended a conference of the California State Juvenile Officers Association at the Miramar Hotel in Santa Monica, the studio announced that Corey Allen had signed to play Buzz and that Marsha Hunt would play Jim's mother in *Rebel Without a Cause*. Hunt, who was also performing in an upcoming play at the Carthay Circle Theater, would apparently have an around-the-clock schedule.

The next day, March 25, the studio announced that Natalie Wood had signed to play Judy in *Rebel Without a Cause*, her twentieth film. The Los Angeles Board of

Education had agreed to let the studio move Wood's school hours each time *Rebel* filmed at night. She would attend class from 3:00 P.M. to 6:00 P.M., with one hour for dinner (the Board mandated hot meals for all minors). Then she could work from 7:00 P.M. until midnight. Wood was to stop work at 10:00 P.M. whenever possible. Under no circumstances was she to work more than an eight-hour day, including makeup time. Tom Hennesy, a social worker, would supervise her on the set and also serve as her teacher. According to the Publicity Department, Wood was already preparing for the rigors of night shooting by taking vitamin "booster shots."

The studio also officially cast Jim Backus and William Hopper as the picture's two fathers. Hopper, 40, son of the syndicated columnist Hedda Hopper, had begun his film career in 1936. His featured roles included *The Maltese Falcon* (1941), *Air Force* (1943) and more recently, *Track of the Cat* (1954). The Publicity Department observed an interesting irony in casting the two men: Jim Backus, who would play Jim's father, had already played Natalie Wood's father in two television plays. Hopper, who would play Judy's father, had played James Dean's father in another television production.

On March 25, with only five days before the start of production, Eric Stacey sent Gordon Bau an unusual memo: *Rebel*'s cast were to wear makeup "at all times." He sent copies to Steve Trilling, Nicholas Ray, David Weisbart, Don Page and Ernest Haller. Stacey almost certainly had James Dean in mind. On the *East of Eden* set, the mischievous Dean had frequently rubbed off his makeup between scenes. This time, the studio was ready for him. Warner Bros. might be making a movie about rebels, but they wanted no real ones on the set.

25

EXIT STERN

On March 25, the Publicity Department reported that Stewart Stern was leaving for New York to discuss staging a play, *The Hell of It*, with a group of Broadway producers. According to the press release, he planned to be away for two weeks. Actually, he would stay away during the entire production of *Rebel*. Stern had personal as well as professional reasons for leaving.

He later recalled:

> Jimmy had confided to me his doubts [about Ray], and I knew if I were there, he would be pulling me into his dressing trailer all the time to ask me what I thought. Given Nick's sensitivity and the importance to him of his relationship with Jimmy and how totally that film would depend on the state of the relationships between the director and his actors, I just felt it would be too destructive if I couldn't control myself about things I saw happening that I didn't like. I decided to stay away.

Stern did not feel comfortable about leaving. He had never been away from a production before. His only consolation was Ray's promise that, should any substantive script changes be anticipated, Ray would telephone him in New York.

Meanwhile, James Dean left to spend the weekend in Palm Springs. He had entered his Porsche Super Speedster in the Eighth Annual Palm Springs Road Races, a two-day event. Dennis Stock, Lilli Kardell (a Swedish movie starlet) and one of her friends went along for the ride. Movie columnist Joe Hyams, a good friend of Dean's, planned to meet them at the track the next day. Dean and his guests planned to stay at the Palm Desert home of his West Coast agent, Dick Clayton.

Before Stern left for New York, he delivered the final version of his script to the Story Department. Except for the elimination of the second father-son argument outside the observatory, the script had changed only to accommodate the objections of Trilling and Shurlock. Stern had worked for twelve weeks on the picture and had earned $12,000.

Five days before the start of production, Ray still had not cast several roles. They included Judy's mother and little brother Beau, Jim's grandmother, Plato's nurse, Ray Framek and a few minor gang members. He had cast several prominent members of the gang: Dennis Hopper would play Goon; Frank Mazzola would play

Crunch, Buzz's vindictive lieutenant; Nick Adams would play Chick; Tom Bernard would be Harry. Jack Grinnage would play Moose, even though the studio incorrectly listed him as Chick in the official credits.

Ian Wolfe, a veteran character actor, would play the planetarium lecturer. Wolfe, 59, had first gained fame as Maggs, Captain Bligh's eyes and ears in *Mutiny on the Bounty* (1935). He had worked with Nicholas Ray before in *They Live by Night* (1949) and *On Dangerous Ground* (1951). Dean's friend, Jack Simmons, would play Cookie, whose only function was to throw the switchblade in front of Jim at the start of the fight. Chili-Picker (Crunch) and Plato had tossed the knife in earlier drafts. Dean had campaigned to get Simmons the role of Plato, and Ray had tested them together, but the results had been disappointing. Dean's only other hand-picked candidate was Christine White for the role of Judy, but she never tested. White had first met Dean in Jane Deacy's office in New York City.

At Palm Springs on Saturday, Dean won his qualifying race. Away from the track, he had also scored a victory with one of the most powerful columnists in Hollywood, Hedda Hopper. Notorious for making bad first impressions, Dean had insulted Hopper at the studio with his bad manners and slovenly appearance. She had even refused to see *East of Eden* until actor Clifton Webb persuaded her. A second, more successful meeting with Dean followed, and now she was profiling him in her syndicated column. "Ex-Farm Boy Now Is Making Hay in Movies" was the title of Hopper's interview with Dean. After discussing his life in Fairmount, his early acting experiences and his current success in *East of Eden*, Dean talked about the future:

> Acting is wonderful and immediately satisfying, but it is not the end-all, be-all, of my existence. My talents lie in directing even more than acting. And beyond direction, my great fear is writing. I can't apply the seat of my pants right now to write — I'm too youthful and silly, but someday...

Despite Hedda Hopper's attention, James Dean's public image might suffer a serious setback if the studio released its latest information on him. Joe Halperin of the Publicity Department was concerned enough to send the text directly to Jack

Hedda Hopper's negative first impression of James Dean changed dramatically after actor Clifton Webb persuaded her to see Dean in *East of Eden*.

Warner. The press release explained that Dean had all his mail sent to the studio, that he looked at it only twice a month, and that he simply threw away the letters he didn't want to open, based on the return address. Halperin's handwritten note to Jack Warner suggested that the proposed release not be given to the columnists because it made Dean look like "an ungracious S.O.B."

On Sunday, March 27, at Palm Springs, Dean finished second in his race. That evening, he drove to Arthur Loew, Jr.'s house in Los Angeles, where he found Stewart Stern. They engaged in some roughhousing, and Stern accidentally put his fist through Dean's glasses. Unhurt, Dean needed new lenses before working at the studio the next day.

On Monday, March 28, two days before filming began, the studio announced James Moore as the film editor for *Rebel Without a Cause*. Working closely with Ray and Weisbart, the editor would arrange the thousands of feet of celluloid, starting with several "rough cuts" and finishing with an "answer print" ready to show in the nation's movie houses.

Meanwhile, W. F. Fitzgerald of the Location Department had bad news for Ray. In Stern's script, Plato breaks the glass in the front door of the observatory to gain access and later climbs up the dome on a Jacob's ladder. The Parks and Recreation Department had said no to both ideas. Frank Mazzola also complained that the studio had not compensated him for his services as gang expert. Weisbart suggested to Steve Trilling that $200 was a reasonable fee, and Trilling told Hoyt Bowers of the Payroll Department to "carry" Mazzola for an extra half-week on salary after he completed his role as Crunch in the film.

March 29, the day before production began, the studio issued a press release: *Rebel Without a Cause* would be the first CinemaScope picture filmed in black-and-white. MGM would follow with *Trial*, "another untinted C'scoper" starring Glenn Ford and Arthur Kennedy, on April 1.

Rebel's production staff was now complete. Don Page, the First Assistant Director, and Robert Farfan, the 2nd Assistant Director, would organize crowd control, keep track of everyone on the set, and direct "second unit" filming of scenes that did not involve the principal actors. Script supervisor Howard Hohler would keep a daily "continuity" record of the production: which scenes Ray had filmed, the camera angles used, the positioning of actors and props, what the weather was like and so on. Matching the action from one scene to another was one of Hohler's biggest responsibilities. He needed an eye for details that even the director might overlook.

Ernest Haller, the cinematographer, would decide how to light and photograph each scene, working closely with Ray. Bill Shurr, the camera operator, would photograph the scenes. Haller also had an assistant, Stewart Higgs. Floyd McCarty, the still photographer, would take photographs of the production. Stanley Jones, the sound man, would insure that the sound recordings were audible and that no extraneous noise (an airplane overhead, a cough from one of the extras) marred the final soundtrack. He also had responsibility for "post synchronization," the re-recording of sound later at the studio. He could expect some difficulty recording James Dean, who frequently mumbled his lines.

Property Master Herbert Plews and his assistant, Robert "Red" Turner, would provide the props required by the script: everything from switchblades and hot rods to a candelabra used in the mansion scene and Plato's gun in the finale. William Wallace, the set dresser, would work closely with Art Director Mal Bert. Wallace would provide the small details for each set: pictures on the wall, table settings, desk lamps and the like. Gaffer Vic Johnson would have two assistants, Claude Johnson and George Wilson, known as "Best Boys." They would help him to manage the complicated electrical needs of the production, both in the studio and on location. They would spend the majority of their time connecting and disconnecting hundreds of feet of heavy black cable.

Leon Roberts and Henry Field would supervise wardrobe selection for *Rebel*: largely T-shirts, blue jeans and whatever else Costume Designer Moss Mabry deemed appropriate. The Wardrobe Department had already begun "soiling and laundering" over 400 pairs of jeans to produce the "well-worn look" that teenagers preferred. Marguerite Royce would oversee the women's wardrobe, including the obligatory poodle skirts. Henry Vilardo would apply makeup, and Tillie Starriett would dress hair.

As *Rebel Without a Cause* prepared to start production, *Blackboard Jungle* was scoring at the box office. *Variety* reported a "Smash $23,000" in Philadelphia, a "Hot 25G" in San Francisco, a "Lush $57G" in Boston, and a "Torrid $65G" in its second week in New York. Despite the storm of moral outrage, *Blackboard Jungle* proved the staying power of delinquency films. Its success was a good omen for Nicholas Ray, whose final distance on his blind run loomed just ahead.

PART III

Production

26

ON LOCATION

Production of *Rebel Without a Cause* began on Wednesday, March 30, 1955, at 7:00 A.M. Cast and crew assembled at the studio, then drove in caravan the short distance to Griffith Park and the Observatory. They arrived at 7:20 and set up for a full day of filming. *Rebel*'s cast, which had experience in both theater and film, understood that film acting was far more difficult. Venable Herndon, one of James Dean's many biographers, described the challenge:

> On stage, an actor has a chance to sustain character, to build moments, to climb toward the climax of a drama that usually progresses chronologically and is actually performed in a continuous time period of only two or three hours. On a movie set, an actor is asked to jump right into the middle of even the most explosive scenes, and the performance is spread out over weeks and months. Most often, too, the story is shot out of sequence.
>
> …Sometimes, when an important actor can only be present for the first, middle, or last weeks of the shooting schedule, all of his or her scenes will be bunched together, regardless of location or light considerations. The resulting sequence solves budget problems, logistical problems, career problems, union problems; but it has nothing to do with reinforcing the flow of the story. Somehow, the director and the actors are expected to overcome this difficulty.

That first day, Nicholas Ray filmed exterior scenes using seven different camera positions. Scenes 75D, 77A-77D and 77G took place on and around a balcony where Jim and Plato go to escape Buzz's gang. In Scene 48, Jim parks his car at the rear of the building. In Scene 104, the Lecturer and the Guide observe Jim and Buzz fighting in the parking lot.

Ray's company included a full production crew, fifteen members of the cast, twenty-five extras and seven "stand-ins." The stand-ins took the places of the actors whenever the cameraman needed to make light readings and set "marks" for the actors. This process, called "blocking," also included positioning the cameras, lights, and other equipment.

After waiting almost two hours for the grips to unload the equipment, Ray and Ernest Haller blocked out the first shot, which was actually a combination of three numbered scenes in Stern's script. Ray rehearsed the actors for twenty-five minutes,

105

The Griffith Observatory, the first location for *Rebel Without a Cause.*

and then the camera rolled: Plato exits the observatory through a doorway; the camera pans with him across the balcony as Jim follows. They look at the mansion, which is off-screen; they watch Buzz and the gang approach below; then they exit left, down the stairs.

After five attempts, or "takes," Ray decided to "print" the fifth and "hold" the fourth. When the lab technicians processed the negative film, they would make a positive print from the fifth take. Ray and Weisbart would view it and the other "dailies" in a screening room that evening. Ray kept the fourth take as insurance in case his first choice contained a flaw that went unnoticed until the screening, or if the printed take was damaged during processing.

After a ten-minute break to reposition the camera, Ray filmed a close-up of Jim and Plato at the edge of the balcony. The shot required six takes. The next shot, Jim parking his car, needed only one. Ray lined up his fourth shot of the morning, in which Moose and Crunch spot Jim from the driveway, and then the company stopped for lunch. The cast got an hour, the crew less than forty-five minutes. At 1:30, the actors rehearsed for fifteen minutes, and Ray filmed the shot he had blocked before lunch.

In the next shot, Buzz is about to puncture Jim's tire as Crunch, Goon, Moose, Chick, Cookie and Harry hover menacingly. Judy and Mil look on in silence, but Helen says a line in French, *"La soleil tombe dans la mer."* Ray printed the seventh take. In the next shot, Buzz actually punctures Jim's tire. Ray was not satisfied with the first take, so cast and crew waited another ten minutes while the prop men changed the tire. Ray liked the second take and printed it.

Scene 104 featured Ian Wolfe as the Lecturer and Dick Wessel as the Guide. Wessel, 42, was a veteran of "B" pictures and a regular in the *Blondie* series. His last screen appearance had been in *Them!* After forty-five minutes of blocking and five minutes of rehearsal, Ray held the second take and printed the fourth. Some of the actors' conversation from the knife fight would be dubbed over, so Ray recorded that part of the sound track separately.

Shooting ended for the day at 5:15 P.M. The caravan left for the studio at 5:40 and arrived twenty-five minutes later. At the end of a long, tiring, ten-hour day, Ray's company had produced two and a half minutes of useful footage. Long after *Rebel*'s cast and crew had gone home, Ray and Weisbart were in a screening room studying the results of their first day's work.

While Ray's crew had labored on location, the studio had also been busy. Stewart Stern's query about the song, "Man in the Moon," had reached Joseph McLaughlin in the Music Department. McLaughlin had identified it as a French folk song with English lyrics by Katherine Davis. The E. C. Schirmer Company of Boston owned the copyright. Warner Bros. would have to ask permission to use the song and pay the appropriate fees. Helen Schoen of the New York office would make the inquiries.

Ray's company returned to the Griffith Observatory at 6:55 the next morning to complete the switchblade fight sequence. Two new actors joined the ensemble. Charles Postal played a teacher, and Cliff Morris joined the gang as "Cliff." Ray would use nineteen camera positions to record the action. During the carefully choreographed switchblade fight, he would alternate between medium shots and close-ups. For six of the shots, he would use two cameras.

Ray filmed the confrontation at Jim's car first: Jim and Plato descend from the balcony; Jim and Buzz trade insults, and Jim questions Judy about the "rank company" she keeps. While Ray was filming, a group of five hundred school children arrived for the early show at the planetarium. They had come to learn about the stars under the planetarium dome, but for a few moments they stopped to watch Ray's actors emote in the parking lot. The Publicity Department was quick to exploit the moment with a press release.

After lunch, Ray filmed the switchblade fight. James Dean and Corey Allen used real knives. It was illegal in California to manufacture or own switchblades, so the Property Department had borrowed thirty of them from Juvenile Hall. The police had confiscated the knives from young hoodlums picked up on various charges. After Frank Mazzola coached Dean and Allen in handling the weapons, they began a carefully choreographed ballet of thrust and parry. The prop man had dulled the blades, and both actors wore chest protectors under their shirts, but there was still some danger. The work was physically exhausting for the two actors, who had to make a convincing display without actually hurting each other. Ray appeared relaxed enough as the cameras rolled, but Dean and Allen quickly showed signs of stress. After several attempts, they still hadn't found the nerve to fight at close range.

When they finally did engage, the safety precautions failed. One of Allen's thrusts caught Dean on the neck just below the right ear. As soon as Ray saw the blood, he stopped filming. The First Aid Man, wearing a bright red windbreaker, rushed to give Dean assistance. Fortunately, the wound was superficial. Neil Rau, a newspaper columnist visiting the set, interviewed Dean while the First Aid Man tended to him.

Visibly nervous, Dean was wiping sweat from his forehead as Rau approached. "Isn't this pushing realism a bit?" Rau asked. For a moment, Dean did not answer. Then he said, "In motion pictures, you can't fool the camera. If we were doing this on the stage we'd probably be able to gimmick it up — but not in a picture. Film fans are too critical these days." Mr. Hill, the First Aid Man, had his own wry observation: "If pictures get any more realistic, they'll be serving popcorn coated with smelling salts in the theaters."

The switchblade scene was not made any easier by the heat. Beverly Long later recalled:

> [The scene] was a bitch to do. I remember it was very hot, really miserable and hot. It was so intricate. Jimmy had so many different shirts he had to take on and off. That shirt would get blood on it, and then another shirt. It seemed like he was constantly changing shirts.

During one of the breaks in the action, Corey Allen found a quiet spot on the front lawn of the observatory. As he tried to focus his thoughts and calm his jittery nerves, he also kept a wary eye on Dean. Allen had made a point of keeping track of Dean on the set, watching him as if he were a real adversary. Suddenly, Dean walked over to him and, without saying a word, handed him a cup of water. The gesture startled Allen, who asked, "How did you know I wanted a drink of water?" Dean answered, "I'm a lot older than you."

The switchblade sequence continued: Buzz taunts Jim as they fight; Plato bursts in with a tire chain; Jim knocks the knife out of Buzz's hand and forces him to give up. At 5:55 P.M., Ray completed his last shot of the day. The company arrived back at the studio at 6:45. After twelve hours, Ray had four minutes and nine seconds of usable footage.

At the studio, Ray received a memo from David Weisbart reminding him to "get a good long shot" of the entrance to Santa Monica High School when the company filmed there in two days. Ray sent Weisbart his own memo regarding a voice coach for Natalie Wood. Jack Warner had complained about the quality of Wood's voice in the screen tests, so Ray had hired his friend, Nina Moise, to work with Wood for a few hours each week. Moise's fee was $15 per hour.

Geoffrey Shurlock, the industry censor, was also complaining. Although he had approved the script changes made since his first reading, "certain details" of the story still troubled him. He telephoned Finlay McDermid, who relayed the objections to Steve Trilling.

Shurlock was concerned, as usual, about sex and violence. Judy's talk with Ray Framek still suggested that she had been soliciting. Although Shurlock wanted the suggestion removed, McDermid believed that Shurlock "could be persuaded" to leave it in. Shurlock had another concern about Judy: the audience might believe that the cigarette she secretly shares in the school corridor is marijuana. McDermid argued that since smoking of any kind was illegal in school, secrecy did not necessarily mean marijuana.

Parts of the switchblade fight troubled Shurlock. Buzz kicks Plato "when he is down." Shurlock disapproved of this poor sportsmanship. He also wanted to avoid glamorizing the violence in the fight. Shurlock still suspected incest when Judy kisses her father and he slaps her. The father, Shurlock insisted, should slap her *before* she kisses him. McDermid admitted to Trilling that he did not understand "what Shurlock's point is here."

Shurlock still disapproved of the chickie run and the dangers it posed to fictional motorists on the highway below the bluff. He also wanted assurance that Crunch, Moose, and Goon only planned to beat Jim, not to kill him. Shurlock felt that Crunch's answer to that question ("You clean out of your head?") still left some doubt. Judy's altered line, "Have you ever gone with anyone who—?" still sounded like an admission of past sexual activity. McDermid suggested completing the new line with a word like "smooched" or "necked" to placate Shurlock.

Plato tells Jim at the mansion, "I think they're going to kill you." Jim answers, "We know." Shurlock suggested adding a line "to indicate that Plato is exaggerating or to show his shock at the idea." In the library, Jim and Judy kiss twice. Shurlock thought that once was enough. Also, he argued, the gang members should not rattle or otherwise "flaunt" their tire chains when they threaten Plato. In Stern's latest draft, Plato shoots at Jim after running into the gang. Shurlock suggested that Plato should not fire his gun deliberately. Instead, "Jim might wrestle with him and the gun go off." When Jim and Judy reappear after being alone together, Shurlock added, nothing in their appearance or actions (adjusting their clothing, etc.) should suggest that they have just had intercourse. Shurlock left McDermid with the usual disclaimer: "You understand, of course, that our final judgment will be based on the finished picture."

On April 1, Ray's company returned to the Griffith Observatory for a third day. One hundred and forty-six extras joined the cast and crew to play students. Ray began with a high-angle shot of Jim's car approaching the building. Another camera filmed the same shot from a lower angle. In the next three shots, the students exit the observatory for the bus and fourteen cars that are waiting in the parking lot. Plato is one of the students, but he keeps looking back at the observatory. When he sees Buzz's gang waiting for Jim, he pushes his way out of the bus. When the teacher on the bus asks where he's going, Plato says, "I forgot something. I'll get a hitch." The bus pulls away, and only Plato, Jim and Buzz's gang remain.

After the parking lot sequence, Ray filmed an "added cutaway shot" of two students running outside the observatory and "skipping school." The company then broke for lunch. In the afternoon, Ray filmed Buzz's gang as they exit the observatory. Buzz and Crunch decide to confront Jim; Buzz and Plato briefly exchange words as they both wait for Jim to come out.

From 2:45 until 3:00, Ray waited for Natalie Wood, who was attending class on the set. After finishing her shot, Ray used two cameras to film more shots of students leaving the observatory. Then, he returned to the switchblade fight location behind the building: Buzz's gang briefly harasses the Guide and departs; the Lecturer sees blood on Jim's shirt and Jim explains, "I scratched my mosquito bites." Filming ended at 7:15 P.M. Cast and crew had worked eleven hours under a hot sun. Natalie Wood had become faint during the day; Dean had sunburn on his face and neck and was advised to stay in the shade now whenever possible. The company arrived back at the studio at 7:35.

Meanwhile, Weisbart had been studying the "dailies." He advised Ray in a memo that many of the shots from the first two days lacked "vitality." He attributed this to Dean's and Corey Allen's poor voice projection. Weisbart also thought that the switchblade sequence needed some close-up "reaction shots" from Judy and Plato. He hoped that Ray had "picked these up" during the day's filming.

In a separate memo, Weisbart informed Ray of Shurlock's latest concerns. He suggested that whenever Ray was about to film one of the "objectionable moments" he should film an alternative version of the scene, "so that we are not forced to butcher the film later on."

27

TRANSFORMATION

According to Nicholas Ray, only three days after *Rebel Without a Cause* began filming, it suddenly faced demise. Jack Warner had approved the first two sets of dailies, but there were strong arguments for backing away from the project. Geoffrey Shurlock's persistent objections to the film's violence and sexual content spelled serious trouble. The nation's unofficial censors also posed a threat, as watchdog groups around the country prepared to attack the picture. *Blackboard Jungle* had sown the wind, but *Rebel Without a Cause* would most likely reap the whirlwind.

Warner apparently called Ray into his office and explained the situation. The studio, he said, might decide to halt production. In Ray's uncorroborated version of events, Ray immediately offered to buy the rights from the studio, find private financing and produce the film himself. He asked only twenty-four hours to come up with the money.

Warner, as the story goes, sent Steve Trilling to the projection room to ask the projectionist what he thought of Ray's film. The projectionist is said to have said that it was the only worthwhile project at the studio. Warner called Ray back and told him to proceed with the film. However, Ray had to discard all the black-and-white footage and start over in color. *Rebel Without a Cause* had suddenly become a prestige picture at Warner Bros.

Perhaps Jack Warner, who was a high-stakes gambler by nature, was just playing a hunch. James Dean had made a huge impression in *East of Eden*, which was doing extremely well at the box office. If Warner transformed *Rebel* from a low-budget exploitation film to a prestige picture on the strength of Dean's popularity, the studio could expect a much bigger take at the box office.

A more compelling reason for the upgrade to color was the fine print in the studio's licensing agreement with the inventor of CinemaScope. The Warner Bros. Legal Department had apparently overlooked a clause stating that all CinemaScope productions had to be filmed in color. MGM had made the same mistake with *Trial*, which had yet to begin production. MGM would opt for black-and-white and drop the CinemaScope format, but Warner Bros. decided to switch to color. Jack Warner sent an urgent memo to David Weisbart: Ray must move quickly to refilm the black-and-white scenes in color, and Weisbart must "not leave the studio" until checking with Steve Trilling or Warner himself as to the progress of the film. "This is a very important picture," Warner explained, and he expected to view the dailies personally with Weisbart "at least until we are on the right track."

Ray looked forward to filming in color, even WarnerColor, the studio's inferior substitute for the Technicolor process. However, the sudden changeover caused some immediate problems. Clothing that tested well for black-and-white might not test as well for color. One of the first wardrobe casualties was a black leather jacket that Dean expected to wear. Ray substituted a red windbreaker, supposedly right off the back of the production's First Aid Man. Ray had it dipped in black paint first to remove the sheen.

The Wardrobe Department also re-dyed all four hundred pairs of jeans, since their shade of blue would "bleed" in WarnerColor. Aside from the bright red coat that Wood was to wear at the precinct station, she had a relatively subdued wardrobe. Ray told her to buy a plain green dress "off the rack" for reshooting the observatory sequence and Dawson High. Ray also decided to move the setting of the picture from Christmas to Easter, a more colorful season in Los Angeles.

The change to color also necessitated a change in film editors. William Ziegler, with more experience editing color than James Moore, would quickly assume his duties.

On Saturday, April 2 at 7:15 A.M., the company arrived at 601 Pico Boulevard in Santa Monica to film the Dawson High sequence in color. One hundred and forty-four extras doubled as the student body. Sixteen cars, thirteen bicycles, five motor scooters, three motorcycles and three school buses occupied the parking lot. Ray filmed only eight shots: in the school quadrangle, Plato arrives on a scooter and stops at the flagpole; a small cannon fires to announce the flag raising; Buzz and his gang stand in the background as the students enter the building; in the corridor, Jim tries to talk to Judy as the students go to their classes; Jim stops to look at the school trophy case. Ray's last shot had the students exiting the building on their way to the planetarium show. The crew wrapped up the production at 5:30 P.M.

Jimmie Fidler's column in *The Valley Times* wasted no time reporting on the new-look *Rebel Without a Cause* for his readers. Much of the news came verbatim from the studio's press release. Philip K. Scheuer's column in *The Los Angeles Times* also spotlighted the upgraded *Rebel* production. Scheuer reported that Ray was trying to distance *Rebel* from the storm caused by *Blackboard Jungle*. Ray's film, Scheuer explained, emphasized the problems in the middle-class home as a cause of delinquency.

After taking Sunday off, the company returned to Santa Monica on April 4. Ray completed ten shots, starting with Jim watching the flag ceremony. Ray decided to move one of the interior shots outdoors. In Stern's script, a school monitor gives Jim directions in the corridor; but Ray had observed a circular plaque at the main entrance and decided that Jim would innocently step on it. Stepping on the school symbol, a minor but telling offense, would emphasize Jim's position as the perpetual "new kid in town." In Ray's new scene, the monitor (Bruce Noonan) then reprimands an embarrassed and apologetic Jim while Buzz and his gang look on disapprovingly. Ray's last shot before lunch had Jim entering the school "in [a] sea of faces."

A second *Rebel* unit simultaneously filmed "wild" shots (film without synchronized sound) at the location. They included a close-up, or "insert," of the cannon firing and long views of the school clock, the raising of the flag, and the arrival of Jim's and Buzz's cars. Stand-ins took the places of the actors. Ray planned to use some of these "wild" shots as cutaways from the main action.

Ray shot interiors after lunch: Jim walks along the corridor; Plato opens his locker and watches Jim, who almost enters the girls' room by mistake. Judy does not smoke a cigarette, since Ray had already sacrificed that scene to the censor. Production wrapped at 6:22, and the company arrived back at the studio at 7:05.

Ray's staff was waiting for him on Stage 6, where Mal Bert's crew had constructed the interior of the precinct station. The design included an open waiting area and seven glass-partitioned rooms, allowing for maximum camera flexibility. Ray and his staff stayed until 8:00 P.M. lining up the first shot for the next morning.

Meanwhile, Joe McLaughlin of the Music Department had learned that a "partial visual vocal" of "Man In the Moon" would cost the studio $750. Ray wanted the song for Judy's back yard scene with her father, but the studio would probably object to the price.

28

RED CHANNELS

The company's first day on Stage 6 was Jim Backus's first day of work. He tried to create a relaxed atmosphere by squinting his eyes and doing his best Mr. Magoo for his co-workers. Even the usually serious and withdrawn James Dean enjoyed the show. The Publicity Department readied a press release. Later, Backus presented Dean with an autographed recording of his famous cartoon voice.

Marsha Hunt should have been on the set that morning to play Jim Stark's mother. Instead, Ann Doran took her place. Doran had just finished a role in *The Desperate Hours* with Humphrey Bogart. At 44, she was six years older than Marsha Hunt. The next day, *The Los Angeles Times* reported that Doran had replaced Hunt "because [the play] 'Anniversary Waltz' is requiring too much of Miss Hunt's time."

There was another, more likely explanation for Hunt's sudden withdrawal. For years, she had been on the infamous Hollywood "blacklist," a *Who's Who* of performers denied work because of their support of "anti–American" causes.

Hunt had been active in fighting the government's investigations of Hollywood "Communists" since 1947. She had signed the *amicus curiae* brief for the Hollywood Ten in 1949. *Red Channels*, a right-wing newsletter subtitled, *The Report of Communist Influence in Radio and Television*, had listed six "charges" against her in 1950. Those charges had effectively put an end to her television career. Hunt had refused to sign a loyalty oath for the Stanley Kramer production, *The Happy Time*, in 1952. She had also refused to place an advertisement in the trade papers expressing remorse for past political "mistakes." Since then, Hunt had not made a single feature in Hollywood. Her blacklisting would keep her off the screen until 1956.

Ann Doran, to the contrary, was a solid citizen in the eyes of the movie colony. The previous July, she had appeared with actor Pedro Gonzales Gonzales and Roy Brewer, president of the Hollywood Motion Picture Alliance, in a patriotic celebration in Silver City, New Mexico. The event, known as "All-Out for All-American Day," had protested the filming of the allegedly pro–Communist film *Salt of the Earth* in Silver City. In November, Doran had been honored for her participation in "All-Out for All-American Day" with a citation at the Statler Hotel in Los Angeles.

Although Ann Doran's Mrs. Stark would be appropriately shrill, Doran projected a far more friendly and relaxed image off-camera. Dressed in an evening gown

Left: Ann Doran, demonstrating a lighter, more playful side. Her role as the shrill, domineering mother in *Rebel Without a Cause* was not one of her favorites. *Right:* Marsha Hunt, a victim of Hollywood's "Red Scare" from 1952 through 1956.

and mink for her opening scene, she plodded comfortably around the set in saddle shoes. Jim Backus already knew how easy she was to work with. According to the Publicity Department, this would be the third time they had played husband and wife in the movies.

Virginia Brissac had the role of Jim's grandmother. She had recently played Walter Pidgeon's wife in *Executive Suite*. Television audiences also knew her from *Dragnet*.

Ray completed nine shots his first day on Stage 6. The first introduced three Mexican children (Skipper Huerta, Stephanie Aranas, and Leonard Martinez) and the two Juvenile Officers who would later interview Jim, Judy and Plato. Robert Foulk played the officer named "Gene." The stocky, balding actor had appeared most recently in two Warner Bros. features, *East of Eden* and *Strange Lady in Town*. Edward Platt, the future "Chief" of television's *Get Smart!*, had the role of Ray Framek.

Ray rehearsed quietly with his actors, first for a half hour, and then for twenty minutes. In between, he kept the three children entertained with comic books.

In the first scene, Jim is playing with a wind-up toy monkey that the Sergeant has let him keep. Spotting Judy, he winds it up and starts it dancing on the floor. Judy shows no interest, but Plato smiles from across the room and the Mexican children respond with glee. Gene kneels down next to them. As one of the children observes that Gene is bald, Ray Framek enters and asks Gene, "What gang does *he* belong to?" Gene answers, "Give him a couple of years."

The actors completed the two-minute, twelve-second scene in one take. However, Ray had taken up the entire morning rehearsing, blocking and re-blocking the action. The company broke for lunch at 12:40. After lunch, Natalie Wood played her first important scene: Ray Framek brings Judy to his office, where she tries to explain why she was walking the streets late at night. The scene required Wood to cry for several minutes without interruption. Because it was such a difficult scene, Ray decided to film it in continuous takes, first as a two-shot of Judy and Ray Framek, then as a close-up of Judy.

After twelve takes, Ray had two that were good enough to print. It marked an impressive adult debut for Wood and seemed to justify Ray's faith in the former child actress. Wood's performance was also something of a record-breaker at the studio. According to the Publicity Department, veterans among the crew could not remember a sustained crying scene of that length (almost five minutes) since Bette Davis apparently set the record with *Winter Meeting* in 1948.

At the end of the sequence, a Woman Officer (Louise Lane) escorts Judy away, still crying because her mother, not her father, is coming for her. Ray finished the day's shooting with five point-of-view reaction shots of Ray Framek as he talks and listens to Judy. Ray completed the filming at 6:35 and set up the next day's first shot.

29

HARD WORK,
HARD FEELINGS

The next day, Mrs. Maria Gurdin, Natalie Wood's mother, arrived on the set. The Publicity Department attributed the visit to social worker/teacher Tom Hennesy, who was supposedly trying to discourage a romance between Wood and Dennis Hopper. Hopper had apparently created the problem by informing Mrs. Gurdin of her daughter's illicit relationship with Ray. Mrs. Gurdin could hardly have been surprised by the news. She and Natalie had frequently argued about Natalie's many lovers and her independent behavior; but neither she nor Natalie's father had any power to control their daughter's life. As Nick Adams observed, "There was little they could do about it. She was bringing home most of the money."

Tension between Ray and Hopper had escalated since Hopper's discovery at the Marmont, and it was beginning to affect the production. One member of the cast later recalled: "Nick tried to get Dennis kicked off the movie, but Dennis was under contract to Warner Bros. and he couldn't. So Nick made things very unpleasant for Dennis." Hopper's action also upset Natalie Wood "because, from then on, her mother was never out of sight. Everyone knew the problems Dennis had created, and he quickly became the goat of the movie."

The animosity between Ray and Hopper undermined the cooperative atmosphere that Ray had been trying to build for *Rebel*. As Steffi Sidney later observed, "Nick wanted a real camaraderie among the kids in the film, but he got just the opposite."

That morning, however, the business of filming took priority over private feuding. Ray completed six shots. In the first, Judy leaves Ray Framek's office while Jim offers his jacket to a shivering Plato. Plato is sitting with his nurse, played by Marietta Canty. Like so many black actresses of her day, Canty had made a career playing domestic servants. Audiences frequently confused her with the more popular Louise Beavers. Canty's recent films included *Father of the Bride* (1950) and *Father's Little Dividend* (1951).

After Plato refuses Jim's jacket, the little Mexican girl hands the wind-up mon-

117

key to Jim, and he hands it back to her. As Judy and the Woman Officer pass in front of the camera, Jim sits in the background watching his parents and grandmother arrive. Ray filmed through the glass partition, as he would do a number of times in this sequence. In the next shot, Jim greets his family with a cynical "Happy Easter."

Ray then set up a shot of Jim and Plato: Jim looks through the partition and complains, "Why didn't you take my jacket?" Just as Ray prepared to film it, Mineo's time ran out for the day. As Eric Stacey had forewarned, Ray's use of minors had already begun to cause delays. The production wrapped at 5:00 P.M.

The next day, April 7, Ray completed the unfinished business, then filmed Plato's interview with Gene. The five-shot sequence took all morning and much of the afternoon. Although Mineo's first major scene lacked the dramatic intensity of Natalie Wood's, it was just as difficult to perform. Mineo portrayed a youth who was far more disturbed and dangerous than the others. He admitted to shocking things, but he needed to gain the audience's support.

In Stern's script, Plato's conversation with Gene provided the balance of sympathy and dread that the audience would need to understand the character. Plato has shot his neighbor's puppies, but he cannot explain why. When Plato's nurse suggests that Gene can help him, Plato responds, "Nobody can help me." His mother is in Chicago, the nurse explains, and Plato's father has not been around "in a long time." Gene asks where Plato got the gun to shoot the puppies. "In my mother's drawer," he answers. When Gene asks if Plato has been to a psychiatrist, Plato asks derisively, "Head shrinker?" Plato's nurse explains that his mother doesn't believe in them, and Gene says, "Well, maybe she better start."

The scene played well. The only problem appeared to be Mineo's Bronx accent, which made "drawer" sound like "draw" and "head shrinker" sound like "head shrinkuh." Mineo's accent was not the only voice problem. William Mueller of the Sound Department had informed Eric Stacey that Dean's "low dialog" in one of the Santa Monica shots was "covered by loud noise." Ray could not reshoot the scene, so he would have to post-synchronize the dialogue. Just before lunch, Ray filmed the "Why didn't you take my jacket?" shot from a different angle.

After lunch, Ray spent forty-five minutes blocking the next shot and a half hour changing the set: Jim and his parents have a heated argument in Ray Framek's office. Ray completed only the first part of Stern's Scene 19. He would film the rest, and Jim's solo confrontation with Ray Framek, the next day. The production wrapped at 6:30 P.M.

Meanwhile, the Los Angeles Police Department had given the studio permission to use the Hollywood Police Station as the exterior for the scenes Ray was filming on Stage 6. The studio had also signed an agreement with J. Paul Getty for the use of his mansion. Ray's company would film there April 16, 18, 19, 20 and 21. Getty would not grant extensions, for he was planning to demolish the building soon after.

On April 8, *Rebel Without a Cause* had been in production for nine days. Ray began work on Stage 6 with a close-up of Judy. She is sitting on a bench and looking at Jim as two policemen bring him into the building. In the next shot, a policeman frisks Jim at the Sergeant's desk. Ray remembered Trilling's objection about placing Jim at the stomping scene. Stern's script had the answer to that objection.

When the desk sergeant asks if Jim was "mixed up in that beating on Twelfth Street," the arresting officer assures him that Jim is "clean" of that charge.

During the brief exchange, Dean improvised: Jim acts ticklish as the policeman frisks him. Ray then filmed a retake of Judy getting up from the bench and leaving with the Woman Officer. This time, Ray had the camera dolly over to the bench to show that Judy has left her compact behind. When Jim sits on the same bench several shots later, he picks up the compact.

Ray filmed two shots of the Stark family arguing about Jim. The work halted for ten minutes until an engine noise outside stopped. The scene continued: Jim explodes, "You're tearing me apart!" Ray Framek brings him into a private office, where he encourages Jim to take out his anger on the desk (Ray deferred the actual desk punching to another day). The production wrapped at 8:00 P.M. after eleven hours on the sound stage.

Meanwhile, Dean's unorthodox acting style was attracting attention in the newspapers. On April 8, Sidney Skolsky wrote in his "Hollywood Is my Beat" column:

> Jimmy, before going into a scene, will take a short run around the sound stage, or Jimmy will jump up and down in one place before going in to play the scene. Dean has to be in action before going into action.

Dean had also been known to lock himself in his dressing room until prepared to play a scene. While making *East of Eden*, he had often wandered away from cast and crew to concentrate, then blown a whistle to signal his readiness. Dean's techniques had become something of a joke at Warner Bros., but he was not the only actor with unusual habits. Corey Allen, concerned that his voice would not project enough masculinity as Buzz, frequently screamed just before going in front of the cameras. When some of the *Rebel* cast began openly mocking Dean and Allen, Ray called the entire company together and issued an ultimatum: respect the working styles of every actor in the picture, or leave the production.

30

LOST TIME

Ray had more work to do on Stage 6 the next morning. His first shots completed most of the precinct station sequence: Jim and his parents prepare to leave. As Jim stops at the Sergeant's desk to collect his valuables, Buzz and the gang enter. They look threateningly at Jim as he passes. In another shot, out of sequence, Jim apologizes to his parents for exploding earlier, and Jim's father offers Ray Framek a cigar. The final shot from the argument sequence, a close-up of Jim's father, required eight takes. Backus spoiled four of them by flubbing his lines.

Next, Ray leaped ahead in the script to Scene 220: Jim comes to the police station after the chickie run looking for Ray Framek. Dean changed out of his rumpled suit and tie and into the faded red windbreaker, white T-shirt and jeans that would comprise his wardrobe for the rest of the film. He played the scene with Paul Bryar as the Desk Sergeant, John Close as an Officer and Peter Miller as the hoodlum who occupies their time while Ray Framek is out on a call.

On Monday, April 11, cast and crew returned to the Griffith Observatory, arriving at 6:55 A.M. Ray had made up one of the three days lost from filming in black-and-white; but because of the switch to WarnerColor and Ray's use of minors, the production was still two days behind schedule. Ray's unfinished business at Stage 6, a shot of Jim's grandmother and the rest of the scene in Ray Framek's office, now had to wait. Ray's company had only a limited number of shooting days at the Observatory and needed to keep to the schedule. Cast and crew worked almost a twelve-hour day to make up the lost time.

Ray re-shot Jim's car arriving, then went inside to film the beginning of the lecturer's planetary presentation. Because the theater allowed so little room for maneuvering lights and equipment, the crew needed almost three hours just to block the first shot. Ray's young actors played a more passive role in that day's shooting, as they listened to Ian Wolfe recite his lines as the Lecturer. At least one member of the cast, Nick Adams, was grateful for the inactivity. Adams had spent the previous day in bed after an attack of malaria. He had contracted the disease while in Panama with the Coast Guard.

Also among the cast was 66-year-old Almira Sessions. Sessions had been a character actress since 1940, usually playing spinsters or "old lady" school teachers. Her films included *Little Nelly Kelly* (1940), *Sullivan's Travels* (1941), *The Ox-Bow Incident* (1943) and *The Miracle of Morgan's Creek* (1944). Now, in *Rebel Without a Cause*, she played yet another "old lady" teacher.

The studio, meanwhile, was working on technical matters. Eric Stacey sent David Weisbart a memo regarding procedure for burning a car in the city of Los Angeles: no more than three minutes of burning in any one hour; all fabric and upholstery to be removed from the vehicle; Shellane fuel only to produce the "flame effect." All this according to the regulations of the city's Smog Control Board.

The next day, Ray's company put in another twelve hours at the Griffith Observatory. Ray completed the lecture sequence. He reshot Jim and Plato hiding out on the balcony and Buzz's gang discovering them. He used two cameras to film the students leaving the planetarium. As one of the cameras pans down from the huge projector, the "old lady" teacher tries to get the students' attention, but finally gives up trying.

Almira Sessions' character was not the only frustrated adult on the set. At 10:00 A.M., as Ray prepared to film a reaction shot of the students, he discovered that Corey Allen and Dennis Hopper had disappeared. By the time they returned, the company had to vacate the planetarium for the real show at 10:45. Ray would have to pick up the shot at a later time. As the production fell even further behind schedule, Ray's already strained relationship with Hopper worsened.

Ray was also having difficulty with the planetarium's special effects. As the teenagers watch Earth being destroyed "in a burst of gas and fire," Ray wanted the apocalyptic display reflected in their faces. He had a lightning effect in mind, but he soon discovered that the planetarium show did not include simulated lightning. Hurriedly, his crew set up their own lightning maker. At the end of the day, Ray lined up the next day's first shot, and the production wrapped at 5:50 P.M. He and his staff drove to the Getty mansion, where they stayed until 7:30. In less than a week, *Rebel Without a Cause* would be filming there, just ahead of the wrecking ball.

The mansion's imminent demise worried David Weisbart. He reminded Ray to concentrate "on all the exterior stuff first." Interiors could always be replicated at the studio, but once the bulldozers demolished the 22-room structure, Ray could not return for retakes. Two days later, Eric Stacey sent a similar memo to 1st Assistant Director Don Page.

Meanwhile, Weisbart and Ray Heindorf, the studio's Music Director, had been discussing musical selections. The studio had to approve any incidental music used in *Rebel*, such as a song on the radio, or students whistling a tune in a school corridor. The Music Department then determined if the songs were protected by copyright and if the studio had to pay royalties. Ray and Weisbart both wanted to use "Man in the Moon," but at $750, it would be expensive. They had also approved "Let's Put Out the Lights," by Herman Hupfeld, and "Song of the Moon," which could replace "Man In the Moon."

At the Observatory the next day, cast and crew worked thirteen hours. Ray refilmed the black-and-white shot of Jim and Plato confronting the gang behind the building. After lunch, the company went back inside, completing the reaction shots and Jim's mooing at Taurus, the Bull.

Ray's approach to filming stressed collaboration, and his young actors frequently experimented and made suggestions. On this third day back at the Observatory, they presented Ray with a new scene. In Stern's script, the gang hovers in the parking lot, waiting for Jim to emerge. Some of the actors suggested a closer view of the gang as its members planned what to do about "Moo." Ray listened, and the actors improvised the scene. A gang member asks, "Hey, what's for kicks?" and another suggests, "How about Moo?" After some discussion, Buzz says, "All right. Moo."

As Ray's young gang members practiced the group mentality that he had hoped for, Dean remained the odd man out. Off camera, he spent much of his time reading (including a book called *How to Build Character*) and quietly adding entries to a Director's Diary he was keeping. At other times, he played the prankster. He had broken his front teeth as a child, and he enjoyed removing his dental bridge for its shock value. He especially enjoyed embarrassing Beverly Long with sexual crudities. One day, while the company was relaxing between takes at the Observatory, Dean picked up a tire iron, walked over to Long and asked her to hold it. "Have you ever felt anything soooo hard?" he asked.

At other times, the little boy in Dean emerged. He asked Long if she wanted to see some photographs. She imagined something pornographic, but discovered instead pictures of him racing his Porsche at Palm Springs.

Dean also offered hair-raising drives around the Observatory parking lot to anyone foolish enough to accept an invitation. Long, like many others, declined. She told Dean that he drove too fast. "I have to," Dean replied. "I'm not going to be around too long."

Dean also enjoyed boxing between takes. He sparred with Perry Lopez, who frequently visited him at the studio, and also with ex-boxer Mushy Callahan, one of Dean's stand-ins. His favorite activity, however, seemed to be ridiculing his rival, Marlon Brando, and his earlier mentor, Elia Kazan. Dean and Nick Adams entertained cast and crew with their spirited impersonations of the two men. An accomplished mime, Dean also did impromptu impressions of Montgomery Clift and Charlie Chaplin.

Few on the set appreciated or understood Dean's unconventional behavior. On April 14, Dorothy Kilgallen wrote in her syndicated column, "Other actors shooting in 'Rebel Without a Cause' break into vivid language at the mention of Jimmy Dean's name. They appreciate his talent, but they don't dig his on-the-set manners." Although many of Dean's fellow actors found him intolerable, Dean's fans held quite a different view. The Publicity Department reported that Dean's fan mail was averaging six hundred letters a week.

April 14 was the company's fourth day at the Observatory. Ray re-filmed the earlier black-and-white scenes. He spent three and a half hours, before and after lunch, trying to reshoot Scene 77G: Buzz punctures Jim's tire, pulls out the knife, and waits for Jim's reaction. Ray needed four separate shots and twelve takes before saying, "Print." James Dean was not even on the set. According to the Publicity Department, he spent April 14 and 15 at the dentist, having his dental bridge repaired. Ray had hoped to finish at the location that day, but now he would have to return. In Dean's absence, the company shut down early. The many small delays were beginning to add up.

Louella Parsons also featured James Dean in her April 14 column: Warner Bros.

would apparently loan Dean to MGM to make *Somebody Up There Likes Me*, the film biography of boxer Rocky Graziano. Dean had both the physical skills and the grace of movement to play a boxer. Jim Backus had observed him sparring with Mushy Callahan at the Observatory, and also doing "beautifully executed leaps, glissades, and *entrechats.*"

Behind schedule, *Rebel Without a Cause* returned to Stage 6 to film the slapping scene in Judy's dining room. Three of the four actors who arrived to work had just joined the cast. William Hopper and Rochelle Hudson played Judy's parents, and Jimmy Baird played her brother, Beau. When Hopper arrived on the set, Wood congratulated him on his performance in the previous night's television production, *No Sad Songs for Me*. Wood had played in the 1950 movie version with Wendell Corey. Rochelle Hudson, a former ingenue of the 1930s, had appeared in *Are These Our Children?* (1930), *She Done Him Wrong* (1931) and *Poppy* (1936). During World War II, she had worked in the Office of Naval Intelligence. Since then she had appeared infrequently in films. Moviegoers had most recently seen Jimmy Baird in *The Seven Little Foys*, with Bob Hope.

Ray completed eight shots, starting with a master shot of the family at the dining room table, then moving to two-shots and close-ups. Three Warner Bros. executives watched the slapping scene in horror, then rushed back to Jack Warner to register their complaints.

Elsewhere at the studio, Joe McLaughlin wrote to Helen Schoen in New York. Ray wanted "one of the girl principals" (probably Natalie Wood) to sing a couple of lines from "Two Sleepy People." McLaughlin thought that the song would cost too much and suggested "Let's Put Out the Lights." McLaughlin objected to "Man in the Moon" for the same reason. He suggested in a memo to Ray that his substitution, "Song of the Moon," would not only cost less, but would suit the scene better.

31

THE MANSION

On its sixteenth day of production, Saturday, April 16, *Rebel Without a Cause* moved to the Getty mansion for five days. All filming there would be at night. Cast and crew left the studio at 3:00 P.M. and arrived on location at 3:30. Ray took two and a half hours to block the first shot. The company took forty-five minutes for dinner, and the cameras rolled at 8:00 P.M.

Maila Nurmi and Jack Simmons of the Night Watch visited the set. They came to watch the performers, and also to admire the famous location where Billy Wilder had filmed *Sunset Boulevard*. Ray was shooting Scenes 257-259 from Stern's script: Plato awakens to find Crunch, Moose and Goon standing over him; he runs to the empty pool, holds the gang at bay, then runs back to the summer house to grab his coat (his gun is in the pocket).

Ray hoped for a productive first evening, but it was not to be. One of the shots required a camera crane to produce a high angle. The fifty-foot crane arrived an hour late, giving Ray only ten minutes to rehearse and shoot the scene before time ran out for Sal Mineo. While Ray was filming the master shot, Mineo became exhausted from running around and wielding a heavy pool hose and collapsed in the middle of the action. Because Ray could not do a retake before Mineo's time expired, he kept the camera rolling, hoping to cover himself with medium shots and close-ups later.

On Sunday, April 17, the company rested. Ray met with Ernest Haller, his cinematographer, to discuss lighting for the remainder of the mansion sequence, the chickie run and the night scenes outside the Observatory. The meeting lasted three hours. Ray felt a special urgency in completing these shots: Daylight Savings Time would take effect in a week, giving Ray one hour less of night shooting with his two minors. The next day, Ray explained to Weisbart about the crane problem on Saturday night. He understood the need to avoid "long takes and excess footage," he explained, and he would "try to make sure" he had good reasons whenever he had to violate those rules.

He sent Weisbart a separate memo regarding *Rebel's* music score, questioning why Leonard Rosenman had not been formally announced to score the film. In making his pitch, Ray cited Rosenman's recent work on both *East of Eden* and MGM's *The Cobweb*.

Weisbart in turn sent a memo to Assistant Director Don Page regarding the swift completion of the night sequences. Eric Stacey, with a similar problem in mind, urged Hoyt Bowers to try to win concessions from the Board of Education: *Rebel* needed more evening hours for Wood and Mineo.

That evening, Ray's company returned to the Getty mansion for a second night. Ray completed twelve shots, starting at 4:25 P.M. and finishing at 2:15 the next morning. The caterers provided 135 dinners and 135 "midnight meals" for cast and crew. In Ray's first two shots, the gang searches for Plato. Jim and Judy break into the mansion with Plato close behind. Jim and Judy climb halfway up a staircase, Plato picks up an "antique Spanish candelabra" and lights the candles. The property man instructed Sal Mineo to take special care of the candelabra. After *Rebel Without a Cause*, the studio planned to use it in the upcoming Liberace movie, *Sincerely Yours*.

The scene on the staircase required three cameras to record simultaneous long shots and close-ups of the action. Ray used a single microphone disguised as part of the staircase. In the scene, Jim and Judy pretend to be newlyweds, with Plato as a realtor trying to rent or sell the place for "only a million dollars a month." The scene extends outside the building as Plato shows Jim and Judy the empty pool. Ray needed the crane for that. In other action, Plato fires at Jim, then shoots Crunch as Goon and Moose react. In the final two shots of the evening, Ray returned to the swimming pool to cover his incomplete master shot from Saturday. He filmed two close-ups. The candelabra survived the evening's work. Cast and crew arrived at the studio at 2:35 A.M.

The next day, Elizabeth Taylor visited the studio. She met her future *Giant* co-star in the Green Room, the VIP dining area of the Warner Bros. commissary. After lunch, Dean gave her the obligatory fast ride around the studio in his Porsche Super Speedster. Studio executives held their breath until Dean returned her safely.

In the evening, Dean returned to the Getty mansion with the rest of Ray's company. Again, they worked late into the night. Jane Deacy visited the set. She had brought Dean offers from three Broadway producers to do plays in 1956, when Dean's contract allowed him time off from the studio.

Ray's first three shots involved Crunch, Moose and Goon. Plato had wounded Crunch the day before, but only now would Crunch get to fall down the stairs. Moose and Goon help him to his feet and exit. Ray followed this with an out-of-sequence dolly shot of Plato, Jim and Judy leaving the house and walking toward the pool.

The major work of the evening was a fifty-foot crane shot of the three teenagers as they crossed the patio. To pick up the actors' voices, Ray used six parabolic microphones. The actors did not improvise on Stewart Stern's dialogue, but Dean could not resist a comic tribute to Jim Backus. To Judy's question about babies ("I don't know *what* to do when they cry, do you, dear?"), Dean replied in his best Mr. Magoo voice, "Of course. Drown 'em like puppies." Later, a humorless studio official complained to Dean that Mr. Magoo was not a Warner Bros. cartoon character; Dean should have imitated Bugs Bunny instead.

After the boom shot, which required five takes, Ray filmed what remained of Stern's mock psychiatric scene. Dean improvised: standing on the diving board, he shouted, "Quick! Fill the pool!" before tumbling in. The last shots of the evening showed Moose and Goon trying to grab the pool hose from Plato. Since Mineo's work for the evening had ended several hours earlier, someone else wielded the hose from off-screen.

On April 20, the company returned for a fourth long night at the mansion. The players had adapted well to the night schedule and the exotic surroundings. They also made good use of their time between takes. Dean, an amateur photographer, rode the camera crane to a height of twenty-five feet and took panoramic shots of the set. He planned to enter the pictures in *Photography Magazine*'s annual amateur contest. Natalie Wood spent her spare time practicing on a grand piano she had discovered inside the house (the one that Plato dives under to escape the gang). She entertained the cast during breaks with impromptu concerts. When Dean requested something that would put him in a serious mood, she played "Crazy Rhythm."

That night, Ray filmed the "summer house" sequence: Jim and Judy pretend to be Plato's parents. He lies at their feet, then falls asleep. As daylight lingered, Ray had to wait longer before he could begin filming. After breaking for a midnight meal at 11:15, Ray filmed one more shot, in which two policemen (Charles Fredericks and Joel Smith) confront Plato outside the mansion. The production wrapped at 1:50 A.M. and everyone returned to Warner Bros. at 2:25.

The studio, meanwhile, was beginning to see the difficulties in scheduling James Dean, especially as the start of *Giant* approached. Eric Stacey sent a memo to Don Page: the *Rebel* company must keep the *Giant* company informed of any changes in Dean's scheduled days off so that he can be made available to *Giant* "for tests, etc."

Meanwhile, Hoyt Bowers had received an answer from Ernest A. Tranqueda of the Los Angeles Board of Education. Tranqueda offered new working hours for Wood and Mineo. The two underage actors could now work nineteen evenings, provided they would not work past 11:00 P.M. except in "extreme" situations. After working until 10.00 P.M. or later, "there must be a ten-hour rest period" before they could be called back to the studio. This rule applied specifically to school days.

There was also some good news about the picture's musical selections. Helen Schoen reported that "Song of the Moon" was almost certainly in the public domain and could probably be used without charge.

While Jim Backus spent the evening moonlighting on Bob Hope's popular television program, Ray's cast and crew spent their fifth night at the Getty mansion. Ray completed nine more shots: the gang looks for Plato; Plato shoots Crunch (again) and takes a shot at Jim; Jim struggles with Plato; Judy runs after Jim and Plato as Moose and Goon attend Crunch. In the final shot of the evening, Jim and Judy enter the library and explore. The production wrapped at 11:15. The caravan returned to the studio at midnight.

32

FURY AND SOUND

On Friday, April 22, at 9:00 A.M., the company returned to Stage 6. Ray had several "pickups" of shots he had been unable to complete two weeks earlier. He began with a shot of Jim's grandmother. She tells Ray Framek that Jim was "always a lovely boy," then scowls as Jim says, "Grandmother, you tell one more lie and you're gonna get turned to stone." Ray completed two more shots before lunch: Ray Framek looks at the Mexican child playing with Jim, then sits on his desk listening to Jim talk about his troubled family life. The company broke for lunch at 1:35.

After lunch, Ray planned to shoot the rest of the sequence with Jim and Ray Framek. The crew was ready at 2:17, but Dean failed to arrive for rehearsal at 2:35. Instead, he stayed in his dressing room drinking wine, playing his bongo drums and listening to Wagner's *Ride of the Valkyrie*. The delay exasperated the crew and threatened to put the film further behind schedule. Finally, Dean walked onto the set to do the shot. Ray discussed it briefly with him, and the camera rolled. Ray cut the first take after thirty seconds for a technical reason; but the second take, including Dean's savage punching and kicking of the desk, was flawless. Dean's performance so astounded the crew that they forgot their displeasure and broke into applause. Dean, however, was in too much pain to notice their appreciation. He had hit the desk hard enough to injure his hand, and his face showed the effect.

Ray later recalled:

> We rehearsed that scene so Jimmy would be able to hit without hurting his knuckles, but when we began to shoot, it was clear that in the intensity of the scene he was hurting himself. I resisted the temptation to cut, and he continued to play the scene. Tears came, and pain, and the scene was very intense and meaningful.

Dean completed the rest of the sequence, including a heart-to-heart talk with Ray Framek at the water cooler, and a shot in which he tries to call Judy from the precinct station. Then, Nicholas Ray took Dean to Riverside Drive Emergency Hospital, where a doctor X-rayed his right hand. Dean had broken a knuckle and badly bruised the hand. A doctor wrapped it in an elastic bandage, which Dean was to wear for a week. Fortunately, the injury would not delay the production.

At 6:00 P.M., after filming the first component of Stern's split-screen montage (Ray Framek on the telephone), the company moved to another set on the sound stage representing the upstairs hallway of Judy's house. Judy comes home after the fatal chickie run. Her brother, Beau, greets her, but her father brusquely orders him back to bed. Scene 211B in Stern's script was a reaction shot of Judy's parents as she slams the door to her room. In the first two takes, Wood slammed the door so hard that the walls of the set moved. Ray finally got the shot right on the fourth take. In the last two shots of the day, Judy's father talks on the telephone. First, he hangs up on Jim, then he completes his part of the split-screen montage. The production wrapped at 8:25 P.M.

As Ray and Weisbart studied the dailies, they discovered a new problem. A number of the shots outside the Observatory had been ruined by noise from the portable generators Vic Johnson had set up. Eric Stacey wrote to Ray Bunnell in the Location Department: find immediate ways to reduce generator noise, even if it required building sound-proof baffles around the generators. Stacey observed that Columbia Pictures had recently sound-proofed their generators and asked Bunnell to inquire at Columbia. If necessary, drawing electricity from power lines "at some locations" might also help to eliminate generator noise.

Later in the day, Stacey sent a directive to several departments, including Sound and Location: the noise problem was in part due to the fact that generators had not been placed far enough away from the set. The company was to try as often as possible to place generators as far away as possible to eliminate the noise problem. Sound mixers, gaffers, head grips and all location men were expected to cooperate in this effort.

Meanwhile, Ray was becoming impatient with the studio's attempts to impose a tighter work schedule on *Rebel*. He wrote a terse memo to David Weisbart and sent a copy to Steve Trilling. The studio, of course, had its own agenda, most of which involved saving money. Eric Stacey sent the following order to Don Page: since so much of *Rebel Without a Cause* was being filmed at night, and since night exterior work involved "a terrific amount of expense," the *Rebel* company was "not to shoot any close shots on night exterior locations" that could be shot just as well at the studio. Mal Bert was to create the necessary interior sets.

That evening, Ray shot more interiors at the mansion. He began in the library, where Jim and Judy snuggle in front of an empty fireplace (the effects people added a flame effect later). Wood felt justifiably nervous before her first serious kiss in the movies. Dean teased her by observing, "You look green, and you know how green photographs in color."

Wood played the scene well, even though a critical two-shot required six takes. Ray added some point-of-view shots, and shots of both Jim and Judy sitting *in* the fireplace, then broke for dinner. After dinner, Ray re-filmed Plato shooting Crunch; Jim and Judy run past him as they follow Plato outside. Ray continued with a series of exteriors filmed out of sequence: Jim and Judy walk toward the mansion before Plato's arrival; Plato runs outside, Jim and Judy follow; Plato fights Crunch, Moose and Goon in the pool; Plato arrives on his scooter and runs to the door; Crunch, Moose and Goon get out of their car to enter the mansion. Ray's final shot of the evening was Jim's car arriving at the mansion. Because the building might not show up well behind the car, he decided to "matte in" the building later at the studio. "Matting in" meant combining a background that had already been photographed (the mansion) with a live-action scene (the car's arrival). The production wrapped at 11:15, and Ray's company returned to the studio.

The Getty mansion had seen its last film crew.

33

LOOPING AND AD-LIBBING

On Monday, April 25, Ray returned to the Griffith Observatory for three more days. He spent most of the first day shooting scenes that were not in Stewart Stern's script: Harry (Tom Bernard) stalks Jim through a corridor as Buzz and the gang wait outside; Plato waits at the pendulum pit in the lobby, then moves away as the gang approaches. Using the scene ad-libbed earlier by his actors, Ray improvised further:

> Before they rumble, the kids are standing around wondering, "What should we do about Moo?" And somebody says, "Moo!" and they start to go around this pendulum saying, "Moo," and this big circular thing [is] swinging around like the rhythm of the earth, and Corey Allen takes out his comb and starts beating a rhythm on the ledge, and then someone takes a set of keys, then a steel comb, a tube of lipstick and so on until they're going around and around beating this rhythm…boom…baboom…boom…baboom.

In the next two shots, the gang performed a "jitterbugging" number around the pendulum pit. Ray hoped to use the beat as a musical bridge leading to the switch-blade fight. For the scene to work, however, he needed suitable music, which he hoped Leonard Rosenman would write. When Rosenman failed later to compose this "be-bop suite," Ray reluctantly excised what had become one of his favorite scenes in the picture.

In the next shot, Plato runs to the exit, finds Buzz blocking it and goes back inside. Jim passes the pendulum, sees the gang and wanders back into the display area. Plato finds him looking at a Tesla Coil display.

The next day, Ray's company moved to Stage 8, where Mal Bert's staff had constructed the kitchen of Jim's house: Jim's family is eating breakfast on his first day of school. As the three adults bicker, Jim sees Judy outside in the alley. The kitchen scene was Virginia Brissac's last in the picture. Stern's script had given her four lines of dialogue, but only two would remain in the film.

On April 27, columnist Army Archerd reported that James Dean and Nick Adams planned to turn their impromptu Kazan and Brando imitations into a nightclub act after they finished *Rebel Without a Cause*. Dean would play Kazan, and Adams would play Brando.

Meanwhile, Finlay McDermid of the Story Department was trying to complete the picture's writing credits as they would appear on the screen. Irving Shulman, who had finished his work on the picture in January, had apparently not responded to the question. McDermid wrote to Shulman asking him to present "a fairly immediate answer to your feelings about the credits." If Shulman did not respond within the required period, the credits would become final.

That morning, Ray's company returned to the Observatory. Ray re-filmed the balcony sequence with Jim and Plato, the gang's arrival, and Jim's encounter with Buzz. This time, Buzz pushes Jim instead of slapping him. Jim threatens Buzz with a tire iron, then flings it over a wall and says, "I don't want any trouble." Buzz pulls a switchblade and Jim backs away.

Ray finished the fifteen shots by 6:20 P.M. The company arrived at the studio at 6:45. All the re-filming in color had left the production five days behind schedule.

Ray finished the switchblade fight the next day. Once again, Dean and Corey Allen put on chest protectors; once again they fought with dulled knives. This time, no one was hurt. Ray also re-filmed the Guide and Lecturer arriving to break up the fight. The taunting of the Guide in Stern's script borrowed from Irving Shulman's scene at Wimpy's, including some of the dialogue.

Ray's improvised version ended as Chick (Nick Adams) lifts the cap from the Guide's head and does an animated impression of Hitler ("Achtung! Achtung! We were just coming out!"). Adams was the most brazen scene-stealer on the set, and his tactics did not endear him to most of the other actors. Earlier, during the switchblade fight, Adams had punched Steffi Sidney in the ribs just as she was to say her one line in the film, "Look out, Buzzie, he's got a chain!" Adams had then shouted the line himself. (Sidney got the line back on the next take.)

While Nick Adams was shouting his lines, Dean and others were still mumbling theirs. Weisbart's latest memo to Ray stressed the need to make the actors project their voices to avoid post-synchronizing in a sound room after filming was completed. "Unfortunately," Weisbart complained, "some of our key scenes are involved."

The Sound Department reported that traffic noise had also created some of the problem. Ray would have to "loop" these shots as well during post-production. Meanwhile, Eric Stacey had given up trying to find an exterior for Jim's house. He informed the Location Department that Ray would film it on Stage 8. Moving this exterior indoors would save the studio money and travel-time. It would also ease Ray's night shooting schedule. Unfortunately, the sound stage could not duplicate the realism of an actual location.

The next day, Ray's company returned to Stage 8. After four days of reshooting at the Observatory, the production had fallen six days behind schedule. Ray completed ten shots, mostly entrances and exits: Jim comes home after the switchblade fight, lingers in the kitchen and hears a crash upstairs (his father has spilled a dinner tray). Jim passes through the living room and goes upstairs. Ray saved the actual "spilling" scene for another day.

After Dean changed clothes and the company broke for lunch, Ray filmed Dean leaving for the chickie run as his father runs down the stairs after him. After failing to stop Dean from leaving, Backus was supposed to take off his apron and run back upstairs. The first of these apparently simple shots required five takes; the second required fourteen. Backus appeared to be the problem in most of the bad takes.

On April 30, Ray moved to a new set on Stage 22 to film the "exterior" of Plato's house. The studio was employing yet another cost-cutting measure despite Ray's protests. Ray completed fourteen shots, covering three of Stern's numbered scenes and part of a fourth: Plato arrives on his scooter and Crunch, Moose and Goon ambush him. Since the scooter was moving slowly, Ray "undercranked" the camera to twenty frames per second, instead of the usual twenty-four. This made the action look faster on the screen. The actors could perform safely, and the audience still had the illusion of normal movement. Plato then runs onto the porch and escapes inside when his nurse comes to chase the three boys away. He goes to his mother's room, gets a gun from under her pillow, and runs out. Ray's last shot of the day was another addition to the split-screen montage: Plato's nurse on the telephone.

On Sunday, May 1, an off-day, James Dean entered his sports car in a race at Bakersfield. He did not inform the studio. He finished third overall and first in his class. During the contest, which took place in a rainstorm, one driver was killed and another injured. The next day, Neil Rau's column reported more Dean news, courtesy of the Warner Bros. Publicity Department:

> The proposed nightclub comedy act of James Dean and Nick Adams is now under consideration by four Las Vegas bistros, it was learned today.
> The act, which started off as a gag on the set of Warner Bros.' "Rebel Without a Cause," went over so funny with the cast and crew of the picture the boys decided to form an act in which Dean plays Elia Kazan and Adams mimics Brando.
> Since Dean goes into "Giant" he won't be able to start his act until 1956. But he and Adams are formulating plans to also include modern comedy versions of "Hamlet" and "Macbeth," and a couple of musical numbers.

Army Archerd started his May 2 column in *Daily Variety* with more bits of news from *Rebel*:

> GOOD MORNING: James Dean's tired of "mumbling and shuffling" roles — wants to do "Romeo and Juliet." Recuping from laryngitis, Dean balked at doing makeup and wardrobe tests for "Giant" on Saturday, his one day off from "Rebel Without a Cause"...One scene of "Rebel" was so dramatic, Jim Backus quipped, "Welcome to the Elia Kazan hour"...However, director Nick Ray manages to keep his sense of humor — while George Stevens keeps a map of Texas as his emblem, and Jack Webb a cornet, Ray has a plucked, rubber chicken hanging from his dressing room...

A flattering portrait of James Dean also appeared in Harold Heffernan's column in *The Valley Times*.

> [Dean] exudes confidence in his histrionic potentials, yet at the same time he gives not the slightest hint of conceit. He's just sold on himself in a nice, quiet way.
> "An actor should never have a best performance," he related seriously in his dressing room between takes. "Once he gets in that category he's a dead duck. He not only limits himself as to his capabilities, but he automatically throws a psychological block at theatergoers.
> "I can honestly say I consider my present role in 'Rebel' better than the Cal part I did in 'East of Eden.' And in each succeeding picture, I shall think of its character as better

than the one before. I must always feel that my best is yet to come. If I can't keep such a thought in mind I'll quit the business."

Dean would be able to put this philosophy to the test in a few days, when Ray filmed the Stark family's confrontation scene. Today, however, the work was less challenging. Dean spent only three hours on the set and worked for only an hour and a half: Jim Stark enters his bedroom, lies down and looks at the moon through his window. A process screen behind the set provided the artificial night and the moon.

The other work of the day centered on Judy, who hears the sound of Jim's telephone call from her bedroom, and on Jim's parents, who have an unpleasant meeting with Crunch, Moose, and Goon. In Stern's script, the three hoodlums knock on the door until Jim's father finally comes out. Nailed to the front door is the bloody carcass of a chicken. As the hoods whistle from out of the dark, Jim's father, "frightened, looks out at the night."

However, since the Production Code forbade any mistreatment of animals, Ray filmed the scene with a live, squawking chicken. Instead of blood, there were eggs. According to a press release, Dean gathered them from the two leghorn hens being used for the scene, then took them to the studio commissary and made an omelet.

On May 3, only Dean, Backus and Ann Doran reported to the soundstage. In the morning, Ray planned to complete the "spilled dinner" scene and Scene 123, where Jim asks his father's advice about the chickie run. After waiting for Dean, who arrived twenty minutes late, they finished the work. From 2:30 P.M. to 6:45, Ann Doran rehearsed her part in the family confrontation scene. Ray would shoot it the next day.

Meanwhile, Sal Mineo and Natalie Wood attended school from 9:00 A.M. to noon. Wood brought along one of her most prized possessions, a suede jacket bearing the signatures of ninety-nine Hollywood stars. The names included Gregory Peck, Ann Blyth, Rudy Vallee, William Hopper, Jane Wyatt, Edward Arnold, Maureen O'Hara and Cary Grant. Wood had kept the jacket from her earliest years in the movies. James Dean had the distinction of being the one hundredth person to sign it. Later, Wood's mother burned in Dean's signature with a hot needle.

The same day, Irving Shulman sent Finlay McDermid a brief, handwritten letter. Without mentioning the credits question specifically, the letter suggested that it had not been resolved to Shulman's satisfaction.

The next day, May 4, David Weisbart sent an eerily prophetic memo to George Groves of the Sound Department regarding James Dean. Weisbart asked Groves to make sure "that all the loops for post-syncing are prepared and kept up to date." This was especially important for the post-syncing that involved Dean. Dean was going immediately into *Giant*, Weisbart explained, "and we may never see him again."

Weisbart sent a second memo to Nicholas Ray: the Griffith Observatory had placed no restrictions on the company's use of the building for exterior night shooting. *Rebel*'s climax, one of the major night sequences in the picture, would take place both inside and outside. The censor, however, was still complaining. Even though Shurlock had recently approved the script's first 48 pages, he did not approve the expression, "Good lord," in Jim's argument with his family. That scene would soon go before the camera, and Ray would not change it.

Ray returned to Stage 8, where a replica of his own living room awaited the actors. Ray's first three shots completed the earlier sequence: Jim comes down the stairs on his way to the chickie run; his father follows; father and mother meet at the top of the stairs after Jim has gone. In the first shot of the new sequence, Jim enters the living room while his father sleeps in a chair. Jim's mother comes downstairs and his father wakes up; they talk about Jim's return, moving gradually toward the staircase landing. Jim sits on the bottom step, then rises as he explains what happened on the Millertown bluff.

34

STERN'S ARGUMENT

On Thursday, May 5, Stewart Stern wrote a letter to Steve Trilling. Stern was not pleased with what he had heard during a recent telephone conversation with Nicholas Ray. Ray's report, and others, had convinced Stern that the studio was systematically "emasculating" the film. Stern argued that "the delicate and tenuous qualities" of his script were being sacrificed in an effort to make the film "conform." The studio, he said, was trying to turn a silk purse into a sow's ear. Stern argued that the strength of his script lay not in the "plot points" of the story, but in the subtle interplay of the characters' feelings. *Rebel* was "from the very start, an unusual exploration of a theme not touched before," he argued, and it should not be tampered with. Stern understood that the studio's cost-cutting accounted for much of *Rebel*'s "emasculation." Cutting lines, shortening scenes, substituting interiors for exteriors, might save money for the studio, but it would achieve only "dullness" for the film. Stern had a specific scene in mind that the studio wanted to excise: when Jim and Plato break the tension by laughing after Buzz's death. The scene, he argued, "showed a reaction to tragedy which is not only bare and honest," but which was completely new to the screen. Plato's boldness in seeking Jim as his father (Steve Trilling's suggestion) also irritated Stern: "I think that under no credible circumstances would he, even in hysterics, refer to Jim as his 'father' here. When I heard the proposed alteration, I was embarrassed and shocked." Stern concluded with an impassioned plea to honor the *Rebel* script as he wrote it: "Our picture is a rebel. Let it have its cause."

Ray, meanwhile, began the day rehearsing the conclusion of Scene 213D, in which Jim grabs his father, drags him across the living room and chokes him in an overturned chair. The three-shot sequence proved to be a harrowing experience for Jim Backus. Dean, who had told Neil Rau, "You can't fool the camera," wanted the same realism here. Backus recalled the experience in his book, *Rocks on the Roof*:

> The crucial scene in *Rebel* was where Jimmy and I had a terrible argument at the top of a staircase, at the climax of which he threw me down the flight of stairs, across the living room, into a chair which went over backward, and tried to choke me to death. There is only one way to do such a scene. I had to remain completely passive and put my trust in Jimmy. If I, for any reason, got tense, we both could have been severely injured or even possibly killed.

135

> I was two hundred pounds of dead weight, and this boy, who could not have weighed
> more than 140 pounds, tossed, carried, dragged and lifted me down those stairs, across the
> room and into the chair over and over again all day long, while they shot their many angles.

During the third take, Dean and Backus broke the railing on the staircase. After the prop men replaced it, the actors repeated the action twelve more times. Dean seemed especially intense during the entire sequence, and held up production twice for brief periods while he collected himself.

Two of Ray's final shots presented different versions of Jim's exit from the house. In the first, he leaves through the French doors; his parents watch him from the doorway, look grimly at each other, and go back inside. In the second, Jim kicks a hole in a portrait of his grandmother on the way out.

Meanwhile, Warner Bros. had learned of Dean's racing at Bakersfield; Louella Parsons reported the studio's displeasure in her column. Angry studio officials feared that Dean might injure or kill himself before *Rebel Without a Cause* completed production.

Eric Stacey still worried about *Rebel*'s night shooting schedule. In his second memo on the subject, he reminded Don Page and Mal Bert that exterior night shooting must be kept to a minimum. Whenever possible, the company was to use process shots or close-ups of small sets instead of night locations.

On Stage 8 the next day, Ray continued work on the confrontation scene. To film Jim's mother coming down the stairs as Jim watches her from the couch, Dean and Ray improvised a daring 180 degree camera rotation. The movement replicated Jim's point of view: he sees her first while lying on his back, then turns his head and body upright. Such a shot usually called too much attention to itself, but Ray believed he could justify it.

He later recalled:

> The shot came to express my feelings toward the entire scene: here was a house in danger of tipping from side to side. It was organic to the scene.

Ray also filmed the shot without the 180 degree tilt and "held" the take as insurance. Because he could not guarantee silent camera movement, he recorded the sound separately. Ray completed two more shots from the confrontation sequence: Jim tells his parents that he wants to go to the police. When his father asks if anyone saw his license plate, he walks to the window, buries his face in his arms and says, "It doesn't matter! It doesn't matter! It doesn't matter!"

In the next shot, Ray added Jim's father to the split-screen telephone montage. Then he moved "outside" to the part of the sound stage that now represented Jim's back yard: Jim's father and Plato collide as Plato comes looking for Jim. The shot required six takes, four flubbed by the actors, and one spoiled by the sound of an airplane. Ray's next two shots took place in front of process screens. In the first, Judy's father sings to her as she looks up at the moon; in the second, Crunch, Moose and Goon are in a car looking for Jim. After waiting twenty minutes for prop men to remove the side door of the car, Ray completed the shot in four takes. The production wrapped at 7:20 P.M.

That night, Dean appeared in "The Unlighted Road" on the *Schlitz Playhouse of*

Stars. He had completed the role two and a half months earlier. Dean played Jeff Latham, an ex-GI who gets a job at a roadside diner, hoping to build a future for himself. Inadvertently, he becomes involved with hijackers, who frame him for the murder of a policeman. Pat Hardy played Ann, Dean's love interest. One scene, in which Jeff describes the policeman's death to Ann, sounded remarkably similar to the scene just played out on Warner Bros.' Stage 8:

> JEFF:
> I'm in trouble. Big trouble.
> ANN:
> What happened?
> JEFF:
> Well, I was out driving tonight, and I was speeding. So a State Trooper took out after me. So he started shootin' at me, and I got scared and I didn't want to stop, but he kept on chasin' me and I heard the car skid off the road.
> ANN:
> Did he see the license number?
> JEFF:
> It doesn't matter. The Trooper's dead. He broke his neck when he went off the side of the road.
> ANN:
> Jeff, no!
> JEFF:
> So, I'm gonna give myself up. They don't know yet it was me, but I gotta do it. I keep thinkin' about it.
> ANN:
> But will they believe you? Will they believe it was just an accident?
> JEFF:
> I don't know. I'll have to take my chances.

Inclement weather canceled the company's first day of location work in Baldwin Hills, the location of Judy's house and the adjacent alley. The company returned to Stage 8, where Mal Bert had created a "wooded" area meant to represent the space between the mansion and the observatory. Plato, the police, Jim, and Judy cover this ground after Plato shoots Crunch. Once again, the studio had moved a night exterior indoors to cut costs. Ray completed the ten shots without serious difficulty. The only snag came when one of the policemen's pistols misfired. The production wrapped at 5:10 P.M.

On Monday, May 9, the production moved to 5975 Citrus Avenue in Baldwin Hills, one of the few exteriors the studio had not tried to move to a sound stage. Ray filmed Scenes 21–25 on the street and in the alley of Jim's and Judy's neighborhood: Judy calls to Beau and lights a cigarette; Buzz's car arrives, overflowing with rowdy teenagers.

The major shots of the day included Judy's walk down the alley with Jim and her brief exchange with Buzz in the car. The first scenes emphasized Judy's dissatisfaction with her life ("Life is crushing in on me...Who *lives*?"); the second revealed her superficial relationship with Buzz: as Jim goes to his car, Judy and Buzz kiss "ardently and without love." When Buzz asks "What's that?" Judy answers, "Oh, that's a new disease."

Except for a hard-starting camera car, an airplane overhead, and the need to change a spotlight, the filming went smoothly. The production wrapped at 6:05.

35

LONELY STREET

On May 10, Ray was still six days behind schedule. He hoped to make up some of the time by working twenty-one hours straight, starting at 7:30 A.M. and ending at 4:30 the next morning. To keep within union guidelines, a second crew would take over after the first twelve hours. Except for Wood and Mineo, the actors would work straight through.

Ray's first location was Baldwin Hills. It was a night scene, but Ray filmed it in daylight: Jim pulls into his garage after the chickie run; he and Plato get out; Plato wants Jim to come home with him. Ray also filmed close-ups of Jim and Judy in the alley and Buzz and Judy in Buzz's car. Ray completed the eight shots by 5:40 P.M.

At 7:30, Ray's cast and a second crew met outside Wattles Park in Hollywood to film the stomping sequence that would open the film: a man with an armful of Easter presents (Harold Bostwick) suddenly comes face-to-face with a gang of nine teenagers. A children's choir sings Easter songs in the background. In Stern's script, the man is whistling quietly as the gang, "who have been hiding in concealment," rise to follow him. When he hears the sound of their footsteps, he stops whistling but speeds his pace until he is running, his arms still filled with Easter packages. When he stops under a street light, the gang surrounds him. With an intimidating smile, Buzz asks him to whistle again. As he tries, Buzz asks for a cigarette. Fumbling in his pocket, the man finds one. "You smoke it," Buzz insists, still smiling. "Smoke it, Dad." As the man, "smiling uncertainly," tries to light the cigarette, Buzz produces a box of matches, lights one, then ignites the entire box. The man shrieks and the gang jumps him. During the attack, one of the man's Easter gifts, a toy monkey, falls to the sidewalk. It is still lying there after both the gang and their terrified victim have fled. Jim Stark, alone and drunk, stumbles upon the scene. He looks at the spilled toys and wrappings on the sidewalk, winds up the mechanical monkey and "watches it dance for a moment."

Ray completed the sequence in eight shots, using the location to improvise on Stern's script. In Ray's version, the man is carrying a potted Easter lily along with his other packages as he gets out of his car. The gang crosses the street and stalks him. Three of the gang members follow along the roof of a building as the others "deploy"

138

around their prey. Ray's cast also improvised on Stern's dialogue, and 2nd Unit Script Supervisor Fred Applegate recorded the minor changes.

James Dean also improvised on his entrance. Around 4:00 A.M., he asked Ray and 2nd Unit cinematographer Ted McCord to simply start the camera rolling. Dean staggered toward the mechanical monkey in the foreground, played with it briefly, then wrapped it tenderly in paper and curled up beside it in a fetal position.

Beverly Long remembered the moment well:

> I remember that we'd been working for twenty-three hours straight that day so we could get the dawn light, and we were really exhausted. But we all stayed, as tired as we were, and sat on the curb and watched Jimmy do that scene. And it was so beautiful that we just *wept*.

Sometime during the day's hectic schedule, Ray and Weisbart had found time to view the latest dailies with Dr. Kelley. Kelley had not visited the studio in two months. Meanwhile, Rochelle Hudson and Harold Bostwick had finished their roles in *Rebel Without a Cause*. Hudson spent a few days visiting her mother in Indio, California, before returning to Hollywood to make a pilot for a television program. Bostwick simply disappeared among the extras.

Wednesday, May 11, was a day of mixed news for Ray. Geoffrey Shurlock had approved the script changes up to page 84. Ray and Weisbart, however, had a serious problem with the Observatory's dome. They still planned to film the picture's climax on top of it, but the actors had no way to get up there. Even a Jacob's ladder would not work. Eric Stacey informed Steve Trilling of the problem and its somewhat expensive solution: build a replica of the dome on one of the studio's sound stages. That set, which had been designed, but not yet built, would take at least a week to make ready, and would cost about $5,000.

That evening, Ray's company returned to Baldwin Hills. The first three shots completed the "Man in the Moon" sequence in Judy's back yard. In the next three shots, Jim drives home with Judy and Plato after the chickie run, returns Judy's compact and backs his car into the garage. In the last shot of the day, Jim's and Judy's fathers meet in the alley, each searching for a lost child. As per the studio's agreement with the Board of Education, Natalie Wood and Sal Mineo attended school from 3:00 to 6:00 P.M., then worked until past 11:00. Filming ended at 2:05 A.M. for the rest of Ray's company.

The next day, another night location fell victim to the budget ax. David Weisbart sent a memo to Don Page: the exterior shots of the police station would be filmed on the back lot. This was to be done following a day of shooting at the studio, "with a second crew if necessary." Eric Stacey conveyed a more specific message to F. C. Fuhrmann of the Location Department: the courthouse building on the back lot's Midwestern Street would be the location for EXT. PRECINCT STATION in Stern's script.

Weisbart also canceled a process shot for one of the planetarium scenes, since Ray had already covered it with a shot in the theater.

The company returned to Baldwin Hills for a second night of work: Jim drives up and finds Judy sitting on a stone wall in the alley. They drive away to the mansion. In the next two shots, Plato arrives at Jim's house on his scooter, then drives away. Ray added two new shots to the script: Buzz drives up to Judy's house during the slapping scene and honks his horn. Judy's father looks through the window as Buzz drives away. In the second shot, Moose, Crunch and Goon arrive in the alley just after Jim and Judy have left. Jack Grinnage (Moose) had some difficulty maneuvering through the narrow street, but the shot came off without incident. In Ray's final shots, Jim's and Judy's fathers talk across their back yards.

According to the Publicity Department, the evening's work in Baldwin Hills had been threatened by a thick bank of fog. Rather than postponing the work and losing more precious production time, Ray positioned a number of wind machines "in a semi-circle around the action" and blew away the encroaching fog. Ray completed the sequence without interruptions.

36

NIGHT WORK

On Friday, May 13, Ray sent an angry memo to David Weisbart: the time restraints that the studio was imposing on his shooting schedule were affecting the production. Citing several recent incidents of interference by "a member of the production staff," and anticipating similar problems on his two major remaining night sequences (the chickie run and the planetarium), Ray asked to be advised of his "limitations" on filming those two sequences. And, he added, "I trust a quiet generator will be placed in such a position as to neither disturb the residents nor require post-sync-ing."

In a less strident memo, Ray asked Weisbart if he might work with Dean, Wood and Mineo the afternoon before taking the company on location to the Warner Ranch, site of the fictional Millertown bluff. Ray expected to film there for two nights. Since the Warner Ranch in Calabasas did not actually have a bluff, Mal Bert would later replicate that on a sound stage. Darkness would help to create the illusion of a steep cliff at the end of the flat plain where the cars assembled.

Ray and Warner Bros. had been debating what kinds of cars to use in the sequence. The studio had first suggested standard vehicles for the teenagers' cars, but Ray had demanded more realism. Finally, the studio agreed to lease twenty customized hot rods through Los Angeles area auto clubs. The cars would line both sides of a narrow runway where Jim and Buzz would race. Jim Stark's car, a sleek, black 1949 Mercury club coupe, was the only other customized vehicle in the picture. George Barris had done the work. He later gained fame customizing the Batmobile for television and Herbie, the Love Bug, for the movies. He also customized the Porsche Spyder that James Dean drove to his death four months later.

Another debate concerned the nature of the race itself. Frank Mazzola, the film's consultant on gang activities, believed that the race lacked realism. In Mazzola's experience with chickie runs, teenagers rarely chose exotic locations for their contests of *machismo*; nor did they race stolen cars. They raced their own cars on any available street. The driver who turned aside first lost his car to the other driver.

It took an hour for Ray's company to drive to the Warner Ranch, some twenty miles from the studio. They arrived at 5:55 P.M. The convoy included equipment and catering trucks, twenty hot rods and two motorcycles. Filming the sequence involved

141

some danger, so a full medical unit was also on the scene. Natalie Wood would be in an especially vulnerable position at the start of the race. She was to stand about twenty yards ahead of the two racing cars. When she signaled the start of the race, the cars would pass very close to her on both sides. Concerned for her daughter's safety, Maria Gurdin watched from the sidelines, along with Natalie's little sister, Lana, and Wood's friend and stand-in, Faye Nuell.

It was cold that first evening at the Warner Ranch, and many of the actors had not brought enough warm clothing. There were blankets in the prop truck, however, and many among the cast and crew wrapped themselves up while waiting for the cameras to roll. Corey Allen was among the actors seeking a blanket, but he got an unwelcome surprise when he stepped inside the prop truck: a half-dozen dummies piled up like corpses, all wearing Buzz's blue jeans and black leather jacket. Their eyes were open, and they all had Corey Allen's face. They were to serve as "stand ins" during Buzz's fiery death.

Although the weather was cold, Dennis Hopper was hot. Since Natalie Wood and Nicholas Ray had begun their affair, the working relationship between the two men had deteriorated steadily. Hopper believed that Ray was treating him unfairly as a result, and that night he was ready to respond in the way he knew best. During the preparations for the chickie run, he challenged Ray to a fist fight. Ray de-fused the situation by telling the headstrong young actor, "You know, someday you're gonna have to figure out how to do things without using your fists, you're gonna have to start using your mind."

Another of Hopper's passions was raging: the need to develop into a real actor. Hopper saw James Dean as his ideal. He had already tried to get Dean's attention on the set, in the commissary and in the studio corridors, but Dean had remained aloof. At Calabasas, Hopper decided to change all that. According to Hopper, he pulled Dean into a car and demanded that Dean teach him everything he knew about acting. Dean apparently agreed, and continued to work with Hopper through *Giant*, their next picture together.

After almost an hour of unloading equipment and blocking, plus an hour for dinner, the company rehearsed for another two and a half hours. Finally, at 10:20 P.M., the cameras rolled. The actors worked almost until dawn. Ray began with a high-angle shot of Jim's car arriving. He used two cameras, but decided to print only the fifth take from the second camera. Then Ray filmed another shot of Jim's arrival from ground level.

Working out of sequence, Ray filmed the scene where Jim drives Judy and Plato away after Buzz's car has gone over the edge. From 1:17 A.M. to 2:17, the company broke for a Midnight Meal. Sometime in the early morning hours, cast and crew saw a sudden flash of light in the eastern sky. Many thought it was an atomic explosion. Steffi Sidney even made a point of checking the next day's newspapers, but she found nothing. Years later, Sidney learned that an atomic bomb had indeed been tested that night in the vicinity of Las Vegas, Nevada.

After the Midnight Meal, Ray used two cameras, one high and one low, for each of the next three shots: Jim and Buzz position their cars; the twenty hot rods line up on both sides of the runway, turn on their headlights (Stern's "flare path"), and the two boys drive toward the bluff. Ray completed the night's work with two "key" shots, which would provide the projected backgrounds for in-studio process shots of Jim and Buzz "driving." The long night ended at 5:50 A.M., Saturday, and the company returned to the studio at 6:30.

Ray's company was idle until 2:30 Saturday afternoon, but the columnists were busy. Sheilah Graham observed that Dean had been working out at a local gym, getting himself in shape for the role of boxer Rocky Graziano in *Somebody Up There Likes Me*, which he hoped to do at MGM. Louella Parsons used her column to scold Dean for his uncomplimentary imitations of Elia Kazan on the set of *Rebel*. She wondered if Dean's comic routines were "too biting for appreciation in certain quarters." Dean, as usual, paid little attention to the commotion. That morning, he had gone to Catalina Island with Tom Hennesy and was learning to scuba dive.

Ray was also in the news. Mike Bessie, an executive with *Harper's* magazine, had come to Hollywood from New York to discuss a book project with him. The book's title was *Diary of a Film: The Origin and Development of Rebel Without a Cause*. Ray planned to write it immediately after he finished the picture.

Saturday's shooting began at the studio. Ray returned to Stage 6 to film close-ups for the mansion sequence. Mal Bert's crew had built a replica of the summer house. In one of the shots, Jim and Judy laugh at the sleeping Plato's mismatched socks. At 6:00 P.M., the company caravan set out again for Calabasas. That night, Dean ate dinner on location with Faye Nuell, Natalie Wood's double, then took her for a drive around the ranch. Nuell was one of the few young women in the cast with whom Dean felt comfortable.

By 8:30, Nicholas Ray was ready to continue the chickie run sequence: Jim and Buzz ask Judy for "some dirt" to get better grips on their steering wheels; Judy gives the signal for the start of the race, and the two cars speed past her. Out of sequence, Buzz taunts Plato before Jim's arrival; Jim and Buzz inspect the cars, then walk to the edge; they get in the cars and back them up to the starting line.

Ray used three cameras for each of the last two shots. In the first shot, the cars go over the bluff (Ray decided not to print it). In the second, the onlookers rush toward the edge, then run back to their own cars to escape before the police arrive. The company stopped filming at 5:35 A.M. It was now Sunday, and the overworked cast and crew finally had a whole day to relax.

37

RECKLESS VIOLENCE

Warner Bros. executives were not likely to relax after reading Bosley Crowther's latest diatribe in the Sunday edition of *The New York Times*. Crowther's subject was screen violence. He supported the position of British censors, who frequently banned American films from their country's movie screens if they presented "reckless violence and needless brutality." Although Crowther defended a limited expression of violence in the movies, he opposed "the pointless, the untrue and the willfully sensational" uses of it. For this reason, he defended films like *On the Waterfront* and *Bad Day at Black Rock*, but condemned *Violent Saturday*, the new Victor Mature picture, because its violent scenes had "no moral purpose or point." He also believed that *Blackboard Jungle* went "to questionable excess" in depicting juvenile delinquency.

How would Crowther and the other critics react to *Rebel Without a Cause*? Would they consider the switchblade fight "reckless violence?" Would they decide that the stomping scene was "willfully sensational?" Would Buzz's violent death in the chickie run have "no moral purpose or point?" How would they respond to Sal Mineo's portrayal of a psychotic 16-year-old and *his* violent death? Although the Warner Bros. front office could not turn back the clock on Ray's production, it might think the time had come to edit out *Rebel*'s own "questionable excess."

On the heels of Crowther's attack came Shurlock's latest script evaluation. On May 16, Shurlock reported to Jack Warner that he had read the changed pages dated May 2, 6, 10 and 13 in Stern's script and had concluded that they seemed "acceptable under the provisions of the Production Code." There were, however, exceptions. Judy's question, "Have you ever gone with anyone who—?" was still "unacceptably blunt talk" about the two teenagers' sexual experiences. Shurlock suggested that the line be rewritten. Also unacceptable was the scene in which gang members attack Plato outside his house. Shurlock suggested that the beating was excessive and that the many punches might be replaced by one. Shurlock concluded, "You understand, of course, that our final judgment will be based on the finished picture."

The same day, Hoyt Bowers sent a memo to Steve Trilling about Natalie Wood's continuing education on the set. The Board of Education had determined that whenever a minor worked on a film "within ten weeks of the close of the school term," that minor "must receive (her) schooling from the Studio for the balance of the

period." This rule pertained especially to students who were high
school seniors. As a senior, Natalie
Wood would be required to continue
her education on the set for four
weeks *after* the completion of the
film.

Despite twelve-hour working
days and the long night at Wattles
Park, *Rebel Without a Cause* had
fallen even further behind schedule.
Ray still had to film the climax at the
Observatory, and he was unsure how
the scene would play. Stern's script
called for police to kill Plato while
he was on top of the dome. In
another proposed ending, Plato did
not die. For either ending, the studio might have to build an expensive dome set.

If Ray planned to retain the
dome ending and do some of the
work on a sound stage, he had to
decide quickly. *Giant* began filming
in five days, and Dean reported to
the picture in June. To save time
elsewhere in the schedule, Ray sent
a second crew to the Precinct Station
set on Stage 6. The four shots they
filmed were part of the sequence in Ray Framek's inner office.

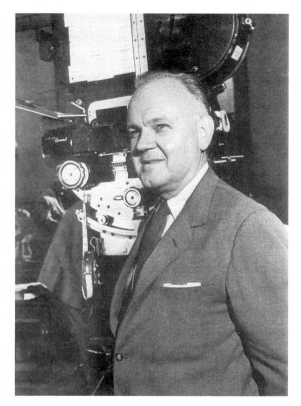

Bosley Crowther, the influential movie critic of
The New York Times, strongly opposed "reckless
violence and needless brutality" on America's
movie screens.

Work at the studio ended at 4:30 P.M. Ray and his staff went immediately to the
Observatory, where they took three and a half hours to set up, have dinner and
rehearse. Ray had fewer than three hours to work with Wood and Mineo. The evening's shots included Plato breaking inside; the police following; Jim's parents arriving with Ray Framek; and Jim and Judy following Plato. Ray's last shot of the evening
presented one of the film's least plausible moments: Plato's nurse arrives on foot in
her bathrobe to tell a startled officer that Plato is loose somewhere with a gun.

Meanwhile, the chain of command had sent Geoffrey Shurlock's message to
Nicholas Ray via David Weisbart. Once again, the key subject was the line, "Have
you ever gone with anyone who...?" Weisbart's recommendation was to use "two
close angles...so that we will be protected in case this deletion has to be made."

On May 17, Ray and company returned to the Observatory for one more night
of shooting. A second unit on daytime duty filmed key shots of the cliff that would
represent the Millertown bluff. A bluff near Palos Verdes, south of Los Angeles, doubled as the fictitious bluff. Later, editor William Ziegler matted in a night sky. At the
Observatory, Ray filmed more exteriors: the police maneuver; Jim and Judy hide in

the bushes before running inside; Jim negotiates with Ray Framek; Plato runs outside with an empty gun.

Dean arrived an hour late. Even when he arrived on time, Ray frequently had to delay production because of all the fans and autograph hunters who now hounded Dean. The studio decided to add extra security, not only for Dean, but to keep back the growing crowds that had come to watch the filming.

Unfortunately, the production kept calling attention to itself. During one particular night of filming at the Observatory, the glare of arc and spot lights convinced numerous residents of Los Angeles that the building was on fire. Telephone operators were kept busy explaining that a movie was being filmed there.

Elsewhere, *Blackboard Jungle* was still making news. The place was Schenectady, New York. The headline in *Variety* read: "Police Seek to Finger *Blackboard Jungle* as Root of Hooliganism." The article read:

> Exhibition of "The [sic] Blackboard Jungle" at Proctor's Theater was blamed for prompting several teenagers last week to form a gang, which proposed to wage a battle with an Albany group. Other juvenile outbreaks were attributed to the motion picture, which deals with delinquency in a public school. Local papers played up the film as an alleged contributing factor.

38

TWO ENDINGS AND
AN ARGUMENT

As the last days of production approached, Ray still had not decided on an ending for the picture. Weisbart reminded him that they might need to film an alternate ending in which Plato does not die. He suggested Scene 311, where the ambulance attendants put Plato on a stretcher, as the logical place to reveal this outcome.

On May 18, Ray filmed one of the possible endings, using the Observatory roof and dome. The studio had not yet constructed a dome on the sound stage, so Ray had to film medium and long shots at the location, then try to complete the matching close-ups indoors. The company worked from 2:10 P.M. to 6:40 P.M. The waning light of dusk represented dawn in the film.

Ray covered six of Stern's numbered scenes with sixteen camera placements: Plato starts toward the roof; he drops his gun, picks it up again and continues up the stairs. As Judy and Jim follow him, they struggle with police. Plato's nurse also follows. Judy trips following Plato, then continues. The police shoot Plato trying to climb up the dome, and he falls to a balcony. Jim holds up the empty cartridge clip in a gesture of frustration and cries out, "*I've* got the bullets!" (Dean's line was a creative gift from Ray's friend, Clifford Odets, Ray's original choice to write the screenplay.)

On May 19, Ray continued work on the dome sequence. He filmed Plato's fall and the others' reactions in medium-long-shot. Jim's parents rush to his side. The attendants carry Plato away on a stretcher and Jim's father comforts his grieving son. Out-of-sequence, Ray filmed scenes of the police preparations, Jim's parents waiting, reacting and running to him, and Plato's nurse still following improbably in everyone's footsteps.

The same day, Stewart Stern wrote a letter to Nicholas Ray. The letter opened the battle over the writing credits for *Rebel Without a Cause*. The studio, keeping its secret bargain with Ray, had explained to Irving Shulman that he could not receive story credit. Stern had also been unaware that "The Blind Run" would be the only source of story credit for the picture. Like Shulman, he had never heard of "The

Blind Run." He now protested Ray's secret agreement and argued that he and Shulman receive co-credit with Ray for the story. Stern argued that until he and Shulman had written their respective screenplays, there was, in fact, no story. Without Shulman's and Stern's contributions to *Rebel*'s story line, there could have been no film.

In determining story credit, the studios operated by the "forty percent" rule. No writer could claim story credit unless at least forty percent of his or her material was the basis for the final screenplay. Except for the name of the main character, Jim, there was almost nothing of "The Blind Run" left in *Rebel Without a Cause*. Ray could claim that the two observatory scenes and the switchblade fight were his ideas, but Shulman could claim equal credit for the chickie run, the film's dramatic centerpiece.

Shortly after writing to Ray, Stern met with him to discuss the issue. It was not a friendly meeting. Ray asked Stern to list Stern's contributions to the film. Ray then claimed that those same contributions were his own. Ray continued to insist that he alone receive story credit. He was willing to share it with Shulman only if Stern agreed to share screenplay credit with Ray. Stern declined, because not a word of Ray's was in the screenplay. He suggested that Ray at least offer Shulman adaptation credit.

On Friday, May 20, daytime filming concluded at the Observatory. Most of the work was indoors. Unfortunately, the building had no sound-proofing, and outside noise ruined three of the first seven takes. Ray also had trouble with his sound system and needed to test it before continuing. Jim's meeting with Plato inside the darkened planetarium occupied most of the company's time.

Ray completed additional exteriors for the dome sequence, plus a scene from much earlier in the film when Jim and Plato watch the perpetual motion pendulum swinging in the lobby.

In the evening, Nicholas Ray, Natalie Wood, Perry Lopez and Marilyn Morrison (ex-wife of singer Johnnie Ray) attended a farewell party for Nick Adams at the Mocambo Restaurant. Adams was leaving the next day for Kansas City to play the role of "Bomber" in Joshua Logan's film of *Picnic*. Adams had worked for Logan before, in *Mister Roberts*.

On May 21, Ray moved the chickie run indoors to Stage 7, the tallest soundstage at Warner Bros. To simulate the edge of the Millertown bluff, the studio carpenters had built a wooden structure elevated a few feet above the floor. Ray planned to film some of the shots from a high angle, looking straight down. Later, William Ziegler would matte in an ocean and shore line, but as Ray filmed, there was only a black velvet drape on the floor to simulate the void below.

The drape, unfortunately, left James Dean without the necessary inspiration to do an important scene. He had to react convincingly to Buzz's death as he looked down at the burning wreck. As usual, Dean kept the entire company waiting while trying to bring forth the emotion. Finally, he noticed a crew member eating an apple and borrowed it. He asked the special effects man to put some studio "blood" on it. Dean concentrated on the apple: *this* was Buzz at the bottom of the cliff.

The last shot of the day involved some minor stunt work for Dean, who had insisted on doing his own stunts throughout the production. The scene called for Jim Stark to roll from his car before it went off the cliff. According to the Publicity Department, a prop man tried to place a mattress underneath the studio "grass" to break the fall, but Dean refused to use it. The prop man told Dean that Errol Flynn used the same mattress to do *his* stunts. Dean still said no. The camera operator undercranked the camera from the normal twenty-four frames per second to eight. When the slow-moving car and Dean's roll onto the grass were projected at the normal running speed, the stunt would appear convincingly fast and dangerous.

The Sunday newspapers continued to feature Natalie Wood. Tyra Fuller did the interviewing. Wood explained that it was easy for her to learn her lines: "I just look at the page, and remember them." Wood was a willing subject for the columnists and the fan magazines. Unlike Dean, who despised Hollywood hype, she genuinely enjoyed it. She also enjoyed the lifestyle that accompanied stardom. She had no causes, no axes to grind against the system. She was the perfect studio product, always properly dressed, always polite.

Despite his contempt for the Hollywood system, James Dean's popularity in the movie capital was soaring. Dean now ranked fourth in *Motion Picture Magazine's* May popularity poll, behind Marlon Brando, Tony Curtis and Rock Hudson. In April, he had not even been on the list. Dean, however, was thinking about Broadway, not Hollywood. Jane Deacy had submitted twelve more plays for his consideration, as Broadway producers waited eagerly for his decision.

Meanwhile, the ending for *Rebel Without a Cause* remained in limbo. As the final days of shooting approached, and with only a partial ending already shot, a concerned Nicholas Ray wrote a memo to David Weisbart. Ray had a number of concerns. First, he wanted the footage for the final planetarium scene put together and ready to view in the editing room "sometime today." Ray wanted to be sure that the footage made clear that the picture ended "at the beginning of a new day." He believed that there were already enough shots, however brief, to convey the sense of dawn, which would be further enhanced by Plato saying, "It's morning." Ray was concerned also that the dome sequence as filmed on location (without the close-up and medium shots to be filmed on the interior mock-up if that ending was used) would require seven or eight more shots to complete. Those shots, Ray explained, "would play against concrete." In conclusion, Ray argued, "I really believe our story is in jeopardy if we play it as a night sequence." Also, it would be less expensive to complete the sequence "as written" rather than filming it strictly as a night sequence "and then discovering we should have done it as day."

May 23 was a day of bits and pieces at the studio. The company began work on Stage 7. Ray required more night "exteriors" to finish the chickie run sequence, including a high overhead shot of Jim and Buzz as they look over the edge of the Millertown bluff. The cast waited for the crew to return from Stage 5, where Ray was filming a process shot of Jim's parents riding in Ray Framek's patrol car: Jim's mother, sitting in the back seat, suddenly recognizes her own responsibility in the night's tragic events:

> MOTHER:
> I don't understand. I don't understand. You pray for your children. You read about these things happening to other families, but you never dream it could happen to yours.

Stewart Stern did not write Ann Doran's lines; nor were they the invention of Nicholas Ray. They belonged to the mother of John Fred Brodl, a 19-year-old Los

Angeles teenager stabbed to death a month earlier by another youth. Brodl and his friends had been racing another car along Hawthorne Boulevard, had exchanged insults with the occupants, then fought in the street. A newspaper reporter had written down the mother's words as she learned of her son's death, and they had appeared in the next day's paper. Someone, presumably Ray, had added them to the script.

After Ray completed more chickie run scenes on Stage 7, the company waited again for the crew on Stage 5. James Dean and Corey Allen "drove" their cars in front of the process screen, with the key shots from the ranch location as background. After the process shots, the company finished the bluff sequence: Jim holds out his hand to Judy and draws her away from the edge.

After dinner and the arrival of darkness, the company moved to the back lot's Midwestern Street, where a courthouse building represented the exterior of the Precinct Station: Jim parks his car outside and starts up the steps just as Moose, Goon and Crunch are coming out. After a quick wardrobe change, Dean climbed the steps a second time: two policemen (Dave McMahon and Bob Williams) bring the drunken Jim Stark into the Precinct Station at the beginning of the film.

Ray filmed two more shots on the back lot. He decided to use the Midwestern Street as part of the stomping sequence: Buzz sits on a fence as he confronts his victim. Since Harold Bostwick was no longer available, Allen recited his part of the dialogue to no one in particular. Later, in the editing room, Ray tried to match this scene with the rest of the sequence.

By Tuesday, May 24, most of *Rebel*'s cast had completed their roles. Corey Allen returned to the stage in *My Three Angels* at the Player's Ring. Beverly Long began a role in *Those Whiting Girls*, the summer replacement for television's *I Love Lucy*. William Hopper completed his role as Judy's father in time to play another father in the "Casablanca" segment of television's *Warner Bros. Presents*. His next role was Patty McCormack's father in the film version of *The Bad Seed*.

That night, Ray completed his last major work on the picture, an alternate ending that replaced the dome sequence. It was an unusually cold night in Griffith Park, and most of the cast huddled in blankets.

Dean, however, had a portable dressing room. At one point, he invited Ann Doran inside to discuss the script. As soon as she entered the trailer, however, she was overcome by a pungent odor she had never encountered before: Dean was smoking marijuana. Doran, who liked neither the smell nor the idea, insisted that they continue their script discussion in the cold air outside.

Ray started filming at 9:00 P.M. and planned to shoot until daylight. In this new sequence, Jim talks to Ray Framek from the door of the building. He gets the police to turn off their searchlights, but when one of the officers sees the gun in Plato's hand, he turns his light back on. Plato bolts from Jim and the police shoot him. Jim holds up the empty clip and cries, "*I've got the bullets!*"

To be sure that he had enough material when he went to the editing room, Ray used two cameras for ten of the nineteen shots. He had the morning light for only the last three. The last was a high angle shot of the observatory as the police cars pull away and an employee (presumably the lecturer) walks toward the building with a briefcase. The man with the briefcase was Nicholas Ray, leaving his director's signature.

The May 24 issue of *Variety* reported that the Winthrop Theatre in Winthrop, Massachusetts, had removed *Blackboard Jungle* from the bill following a request from the city's Board of Selectmen. The theater was showing *The Far Country* in its place. Meanwhile, Warners' Publicity Department announced that all three television networks were trying to sign James Dean to perform a series of Shakespeare plays for the fall of 1956. One network had offered him six plays at $10,000 each. Dean would be on leave from Warner Bros. during all of 1956.

For two days, the Sound Department had been sending Ray memos about post-synchronization for *Rebel Without a Cause*. Re-recording dialogue marred by poor voice projection or external noise was tedious and uninspiring work. Unfortunately, hundreds of shots would have to be post-synched, and Ray's actors needed to return to a recording room at the studio to complete them.

On the second-to-last day of production, Ray busied himself with more process shots on Stage 5. The first shot was a close-up of Buzz screaming as he goes over the cliff in his car. In the next shot, he is sitting in the car before the race giving instructions. Jim, sitting in his own car, listens without attention and smokes a cigarette. Other process shots involved the police as they spot Jim's car outside the mansion and call headquarters. Jim and Judy re-enact their driveway scene in the alley between their two houses. Ray filmed some of the sequence against a process screen, the rest as a sound stage "exterior." Ray's original Baldwin Hills sequence had run too long, and since he had neither the time nor the studio's permission to return there, he had to reshoot the entire sequence on the sound stage.

The last two shots of the day required only a minimum backdrop and a night sky. Ray would insert them into the final observatory sequence: Plato's nurse leans over his body as Jim zips up the red jacket that Plato now wears; out of sequence, the nurse cries, "John!" just as the police shoot him.

Thursday, May 26, 1955, was the last day of filming for *Rebel Without a Cause*. Ray's cast and crew spent most of it going back and forth between sound stages. Work on Stage 5 began at noon with the completion of the alley scene. From there, Ray moved back to a process screen of the observatory: Jim puts his arm around Judy and tells his parents, "Mom, Dad — This is Judy. She's my friend." More creative geography returned Jim and Judy back to the edge of Millertown bluff, which was still on Stage 7, and then to a partial replica of the library at the mansion (Stage 5), where Ray filmed an "added cut" in front of the fireplace. Ray returned to the bluff and Stage 7: Jim and Buzz take turns exiting first on the way to their cars. Back at the observatory process screen (Stage 5), Jim shouts, "*I've* got the bullets!" again through eight takes. Ray then filmed an insert of Buzz's sleeve caught on the door handle. After that, Ray returned to the planetarium process screen as Jim removes the bullets from Plato's gun. At the end of the day, the company returned to the alley set to reshoot that entire scene, which had gone unrecorded due to a faulty camera magazine.

At 2:45 A.M., Nicholas Ray was probably too tired to appreciate the irony of ending *Rebel Without a Cause* with a retake. Two months earlier, that was how the picture had re-started, with the shift from black-and-white to color. Forty-seven shooting days later, with his picture eleven days behind schedule, he had a lot to look back on. The production had amassed 194 minutes and 17 seconds of film, which

William Ziegler would trim finally to 115 minutes. Ray and his assistants had blocked and filmed over six hundred shots at eight separate locations and on six sound stages.

Nicholas Ray and James Dean were among the last people to leave the various *Rebel* sets that morning. They wandered around the sound stages together, reminiscing. They had developed a unique creative partnership during the past eight months, but now it was over. Only the guard at the studio gate remained as Ray and Dean left the studio. For a while, they rode in tandem, Dean on his motorcycle and Ray in his automobile. On Hollywood Boulevard, Dean demonstrated a stunt, lying flat across his motorcycle, arms outstretched, as if he were flying. At the next stoplight, the two men considered going their separate ways, then decided on an early breakfast at an all-night restaurant.

PART IV

Post-Production and Beyond

39

TWO ASSIGNMENTS

Post-Production began on Friday, May 27, in Projection Room 14. Nicholas Ray's footage for *Rebel Without a Cause* was almost complete, but it was not a film. Thousands of disconnected images awaited the editor, and many tedious hours of post-synchronizing, or "looping," awaited the actors. Whatever the reason — noisy generators, mumbled dialogue, or airplanes overhead — *Rebel* had an astonishing number of scenes that needed re-recording.

The post-sychronizing process was simple enough: the film ran in a continuous loop as the actors tried to match their voices with the movement of their lips. Natalie Wood and Sal Mineo spent four hours that first day. Ray and Weisbart supervised the process, along with the sound mixer, a boom operator for the microphones, and two sound recorders.

Post-Production was anti-climactic but necessary work, part of the artistic process that Nicholas Ray needed to oversee. Yet, in the studio's view, his work had already ended. Steve Trilling's memo to Roy Obringer made it official: Nicholas Ray was to be notified through his agent that his services for *Rebel Without a Cause* had been completed and he was now "closed from salary."

Obringer also received a memo from William T. Orr regarding a start date for James Dean on *Giant*: June 3. Dean was to be kept "on salary" on *Rebel Without a Cause* until June 2 despite the fact that the pre-production period for *Giant* and the post-production period for *Rebel* would overlap. It also meant that Dean's week of "free services" to the studio would be canceled.

After the long Memorial Day weekend, post-synchronizing continued on Tuesday, May 31. Dean joined Wood and Mineo in Projection Room 14. Wood and Mineo worked eight hours, Dean four and a half. His contract with the studio and his own artistic interest in Ray's film should have committed him entirely to *Rebel* at the start of post-production. However, the need to prepare for his role in *Giant*, which was already filming in Virginia, had created a special dilemma. Dean was now working on two films simultaneously. He was interpreting two characters. He was also dealing with two directors whose approaches to filming could not have been more different. Ray gave his actors the freedom to develop their roles as they saw them, while Stevens liked to control everything in the production. Ray had not kept Dean from racing while *Rebel* was filming, but Stevens was adamantly opposed to it during *Giant*. After Dean raced at Santa Barbara over the Memorial Day weekend, Stevens telephoned him and banned him from further racing until Dean had completed his role.

On Wednesday, June 1, the third day of post-production, Dean arrived three hours late to post-synchronize dialogue in Projection Room 14. He had spent the time in Wardrobe doing makeup tests for *Giant*. Dean's overlapping assignments prompted a memo from Steve Trilling to Hoyt Bowers: on those days that Dean was called to do post-production work for *Rebel*, he was to be paid for that time regardless of his commitments to *Giant*. He was, in effect, to collect two salaries.

As Dean struggled with the mounting pressures of working on two pictures, he seemed to have found a surrogate mother in Ann Doran. At three o'clock one morning, he arrived outside her house. Instead of knocking at her door, he called out, "Mom! Mom!" (He also referred to his New York agent, Jane Deacy, as "Mom.") Doran opened her window and saw someone standing on the front lawn. When she asked who it was, Dean shouted, "It's your son Jimmy." Doran opened the door, invited him in and made coffee. They sat on her kitchen floor until daylight. Dean confided in Doran as if she were his real mother. (Mildred Dean had died when he was nine years old, and he had never overcome the loss.) Doran understood that Jim Stark's loneliness and confusion were also James Dean's. He visited "Mom" several more times before leaving for Texas.

Meanwhile, Eric Stacey reported to Trilling on the progress in Projection Room 14: post-production synchronization (dubbing) had been completed through the mansion sequence. This was especially good news for Sal Mineo, who needed to return to New York "to take his final examination exams."

By June 3, after six and a half more hours of post-recording, Dean and Mineo had wound up their current work in Projection Room 14. Natalie Wood finished the next day. Ray, off salary, supervised Wood's post-recording.

On Monday, June 6, Warner Bros. assigned tentative writing credits for *Rebel Without a Cause*. Finlay McDermid of the Story Department informed Stewart Stern, Irving Shulman and Leon Uris of the studio's decision. Stern received screenwriting credit, and Shulman received credit for adapting "The Blind Run." Leon Uris received no credit. Ray received sole story credit, as the clause in his contract dictated.

The studio's notice required Stern, Shulman and Uris to respond to the assigning of credits within two days. After that time, they could no longer protest the studio's decision. After learning of the clause that would deny Shulman partial story credit, Stern had done what he could for Shulman in getting him adaptation credit. He still believed that Shulman deserved to share story credit with Ray, but he was unwilling to share screenwriting credit with Ray as the price. Shulman had to present his own case now.

That evening, the process of editing *Rebel Without a Cause* officially began. To a bewildered Nicholas Ray, it was a process begun in unnecessary haste. When he and Weisbart met with William Ziegler, Ray strongly questioned the studio's decision. He expressed his fear that the studio would haphazardly assemble the film, and he argued for more time.

The next day, June 7, Ray appealed directly to Jack Warner. The two men had not been on the best of terms during *Rebel*'s production and had not spoken to each other for some time. Despite that, the tone of Ray's letter was as direct as the problem: the studio's policy of expediency in filming, and now editing, *Rebel Without a Cause* posed a threat to the artistic integrity of the film. Acknowledging that Warner had been unhappy with Ray "the last time we met any closer than bowing distance," and acknowledging also that *Rebel* did indeed have a great deal of excess footage, Ray appealed to Warner not to assemble the film in such haste. Ray and Weisbart needed time, Ray argued, "to put together a version which...will represent the best of the material on hand." Ray's own time limits made this request all the more urgent, "for I'm due on another picture immediately."

On June 8, Dean and the cast of *Giant* left by the Southern Pacific Railroad for Marfa, Texas, a small desert town about sixty miles from the Mexican border. They would spend six weeks on location. On the 9th, Weisbart sent Dr. Douglas M. Kelley a check for $350.00, along with a letter thanking Kelley for his help on the picture.

Meanwhile, as the storm stirred up by *Blackboard Jungle* once again threatened to engulf *Rebel Without a Cause*, Erskine Johnson's column in the *Los Angeles Mirror-News* featured James Dean in a spirited defense of the film:

> There's a new burst of celluloid juvenile delinquency coming up on the screen in "Rebel Without a Cause" that may again bring out the "excessive violence" blue pencils.
>
> This time it's James ("East of Eden") Dean packing a switch-blade knife and, in one scene, hurling his father down a flight of stairs following an argument.
>
> But if the censors black out the violence Dean thinks "they'll be doing the country an injustice."
>
> It's Dean's private theory after playing the role:
>
> "Since juvenile delinquency is based on violence, it is justified violence. We picture a very real situation that exists in this country — something that should be stamped out. Movies like 'The Blackboard Jungle' and 'Rebel' can help."
>
> Any arguments?

40

INQUISITION

On June 15, as Warner Bros. moved ahead with its plans to edit *Rebel Without a Cause*, Ray continued to object. Studio officials expected to view a rough version of the film at 8:30 that evening. Ray, who had not even seen the rough cut, sent an urgent wire to Steve Trilling. He repeated his warnings about *Rebel's* careless edit and put himself on record: as the film stands, it "cannot in fairness to the studio or me…[be] considered as my cut version."

The studio's hurried assembling of *Rebel Without a Cause* was not entirely its own fault. Senator Estes Kefauver of Tennessee had just begun a one-man inquisition on the subject of movie violence and juvenile delinquency. A Mr. Perian, presumably from Kefauver's office, had been pressuring the studio to screen the picture as soon as possible. For Jack Warner, who had seen only the dailies, it was also much too soon. Finlay McDermid informed him that *Rebel* was still "in little pieces" and without a music score. McDermid did not even have a plot synopsis ready. Warner, who was leaving that day for Washington, would have to defend the picture in front of Kefauver's subcommittee without ever having seen it in finished form.

As the news of the Kefauver inquiry reached Nicholas Ray, he wrote again to Jack Warner. Ray had seen an article in the morning paper condemning *Rebel* "as too lurid or too full of violence." The critic, Ray observed perversely, was "someone named Bobo." Ray learned from the same article that Jack Warner was "to appear before a Senator who provided a prologue for the type of film we have tried to avoid," one which "even our Trades term brutal and without explanation." Ray suggested to Warner that those criticizing *Rebel Without a Cause* might be "confusing our picture with the title of the book."

The "Bobo" to whom Ray referred was James Bobo, the chief counsel for Kefauver's subcommittee. The senator who had provided a prologue for a film that the trade papers had found so unredeemable was none other than Kefauver. The picture was an exploitation film, *Mad at the World* (1955), starring Frank Lovejoy and Cathy O'Donnell. Kefauver's prologue described it as "a motion picture that strikes close to the heart of a problem that is the tragic concern of a special committee upon which I serve." The book to which Ray referred, and which Kefauver was "confusing" with

Ray's film, was Robert Lindner's story of Harold, the psychopathic prison inmate.

On the first day of the hearings, Wednesday, June 15, Kefauver's small panel listened to the testimony of two psychiatrists from the Hacker Foundation, the same group that had sponsored Robert Lindner's lectures in Los Angeles in November of 1954. Although the psychiatrists attempted to minimize the impact of screen violence on America's impressionable teenagers, Kefauver insisted that "indiscriminate" scenes of brutality and violence "constitutes at least a calculated risk" for the nation's youth that it "cannot afford to take."

Kefauver cited as evidence the continuing fury over *Blackboard Jungle*. MGM executive Dore Schary defended the film as a reasonable attempt to come to grips with a serious social issue. When Kefauver tried to link *Blackboard Jungle* to a news story of school girls in Nashville setting fire to a barn, Schary replied, "There's no fire in the picture. They can't pin that on us." Others testifying in defense of Hollywood included Y. Frank Freeman, President of Paramount Pictures; Jerry Wald, now an executive producer at Columbia; George Murphy, actor and MGM public relations director; and actor Ronald Reagan.

Senator Estes Kefauver's hearings on violence in motion pictures put heavy pressure on the industry to suppress the trend that films like *The Wild One* and *Blackboard Jungle* had begun. (University of Tennessee)

The next day, Thursday, June 16, Jack Warner appeared before Kefauver's subcommittee. As if to intimidate the moguls, Kefauver had filled the cramped hearing room on the fifth floor of the Federal Building with lurid movie posters, the supposed proof of Hollywood's bad judgment. Kefauver listed twelve current films that he claimed were too violent, too sexually oriented or too pro-criminal. *Blackboard Jungle* headed a list that included *Black Tuesday, Hell's Island, The Prodigal, New Orleans Uncensored* and *I Died a Thousand Times*, a remake of *High Sierra*. Kefauver's dirty dozen list included the unreleased *Rebel Without a Cause*. As Warner presented his testimony, the following exchange occurred:

> Kefauver: "We've had some calls on *Rebel Without a Cause*."
> Warner: "Whoever called must be working with radar. I haven't seen it myself yet."

Warner suggested jokingly that one of the studio's competitors might have filed the complaint against *Rebel*. He added, "You shouldn't believe everything you hear, Senator."

Most of the other witnesses were more contrite. Although they argued that juvenile delinquency developed in the home, not in the movies, they admitted to past "mistakes" and promised to make fewer in the future. Geoffrey Shurlock testified that the trend away from such exploitative films had already begun. But William Mooring, the editor-critic for the Roman Catholic Diocese of Los Angeles, disagreed. Movies that emphasized "crime, brutality and sex," he said, were undermining young people's regard for law, order and morality.

On Friday, June 17, the Kefauver hearings continued into a third and final day. Roger Albright of the Motion Picture Association defended the industry's position against lurid advertising: "This generation is confronted daily with stories of rapes, abortions and heinous sex crimes in the news columns of daily newspapers," he explained. Such material was also prevalent in current novels, Broadway plays, and even "reputable" magazines. Hollywood, he insisted, was "far behind this parade" and proud of it.

As the hearings ended, Jack Warner may have wondered how well he had succeeded on *Rebel*'s behalf. Although he and the other industry spokespersons had confronted the allegations squarely, and even cast some doubt on Kefauver's judgment in promoting *Mad at the World*, they could not guarantee the public's reaction. Despite his best efforts, Warner might not have distanced *Rebel Without a Cause* far enough from the opinion that *any* film about juvenile delinquency was just another *Mad at the World*.

As if to add insult to injury, an advertisement for *Mad at the World* appeared in *The Los Angeles Times* the day after the hearings closed, complete with Kefauver's glowing endorsement.

41

ROUGH CUT

On Monday, June 20, Don Page informed David Weisbart that Page would film added shots of the chickie run on Stage 7. The new scenes, which emphasized action, had developed out of discussions between Page and Steve Trilling. The scenes included shots of wheels spinning as the cars take off, the cars racing past the spectators and the cars going over the edge.

Page would also film nine inserts, including some that Ray had already done: Buzz's sleeve caught on the door; the radio in Jim's car; Plato's hand holding a check for child support; Jim's hand holding Judy's compact; Jim's hand removing the clip from Plato's gun; a car's speedometer.

On June 23, Page filmed the added scenes for the chickie run sequence. The cars went no faster than fifteen miles per hour, but Page undercranked the camera to make them appear three times faster on screen. Page completed the twenty-one shots by mid-afternoon, then filmed the inserts.

As part of his own post-production process, Nicholas Ray was keeping extensive "cutting notes." He already had more than a page on the chickie run alone (reel #10). Most of Ray's suggestions involved trimming existing scenes within the sequence. He also suggested intercutting Judy's and Plato's "hamburger" chat about Jim with shots of Jim and Buzz checking out their vehicles and preparing for the race. In the scene where Jim and Buzz stand at the edge of a cliff, sharing a cigarette, Ray suggested holding off a process shot of the ocean below until Jim picks up a rock and throws it over the edge. "Just as it leaves his hand, cut to the process shot and stay in this shot until Buzz takes the cigarette out of Jim's mouth." Ray also wanted to shorten the preparations for the race (lining up the cars, kids milling about) after Jim and Buzz finish their meeting at the cliff.

In reel #11, which follows the race, Ray wanted Crunch's line, "Down there is Buzz," deleted (it wasn't). He also wanted to "lose" shots of Jim and Judy looking at each other after Buzz's death as Jim leads Judy away from the cliff. "The first apparent contact should be when their hands touch." He also wanted to shorten shots of Jim putting his car back in his garage. "When Plato leaves we should dissolve to Judy's house."

Ray also had some suggestions about the confrontation scene in the Stark fam-

161

ily's living room (reel #12). Again, the emphasis was on trimming the beginnings and endings of shots in the sequence, especially following the shot where Jim tries to strangle his father. Ray also wanted to play the last part of the sequence (Jim's parents at the open French doors after Jim runs out) without dialogue. "This little area," Ray suggested, "would be much more effective played silent."

Meanwhile, the fallout from the Kefauver hearings still hung like a dark cloud over the studios. Following a closed-door meeting of the Motion Picture Association and studio publicity and advertising departments, the director of the MPA's Advertising Code, Gordon S. White, publicly warned the studios to "exercise restraint and good judgment" in their future advertising. White exhibited some of the lurid advertising material shown at the Kefauver hearings. He offered to help the studios in convincing their advertising agencies to become more responsible.

The nation's press continued to follow the story. The headline in *The New York Times* on June 26 read: "Film Men Warned to Curb Violence."

The article read in part:

> While it is apparent that Hollywood rode out the investigation in good shape, it was also apparent that the industry is on the hot seat once again. Unless a conscious effort is made to eradicate, or at least minimize, the vulgarity, lewdness and senseless brutality that has characterized some movies during the last year the industry will have another crisis to face. The mere fact that the industry was required to defend itself before a subcommittee of the United States Senate gave Hollywood a black eye. The fact that the hearing was inconclusive is no cause for optimism in Hollywood because its critics now have fresh ammunition to fire. And it is a sure bet the critics won't remember Senator Kefauver's comments on the beneficial aspects of movies the next time a film comes along that does not square with their way of thinking.

Rebel Without a Cause was almost certain to be that film. When Jack Warner finally did see the rough cut, he would be looking for the same elements of violence and lawlessness that drew such heavy fire from Senator Kefauver.

On the evening of June 30, Warner finally saw *Rebel Without a Cause*. To prepare for the great moment, William Ziegler had made more changes, including speeding up the end of the switchblade fight, trimming the hamburger sequence (with Plato and Judy), "pick[ing] Judy up a little quicker when Dean kisses her on the forehead" (in the alley scene) and making sure that Plato has wounded, but not killed, Crunch at the mansion. The day after the private screening, Warner sent a glowing telegram to Ben Kalmenson, the studio's General Sales Manager in New York. "The picture itself," Warner exclaimed, "is excellent." He described Dean's acting as "beyond comprehension."

Warner also sent a memo to Steve Trilling. As pleased as he was, Warner was concerned about Leonard Rosenman's score for the picture. The music, he argued, was "one of the most important factors in the picture, especially the last third." He cautioned Trilling not to "let them go 'arty' on us." Warner's only objection to the previewed film was that there were still places "to make it move" through tighter editing. He wanted to see the film again before he left for his summer vacation in Europe.

On July 2, Richard Dyer MacCann, the influential film critic of the *Christian Science Monitor*, sent David Weisbart an advanced copy of a piece on *Rebel Without a Cause*, based on MacCann's visit to the set in May. Weisbart thanked him for his letter and updated him on the film's progress. The picture, Weisbart said, "has just about all the qualities we hoped it would have — the qualities you so clearly articulated in your column."

On July 5, Weisbart required more inserts for *Rebel*, some of which Ray had mentioned in his cutting notes. Since the picture no longer had its own crew, he had to borrow crews whenever they were available. Weisbart informed Eric Stacey and presented a list of seven inserts, including retakes of previous inserts: Jim holding Judy's compact on the bench at the Precinct Station; Jim turning off the car radio after hearing the gang's warning; Buzz's sleeve caught on the door handle. The newer inserts included several shots of Plato's black address book and one of the bulletin board at Dawson High announcing the planetarium field trip. Weisbart wanted Ziegler present during filming to be sure the inserts matched the existing scenes.

Despite his enthusiasm for *Rebel* as a whole, Weisbart still had a problem with one sequence: Plato showing Jim and Judy where to put children when they were "noisy and troublesome." Weisbart reminded Steve Trilling that this sequence had been suspect when they first read it in the script. Even after removing the mock-psychiatric scene on the diving board, Weisbart argued, what remained was still "excruciatingly slow" and acted "as a roadblock in the telling of the story."

Weisbart suggested eliminating the entire scene on the mansion staircase and the first part of the pool sequence by cutting away from the opening matte shot of the mansion to a closer shot showing Jim's car and Plato's scooter. The audience would hear the teenagers' voices in the background, and the camera could then cut to Jim, Judy and Plato as they run to the summer house from the pool. Weisbart estimated that this editing could remove "four or five minutes of very unnecessary footage."

On July 7, Stacey found time to complete the inserts on Stage 22. Weisbart and Ziegler supervised the filming. An assistant director, cameraman, prop man and wardrobe man were the only crew. Three extras provided the hands to be photographed. The work took five hours to complete.

On July 9, Corey Allen came to Projection Room 14 to post-synchronize dialogue. He worked for seven hours. Leonard Rosenman, meanwhile, was returning from a two-week vacation in San Francisco to begin work on the music score. The day after Rosenman returned, Dean returned from Marfa, Texas, following a month of location work for *Giant*. Richard Dyer MacCann's column in the *Christian Science Monitor* featured an essay that day on Dean and *Rebel Without a Cause*:

> There seem to be a good many versions of James Dean's approach to life, and it may well be that most of them are founded, more or less, on fact. Newcomers in Hollywood are likely to be misinterpreted, in any case. Some of them encourage conflicts in interpretation as being dramatic and likely to focus attention on the subject.
>
> I can report on only one or two aspects of this controversial young man, based on a single encounter on the set. I got an impression of powerful intensity (so necessary for survival in show business) and of keen intelligence.
>
> That Mr. Dean is going to continue to be a major character around town seems certain. Groomed for stardom by Elia Kazan's New York Actors Studio, active on Broadway and in television, he has already been selected for a George Stevens film (Edna Ferber's "Giant"), which is at present one of the undeniable accolades in Hollywood...

Mr. Dean, like Marlon Brando, does not normally shamble or mumble. He knows a thing or two about the rising generation, and has discovered that most of them do not stand like ramrods or talk like Demosthenes; therefore, when he plays such roles he tries to imitate life. His newest Warner Brothers picture, "Rebel Without a Cause," handles juvenile delinquency without gloves. It will no doubt take full account of these characteristics, even though he is particularly concerned at present to avoid acting like that other Kazan protégé with whom he is so often compared. It is the romanticized conception of the juvenile, Mr. Dean says in round, clear tones, "that causes much of our trouble with delinquency nowadays."

"This picture?" The new bobby-sox idol leans on a nearby floodlight with one hand, adjusts his horn-rimmed glasses with the other, and stares somberly at the floor, framing his words. "I think one thing this picture shows that's new is the psychological disproportion of the kids' demands on the parents. Parents are often at fault, but the kids have some work to do, too."

"But you can't show some far-off idyllic conception of behavior if you want the kids to come and see the picture. You've got to show what it's really like, and try to reach them on their own grounds."

"You know, a lot of times an older boy, one of the fellows the young ones idolize, can go back to the high school kids and tell them, 'Look what happened to me! Why be a punk and get in trouble with the law? Why do these senseless things just for a thrill?'"

"I hope this film will do something like that. I hope it will remind them that other people have feelings. Perhaps they will say, 'What do we need all that for?'"

"If a picture is psychologically motivated, if there is truth in the relationships in it, then I think that picture will be good."

42

FINAL PREPARATIONS

Nicholas Ray had only a week before reporting to his next assignment, directing Cornell Wilde and Jane Russell in *Tambourine* (later titled *Hot Blood*) for Columbia. He spent his remaining free time making notes on Ziegler's rough cut of *Rebel*. On July 12, he submitted six pages of suggested changes to David Weisbart, with the promise of "more later."

Since the studio had decided to drop the stomping scene, (perhaps as an offering to Kefauver), Ray made suggestions for a new opening. The picture would begin with Jim Stark's stumbling arrival at the stomp scene, then move to the precinct station using the police siren as a transition device, "dissolving and blending into Jim making a siren noise in the shoeshine chair." Ray believed that the current edit (the one Jack Warner had seen and admired) was particularly weak in this opening sequence. Jim Stark, Ray argued, should "introduce our other principals" through his actions at the precinct station—mocking the police siren, playing with the Mexican children, walking past Judy to offer his coat to Plato. "The present scheme," he concluded, "is disturbing."

Ray also complained about Plato's interview in the precinct station. He wondered if the nurse's reference to Plato's birthday amounted to over-explaining the character. "Can't we lose the birthday beat?" he asked. He also objected to placing Ray Framek in the group shot when Jim's mother asks him to stop humming. Ray suggested using another shot of the Starks without Framek: "There seems to be the intent to lose the humming on him, which has more to do with the scene than what the characters are saying."

Ray had another problem with unwanted sound: his own voice. The microphone had picked up Ray's prompts to Natalie Wood in the alley scene where Jim first speaks to Judy. Ray suggested covering his voice with the sound of a car horn or an ad-libbed line. He suggested also cutting away to Wood when she tells Jim, "I bet you're a real yo-yo," then cutting back to Jim when he says, "I love you, too."

Ray had no major suggestions for the Dawson High sequence except to observe, "We're a little brief on the cannon." The last shot in the exit sequence also seemed static. As a result of Ray's critique, Ziegler edited out the exit shots: Jim Stark now looks at the bulletin board announcing the field trip, and the scene dissolves to the outside of the observatory.

Ray also had complaints about the first sequence inside the planetarium. Sal Mineo's Bronx accent ("It's hard t' make friends wid dese guys.") required post-syncing. He wanted Plato to say "What?" after Jim looks up at the planetarium sky and says, "Boy!" He wanted Judy to say "*Gesundheit*" when someone in the audience sneezes. The "end of the world" visual effect left Ray unimpressed. He hoped that Leonard Rosenman could "get us a more startling effect" when he wrote the music for that scene.

Ray thought that the time between the planetarium show and the switchblade fight moved too slowly. He had hoped to enliven the transition with the jitterbugging scenes. Without Rosenman's "be-bop suite," however, he had decided to drop it. Now, he wanted to improve "setting up the opponents," which the current edit did not do. The chickie run also needed work. Ray wanted a better match between a long shot of Wood's double, Faye Nuell, running toward Buzz's car, and Wood's entry in a medium shot. He wanted to re-record Judy saying, "Good luck, Buzz," just before they kiss, or drop the line. Jim's call to Judy, he thought, should come when she and Buzz are kissing. He also wanted to cut out Crunch's line, "Down there's Buzz!" after the crash.

For the Stark family confrontation, Ray wanted to "lose seeing the camera tilt in the one shot shooting toward the stairway as Jim goes on [the] steps." He still wanted to "lose" a close-up of Jim's mother shouting, "You want to kill your own father?" He wanted Jim's parents to stand in silence beside the French doors as they watch Jim disappear into the night.

The alley love scene also concerned him. Sharing Stern's objections about expediency, and unwilling to cave in to the censor on every issue, Ray was still fighting to keep Jim's and Judy's discussion about trust and sexuality ("Did you ever go with anyone who—?"). "We must not cut the content of this show, for [the] sake of time and smoothness," he told Weisbart. Ray admitted that Judy's sexual admissions were "harsh," but that their use in developing her character were essential to the film. "They are true," he argued, "and show more growth than anything else that happens to our two leads together."

On July 22, the *Mirror-News* reported that since James Dean's return from Texas, the columnists had been contacting anyone who even remotely knew him for anecdotes and scraps of information. *Rebel*'s former cast members were the most likely subjects, and Jim Backus had been the most willing. According to the *Mirror-News*, reporters had asked him so many times to describe Dean that he now had a stock response: "Let me put it this way—he's a far cry from Vic Mature."

Publicity for the picture was proceeding. On August 1, the studio sent a "cutting print" and "cutting work track," the intermediate stages of the film that Jack Warner had seen a month ago, to Ben Kalmenson in the New York office. Kalmenson handled publicity for the studio on the East Coast. He used these working drafts of picture and sound to generate a publicity campaign. The Music Department was also working on the picture's incidental music. Helen Schoen requested a "cue sheet" for *Rebel* on August 2. A cue sheet gave a description of each musical selection in the film and its duration. Unfortunately, Schoen had to wait, since Leonard Rosenman had only begun scoring the film.

On August 5, *Rebel*'s cast prepared for more post-recording. George Groves of the Sound Department informed Eric Stacey that Natalie Wood, Sal Mineo, Dennis Hopper, Frank Mazzola, Beverly Long, Jack Grinnage and Steffi Sidney were to report August 9 and 10 to Projection Room 14. Joel Smith, who played a policeman, also had lines to post-sync. Groves believed that these two sessions would conclude the extensive post-recording for *Rebel*.

The studio had scheduled James Dean for post-recording on August 6, but he did not report. When the studio called him at home, he refused to come in. It was Saturday, he was tired after his location work on *Giant*, and he resented the studio's encroachments on his limited free time. Since the entire sound crew had reported, the studio had to pay them. The crew remained "on

Leonard Rosenman (**right**) composed the music for the first two of James Dean's three films.

call" during the day in the hope that Gary Cooper would come in to post-synchronize dialogue for his current picture, *The Court-Martial of Billy Mitchell.* Cooper, however, was also unavailable, leaving the crew without work. On August 8, Dean did report to the projection room and worked for almost five hours.

On August 11, Dorothy Kilgallen's column featured *Rebel Without a Cause*, but Warner Bros. could hardly appreciate her commentary. She wrote:

> Parents worried about juvenile delinquency will hit the ceiling when they see the bloody switchblade scene between teenagers in "Rebel Without a Cause." One Hollywood citizen who caught the film commented: "'Blackboard Jungle' was just a mild trailer for this one."

On August 12, the studio completed a list of "Cast and Credits" for *Rebel Without a Cause*. Irving Shulman had not filed an objection within the deadline and had received only adaptation credit. In a less important oversight, the studio still identified Jack Grinnage incorrectly in the acting credits, listing him not as "Moose," but as Chick, the smaller role played by Nick Adams.

While waiting for Leonard Rosenman's score, the Music Department kept busy. They had identified all the incidental music selections for *Rebel*, including "Got to Be This or That," "Zing Went the Strings of My Heart," "I'll String Along with You" and "Five O'Clock Whistle." The songs "Man in the Moon" and "Song of the Moon" were moot issues. William Ziegler had edited out the entire backyard scene with Judy and her father to shorten the film's running time and speed up its pace.

The Research Department had also been busy adding celestial information for the planetarium lecture. On August 24, Ian Wolfe reported to Projection Room 14 to record the "wild" dialogue that Ziegler would post-record over reaction shots of the students. The dialogue included the description of Taurus, the Bull, that prompted Jim to make a mooing sound. Wolfe worked for two and a half hours. Meanwhile, in the Trailer Department, the task of producing *Rebel*'s publicity film ended. The trailer, featuring clips from key scenes, would play in hundreds of theaters prior to the picture's general release.

Leonard Rosenman's score was also nearing completion, but it was creating some special problems for the studio's musicians. On August 26, *The Los Angeles Times* reported:

> The music for "Rebel Without a Cause," written by Leonard Rosenman, is so unusual and difficult that director Ray Heindorf at Warners has arranged for three different recording sessions three weeks apart, in order to give plenty of time for rehearsals. The score involves not only solos but combinations of solo renditions which will have to be handled in the recording.

43

PREVIEWS

On Thursday, September 1, Warner Bros. previewed *Rebel Without a Cause* in Huntington Park, a suburb south of Los Angeles. Studio officials struck a pose of confidence to mask their apprehension. They knew that the audience would make instant comparisons with *Blackboard Jungle*. Teenagers would demand action and a realistic look at youth. Adults would demand a "responsible" film that would not lead their children toward crime or violence. Watchdog groups would monitor the film for gratuitous sex or violence. *Rebel* could not hope to appease them all.

Beyond the *Blackboard Jungle* controversy, the usual concerns still applied. Would audiences believe the picture? Would they boo, walk out, or laugh in the wrong places? If *Rebel* had any serious flaws, the studio wanted to discover them now, while there was still time to make changes.

At the first preview, only one major problem arose. As Jim Stark squirms in pain after punching the desk in Ray Framek's office, the audience began to laugh. It was nervous laughter, the kind that often masks intense emotion. Many in the preview audience clearly identified with Jim's frustration and pain, but they could not show it in a public place. Still, the studio feared that the laughter might rob the scene of its integrity. Leonard Rosenman quickly composed music to accompany the moment. Rosenman later recalled:

> As soon as they heard the music [the audience] shut up. It was as if the music was a second voice saying, 'Wait a minute, take another look at this scene. It isn't funny…' And that's the only function of music in that scene — to keep the audience from laughing.

The next day, Steve Trilling wrote to Stewart Stern, who was in New York. Recalling Stern's fears of the picture's "emasculation," he said, "You will be proud of the *Rebel* which was previewed last night." Stern responded with appropriate gratitude and signed his letter, "from your own difficult Rebel, Stewart."

Trilling also sent a telegram to Jack Warner and the New York office, anticipating greater star power for Dean while praising the film and predicting "tremendous boxoffice." Trilling promised to send a print to New York "as quickly as possible."

Unfortunately, *Rebel*'s potential in overseas markets was less heartening. The same day that Trilling sent Warner his optimistic telegram, he received a letter from Wolfe Cohen of the New York office. Cohen praised the publicity trailer for *Rebel*, but he wondered how countries with strict censorship boards would react to the film. As evidence, he presented a letter from the Chief Censor of the Commonwealth of Australia, who feared that *Rebel*, like *Blackboard Jungle*, might have too much "shock value" to succeed there.

On September 3, two days after *Rebel*'s successful preview, the issue of violence and film censorship once again surfaced. Claire Booth Luce, the U.S. Ambassador to Italy, refused to attend the Venice Film Festival because one of the American entries was *Blackboard Jungle*. Mrs. Luce did not characterize her action as a form of censorship, nor did she demand that the United States withdraw *Blackboard Jungle* from the festival. She did, however, condemn the film for its violent content and for "portray[ing] the United States in an unfavorable light."

Meanwhile, post-production continued at the studio. On September 6, William Mueller informed Weisbart of changes brought about by the September 1 preview. The changes took up two full pages: the film needed new dialogue for Jim as he apologizes for being late at the planetarium; more "wild" dialogue from the gang as they wait for Jim after the show; a brief conversation during the coin toss at the chickie run; and an added line from Jim as he gets up from the living room couch to greet his mother (this to cover the noise of the camera dolly).

Other changes included Jim's lines at breakfast about being nervous; the conversation between Judy and Buzz in Buzz's car; the gang's responses to Jim's mooing; Jim's conversation with Plato on arriving at the Millertown bluff; more dialogue at the chickie run and the talk between Jim and Plato inside the planetarium as Jim tries to turn on the lights (the machinery noise had drowned out the original lines). Studio writer Sam Rolfe created all the new dialogue. Mueller scheduled the post-recording work for Friday, September 9.

On September 7, Trilling responded to Wolfe Cohen's concerns about *Rebel Without a Cause* overseas. Trilling observed that the first preview had "none of the 'shock' reaction" that would normally accompany "the showing of a gangster or 'Blackboard Jungle' type picture." *Rebel*, he argued, "completely lacks any of the homicidal tendencies indicated in other films," while still dealing seriously with the problems of teen delinquency and parental neglect.

Yet, Trilling understood that the foreign censors presented obstacles for *Rebel*. He concluded that those scenes most likely to cause trouble overseas, such as the switchblade fight, might be removed.

In the cutting room, Weisbart and Ziegler made further adjustments. They added the sound of a bugle to the flag-raising scene and inserted extra shots of the Lecturer during the presentation. Weisbart also suggested major work following the "What do you want to do?" scene that Ray's actors had created, removing shots that slowed the film's pace leading up to the switchblade fight.

On Friday, September 9, James Dean requested a postponement of his next post-recording session until Monday, September 12. Eric Stacey informed Tom Andre, 1st Assistant Director on *Giant*, that the date agreed upon was absolutely the last day Dean could do the work. If he could not report during the day, then he had to report at night. Dennis Hopper, also in *Giant*, had the same deadline.

Meanwhile, six others from *Rebel*'s cast returned to Projection Room 14. Natalie Wood and Corey Allen re-recorded the dialogue from their scene in Buzz's car; Dennis Hopper and Frank Mazzola re-recorded their dialogue outside the Precinct Station; Sal Mineo tried to tone down his Bronx accent in the first planetarium scene; and Bruce Noonan, the school monitor, added some off-camera dialogue as Jim Stark steps on the school insignia.

On Wednesday night, September 14, Nicholas Ray and Lew Wasserman flew to New York, where they planned to stay through Sunday. After a meeting with Mike Bessie of *Harper's* to discuss Ray's proposed book, Ray would fly to Paris to scout new talent, then go on to London to meet with the British Board of Censors. Because the British censorship laws were so strict, Ray would have a difficult time getting the film accepted without significant cuts.

On September 16, Warner Bros. announced that "James Dean plans to go on a racing kick when *Giant* ends." The studio also announced a definite release date for its 504th feature film, *Rebel Without a Cause*. The picture was set to premiere October 29. Carl Schaefer of Warner Bros.' New York office wrote to Arthur S. Abeles, Jr., the company's representative in London, regarding Ray's upcoming European trip. Abeles and Ray would meet with Arthur Watkins of the British Board of Censors. They hoped to convince Watkins that *Rebel Without a Cause* was not another *Blackboard Jungle*, but "a sincere and intelligent story which very definitely has an excuse for being made."

On September 17, James Dean took time off from filming *Giant* to make a public service commercial with Gig Young for the National Safety Council. Dean discussed his racing career, dispelled a few illusions about the dangers of racing, and concluded with a personal appeal to the audience, delivered flippantly: "Take it easy driving. The life you save might be mine."

In the evening, Dean attended a second preview of *Rebel* at the Westwood Village Theater. Jack Warner and Steve Trilling also attended, along with a number of Dean's friends. The word was out about Dean's new film, and the young performers who frequented Googie's and Coffee Dan's had been reading every newspaper advertising a studio preview in the hope of catching his performance. Dean still enjoyed watching people watch him on the screen. He still seemed in awe of his own abilities. At one of the screenings, Sal Mineo looked back and saw Dean "giving that grin of his, and almost blushing, looking down at the floor between his legs."

The day after the Westwood preview, Steve Trilling made cutting notes. Most of his suggestions involved speeding up the action (the switchblade fight, Judy's argument at home, the planetarium ending), deleting lines (Judy saying, "I never felt like this before," in the library scene) and removing shots (Jim tapping the helmet of a suit of armor at the mansion).

Ray was anxious to hear news of the screening. From Paris, he cabled Trilling at the studio. Trilling's response was what Ray might have expected: audience reaction was excellent, but the film still needed further trimming, "particularly the knife fight and alley love scene."

Based on the previews and Dean's popularity, Warner Bros. expected *Rebel Without a Cause* to be a major box office attraction. The Publicity Department was already gearing up for the advertising campaign. On September 21, a two-page ad for *Rebel* appeared in *Variety*. The copy read: "The overnight sensation of 'EAST OF EDEN' becomes the star of the year!"… "Warner Bros. put all the force of the screen into a challenging drama of today's juvenile violence!"

That same day, James Dean purchased a new sports car, a Porsche 550 Spyder, which he planned to race as soon as *Giant* completed filming.

44

DEATH IN THE AFTERNOON

On Thursday, September 22, Dean spent his last day on the set of *Giant*. Freed from George Stevens' directive against racing, he looked forward to testing his new Porsche in a race at Salinas. The race ran October 1 and 2. Although his work on *Giant* was over, Dean still carried some of the picture with him. To help Dean portray Jett Rink at the end of the film (the story covered twenty years), the Makeup Department had given him the appearance of a middle-aged man, complete with receding hairline. People off the set who had not followed his role closely found his appearance alarming. Even people he knew were shocked. He looked old. He *was* old. He was about to die.

The day after his work on *Giant* ended, Dean received a chillingly accurate premonition of his death from a man he had never met before. At 10:00 P.M., Alec Guinness was standing in the parking lot of the Villa Capri Restaurant, Dean's regular eatery and hangout on the Sunset Strip. Guinness and his companion, screenwriter Thelma Moss, had been unable to get a table and had left in a huff. Dean had followed them outside and graciously invited them to join him at his table.

On their way back through the parking lot, Dean stopped to show Guinness his new Porsche Spyder. Competition Motors had just delivered the car, wrapped in cellophane and tied with a ribbon. A bouquet of red carnations adorned the hood. Guinness asked how fast the car would go, and Dean told him proudly, "She'll do a hundred and fifty." Tired and not in the best of moods, a less-than-diplomatic Guinness looked at the car and said to Dean, "Please, never get in it." Glancing at his watch, he continued, "It is now ten o'clock, Friday, the 23rd of September, 1955. If you get in that car you will be found dead in it by this time next week."

Dean did not know how to react. He laughed and said, "Oh, shucks! Don't be so mean!" Guinness quickly apologized and followed Dean into the restaurant, where the subject of the car did not come up again. After an hour of dining and jokes about Lee Strasberg and the Actors Studio, Guinness and Thelma Moss said goodbye to James Dean, never to see him again.

On September 25, Dean spent his last Sunday afternoon at a party in his honor at the Chateau Marmont. His New York agent, Jane Deacy, hosted it. She had come to Hollywood to negotiate a new contract with Warner Bros. for her fast-rising client.

In the evening, Dean visited Arthur Loew, Jr. Eartha Kitt arrived unexpectedly and greeted Dean warmly. But she, too, had a premonition. "Something's wrong," she told him. "You're not here."

On Monday morning, Dean drove his Porsche Spyder to Compton, just south of Los Angeles, where George Barris had a customizing shop. The man who had customized Jim Stark's 1949 Mercury painted "130" on the hood and both doors of the sleek, silver car. He also painted "Little Bastard" on the boot. In the afternoon, Dean discussed his new Warner Bros. contract with Jane Deacy. In the evening, he took a friend, Janette Miller, for a chilly drive over Topanga Canyon (west of Los Angeles) and into the San Fernando Valley.

Dean and Lew Bracker spent Tuesday afternoon with Jane Deacy discussing Dean's idea for an independent production company. Bracker would produce the features, and Joe Hyams would write. After the meeting, Dean and Bracker went to the movies. The picture was *Magnificent Obsession*, with Rock Hudson and Jane Wyman. The next night, Dean went once more to the movies. He and Lew Bracker accompanied Ursula Andress, Dean's most recent high-profile girlfriend, to see *I Am a Camera*. The picture starred Julie Harris, Dean's co-star in *East of Eden*. It was the last movie James Dean ever saw.

On Thursday, the 29th, Dean paid an early visit to Janette Miller. He asked her to take care of his kitten, Marcus (a gift from Elizabeth Taylor) while he was away. He spent the rest of the day trying to convince his friends to accompany him to the race. Lew Bracker could not go; he had tickets for a football game. Joe Hyams was leaving for Mexico. As Dean was asking Ursula Andress, a rival suitor, John Derek (her future husband), drove up. She declined. Dean asked his father, Winton, but he declined also. A photographer friend, Sandy Roth, finally agreed to go, as did Bill Hickman, Dean's dialogue coach on *Giant*. Hickman was the "Big Bastard" to Dean's "Little Bastard."

At 6:00 P.M., Dean took the Spyder out for a test drive. Hickman went with him. They drove almost as far as Santa Barbara, then returned to Los Angeles around 11:00 P.M. Dean had a late dinner at the Villa Capri and returned home at 3:00 A.M.

At 8:00 A.M., Friday, September 30, Dean arrived at Competition Motors before starting out for Salinas. His mechanic, Rolf Weutherich, made a final check of the engine and declared the car track-worthy. Normally, on the way to a race, Dean towed the car behind his sta-

British actor Alec Guinness chillingly predicted James Dean's death in an auto accident almost to the hour.

tion wagon; but he decided to put more miles on it and get more experience behind the wheel. Weutherich would sit beside him in the Spyder, while Roth and Hickman followed in the wagon.

At noon, Dean's father arrived. Dean offered him a short ride, but Winton Dean declined. They adjourned to the Farmer's Market in West Hollywood for coffee and doughnuts. Then, in early afternoon, the two-car caravan started the long drive that was expected to bring them to Paso Robles near dinner time.

At around 3:30, a Highway Patrol officer ticketed Dean for speeding on Highway 99. Dean drove on north to Bakersfield, then west on Highway 466. At around 5:00 P.M., he stopped at Blackwell's Corners, a small gas station and grocery at the intersection of Highway 33 and 466. Paso Robles lay sixty miles ahead.

At around 5:45, Dean's sleek Porsche Spyder, its low profile masked even further by a setting sun, approached the intersection of Highway 41 and Highway 466. A 1950 Ford Tudor station wagon was turning at the intersection. Its driver, a college student named Donald Turnupseed, did not see Dean's car until it was already in his path. Dean accelerated to slip around the Ford, as he might in a race, but the cars collided. The Spyder flipped over several times and came to rest across the intersection. The driver of the Ford suffered only minor bruises. Rolf Weutherich, who was thrown free of the car, was seriously injured. Dean, bearing the full force of the collision and trapped in the Porsche as it cartwheeled across the highway, sustained

September 30, 1955; James Dean's promising film career ended in the twisted wreckage of his racing car.

fatal injuries. His body was still entangled in the wreckage when an ambulance arrived. The doctor who examined Dean made his grim report: Dean had suffered "a broken neck, multiple broken bones, and lacerations over his entire body."

By 6:20, the police had arrived. An ambulance took the injured Weutherich and Dean's body to War Memorial Hospital in Paso Robles, twenty miles away. Hickman and Roth followed in the station wagon. A doctor declared Dean "Dead on Arrival" and attendants moved his body to the nearby Kuehl Funeral Home. One of the hospital staff had the onerous task of telling Warner Bros. that its newest and most bankable movie star was dead.

The call, relayed through the hospital switchboard operator, reached a security policeman working the night watch at Warner Bros. He called the Publicity Department and reached Steve Brooks, the only one there. Brooks called War Memorial Hospital to confirm the news, then phoned Henry Ginsberg, the producer of *Giant*, who was at home in Palm Springs. Ginsberg called Famous Artists, the agency that employed Dick Clayton. Clayton telephoned Jane Deacy at the Chateau Marmont, and they drove to Winton Dean's home, hoping he had not already heard the news over the radio. He had not.

Ginsberg also called Stewart Stern, who was back from New York. "The boy is dead! The boy is dead!" Ginsberg cried. Stern, like many who would hear the tragic news that night, was inconsolable. For a while, he wandered aimlessly along the Sunset Strip, then went looking for his cousin, Arthur Loew, Jr., at whose home he had first met James Dean.

Ginsberg's next call was to George Stevens at the studio. He was in a screening room at work on *Giant*. Elizabeth Taylor, Rock Hudson and Carroll Baker were with him. In the middle of the screening, Stevens picked up the telephone, listened a moment in silence, and turned ashen. He stopped the projector. When he announced the news, Elizabeth Taylor collapsed.

Elsewhere in Los Angeles, others were learning of the tragedy. Jim Backus and his wife Henny heard it on their car radio. Beverly Long and her boyfriend were about to leave for Las Vegas (to elope) when a friend called. Dennis Hopper was watching a play with his agent, who took the call in the theater lobby. He returned to break the news to Hopper, who suddenly struck him and said, "Liar!" Perry Lopez was at a party, having a drink. When he heard the news, he upended his glass and walked out without a word.

In New York, Natalie Wood, Sal Mineo and Nick Adams were having dinner with Richard Davalos and his wife after watching Davalos perform in Arthur Miller's play, *A View from the Bridge*. Davalos had played Dean's brother in *East of Eden*. They were talking about James Dean. Mineo mentioned that Dean planned to go racing that weekend. When the others expressed concern for Dean's safety, Davalos reassured them that Dean "knows what he's doing."

Later that night, Nick Adams learned of Dean's death from Natalie Wood's studio chaperone, Maggie Waite. Waite urged Adams not to tell anyone yet, especially Wood, who needed her sleep before the next day's live telecast of *Heidi* on ABC. In Brooklyn, Leonard Rosenman was visiting his parents when Jane Deacy called. "I want to tell you that Jimmy was killed in an automobile accident tonight," she said, and sobbed.

Nicholas Ray was in London, where it was already Saturday. Although he had come to London to discuss *Rebel*'s problems with the British censor, Ray was also looking ahead to a long-range creative partnership with Dean. They had already chosen their next project, "Heroic Love," written by an Arizona teacher named Edward Loomis. Ray would direct and Dean would play an ex–GI who wants to settle down and study law until he becomes involved in scandal.

Ray received the news from Roger Donoghue, a friend who had often visited Ray on the set of *Rebel*. Ray asked if he was sure, and Donoghue said that he had checked with both wire services. Ray said, "I'll talk to you tomorrow," and hung up.

Outside the movie community, James Dean's death created no major shock wave. While his family and friends in Fairmount grieved and young fans who had seen him in *East of Eden* tried to measure their own loss, others had never even heard of him. Still others confused him with Jimmy Dean, the Country-Western singer. There was as yet no youth cult to worship James Dean.

45

DAMAGE CONTROL

At Warner Bros., despite the shock of Dean's death, the normal activities continued almost without interruption. The only problem that Saturday morning was on the set of *Giant*. Elizabeth Taylor arrived late and informed Assistant Director Tom Andre that she did not feel well. Still upset over Dean's sudden death, she had come to work only at George Stevens' insistence. In the makeup room, she threw up. The First Aid Man gave her something to calm her stomach, and she reported for work finally at 11:45 A.M.

Taylor held up through all of her long shots, but the close-ups clearly showed that she was ill. When Stevens insisted that the work continue, they exchanged angry words. He could not understand why she wasn't ready to work, and she could not understand his insensitivity to Dean's death. Enraged, she left the set for the rest of the day. That evening, when Stevens screened the dailies, he decided that Taylor would have to come in again on Monday.

There were no shouting matches over James Dean in the Warner Bros. front office. The executives were too busy worrying. Their biggest new star was dead. *Rebel Without a Cause*, one of their most promising new pictures, was suddenly in jeopardy. With less than a month before the picture's release, they had several decisions to make. Their first problem was *Rebel*'s advertising campaign, which had already begun. References to Dean as the studio's "rising star" now seemed inappropriate. Should they redesign the film's press book, which featured all the film's advertising art and copy, in light of the tragic event? Should they postpone the picture's release out of respect to Dean's memory, or should they move up the date to take advantage of this sudden windfall of free publicity? Would the studio appear ghoulish or insensitive to take advantage of such publicity?

On Sunday, October 2, the day before George Stevens expected Elizabeth Taylor to return to work, she entered the UCLA Medical Center. She stayed there for two weeks, suffering severe abdominal pain from a twisted colon.

Meanwhile, James Dean's reckless lifestyle, and how it might have led to his death, had become Hollywood's topic of the moment. The front page headline in *The Los Angeles Times* read: "Death Premonition by Dean Recalled":

Hollywood friends, shocked and saddened by the death of James Dean... recalled yesterday that he was always in a hurry because he believed he might not live very long. The actor, a nonconformist in his private life, spoke often of this 'premonition of death' and it came to be an accepted part of his unpredictable character, they said.

On October 3, Dean would have begun rehearsals for a Hallmark Hall of Fame television program, "The Corn is Green." His co-star would have been Judith Anderson. The production temporarily suspended all activity. On the 5th, Dean's obituary appeared in *Variety*. On the same page, the studio revealed its decision about *Rebel Without a Cause*:

Death of James Dean in an auto accident on the Coast over the weekend has not upset Warner Bros. plans for the release of the two pictures in which the 24-year-old actor had starring assignments. "Rebel Without a Cause," a juvenile delinquency yarn, is set for release next month. Since most of the publicity and advertising on the picture had been completed, the company does not contemplate making any big changes in the text of the bally matter.

All publicity stories in which Dean is referred to in contemporary terms will be changed, of course. After conferring with circuits which had booked "Rebel," Warners decided to go ahead with the ads which prominently feature Dean in both art and copy. Only change in the ads will be the elimination of a line of copy which reads: "The overnight sensation of 'East of Eden' becomes the star of the year!"

As further proof that the studio wanted to speed ahead with *Rebel*, it announced a trade screening for October 20th. The screening allowed the film's exhibitors nationwide to get an early look at the picture. A full page ad for *Rebel* would also appear, as planned, in the October issue of *Seventeen* magazine.

The studio's only fear in releasing *Rebel Without a Cause* on schedule was the possibility of nationwide hysteria among the nation's young female moviegoers. An anonymous studio official reassured the readers of *The Valley Times* that the country would not witness any of the unrestrained public grief that accompanied Rudolf Valentino's death almost thirty years earlier: "The moviegoing public is matured, grown-up and doesn't take its idolatry so much to heart." *The Valley Times* added, "It is understood also that [the studio's] ad campaign and picture's billing will not be changed to soft-pedal the fact that the story is built entirely around the eccentric 24-year-old star whose tragic end had been predicted by several Warners executives watching him carom in and out of their gates in his fast racing jobs."

On October 7, David Weisbart sent a memo to William Hendricks, head of the Publicity Department. The memo contained a list of those who had provided advice and technical assistance during the making of *Rebel Without a Cause*. Weisbart suggested that the studio might invite these people to special press screenings of the picture. The list included Judge McKesson and the psychologists, social workers and probation officers at Juvenile Hall; Dr. Douglas M. Kelley of Berkeley; and members of the California Youth Authority.

Leonard Rosenman had made his own list of names, some of whom were in music publishing and, as Weisbart observed, "could conceivably help the picture by calling attention to the music." Rosenman also wanted to send a pair of tickets to Marlon Brando.

On Saturday, October 8, James Byron Dean's family and friends laid him to rest in Fairmount, Indiana, where he had grown up. At 2:00 P.M., they held a funeral service at the Back Creek Friends Church. Three thousand people attended, several hundred more than the population of the town. The studio sent Henry Ginsberg (the producer of *Giant*) and Steve Brooks. Stewart Stern, Jack Simmons and Dennis Stock represented the *Rebel* company. Elizabeth Taylor sent flowers, ordered from her hospital bed. After the funeral service, Dean was buried in the Winslow family plot.

"The greatest young actress since Helen Hayes" was the way Nicholas Ray described Natalie Wood in the October 9 issue of *Spokesman Review*. "The history of Hollywood is filled with young boys and girls who were never able to handle mature roles and have since been forgotten," he added in reference to Wood's convincing portrayal of Judy in *Rebel Without a Cause*. He predicted that Wood "will be one of the great stars of screen and stage within five years." He made no mention of James Dean in the interview, given before Ray had left for Europe.

On October 10, *The New York Post* reported that *Rebel Without a Cause* would have its premiere at the Astor Theater in that city following the current run of *The McConnell Story* with Alan Ladd and June Allyson. The same day, two copies of *Rebel*'s dialogue transcripts arrived at the Story Department. They represented the only written record of what was actually spoken in the film.

Despite the studio's attempts to downplay James Dean as another tragic Valentino, the *Los Angeles Mirror-News* had been building up that very idea in its columns. One irate reader who knew Dean before his sudden fame was quick to dispute the comparison:

> I've read your recent columns about James Dean with interest. In the first place you are making a macabre "Much Ado About Nothing" over all this. There couldn't possibly be mass mourning (of the Valentino type) because people simply didn't know who he was.
>
> In person he looked as unlike a movie star as you can imagine with rumpled hair, dirty jeans and eyeglasses.
>
> Those of us who knew Dean in New York know that there was a monotonous sameness about everything he did. I believe his unreleased movies will bear this out.
>
> Interesting, isn't it, that Dean was much happier a few years ago when he was working in the CBS parking lot. Fame made him uncomfortable and did strange things to him.

46

REAPING THE WHIRLWIND

On October 11, Albert Howson informed the New York office that the New York Board of Censors had passed *Rebel Without a Cause* "without eliminations," meaning that the studio could show the film in New York theaters without deleting any specific scenes or dialogue. Meanwhile, the publicity buildup for *Rebel* continued. That night on ABC television, *Warner Bros. Presents* aired an episode of *Cheyenne*, the popular Western series starring Clint Walker. Gig Young hosted a fifteen-minute promotional spot, "Behind the Cameras," which featured *Rebel Without a Cause*. Unlike many of the studios, Warner Bros. understood the potential of television. Television viewers were likely to be movie viewers, and television reached into thousands of homes.

On October 12, Warner Bros. previewed *Rebel Without a Cause* at the Downtown Paramount Theater in Los Angeles. The newspaper writers attended, along with the major critics of national magazines and wire services. Jack Warner personally represented the studio. The next day, Warner wrote to Ben Kalmenson in New York about the success of the preview. He observed that none of the news media representatives had left early. "This is very unusual," he said. "They milled around in [the] lobby for over [a] half hour after [the] preview was over and heaped praise upon praise not only upon Jimmy Dean and Natalie but [the] entire picture." Warner added that "[The] audience [was] absolutely captivated by [the] dramatic power and emotional impact of [the] picture."

That evening, Nicholas Ray flew to London from Germany, where he had spent the last two weeks visiting a friend, Hanna Axmann. He was scheduled to meet the next day with Arthur Watkins of the British Board of Film Censors. Ray had sent a post card to Steve Trilling regarding positive reaction to the picture overseas. On his arrival in London, he mailed another post card to Trilling. The death of James Dean was weighing heavily on his mind as he prepared for the meeting with Watkins. "Much as I love the picture," he admitted, "it's a little like going to a funeral."

On October 14, Ray and Warner Bros.' London representative, Arthur Abeles, screened a print of *Rebel Without a Cause* for the British censors. Abeles hoped that Ray's passion for the film would convince the British not to judge it too harshly. Yet, as Ray left the screening room, he knew he had failed. Before the film could play on

British screens, Ray would need to trim or cut out entirely many of the film's most important moments. To Ray, that meant nothing less than destroying the film.

Three days later, the British Board of Film Censors put its objections to *Rebel Without a Cause* in writing. Arthur Watkins informed Abeles that "*Rebel Without a Cause* contains, in our view, much that would have a harmful influence on young people." The Board would not certify the picture for British distribution until "essential" cuts were made. Those cuts included some of the most powerful scenes in the film: Jim punching and kicking Ray Framek's desk; the switchblade fight (if not removing it completely); Jim choking his father; Buzz's fiery death at the end of the chickie run. The very idea of such a race troubled the censors. "The less we have of this whole unpleasant idea of young people meeting together to witness a contest which could end in the death of one of the participants, the better," said the official report.

Watkins offered an "X" (adults only) certificate for the picture if the studio made the necessary cuts, and he suggested the possibility of even more cuts later. Because of the Board's unfavorable reaction to *Rebel Without a Cause*, Watkins added, it could not even grant a certificate for the picture's trailer.

The British Board's decision was a serious setback for the studio's European marketing plan. If teenagers could not watch a film designed primarily for them, the film's audience evaporated. If the studio agreed to even more drastic cuts so that teenagers *could* see it, would there be anything left to entice them into the theaters? For Ray, the news was particularly depressing. His emotional balance, already burdened by Dean's death, could not easily bear this second shock.

In the United States, word of Dean's performance in *Rebel Without a Cause* was spreading. Columnist Dorothy Kilgallen predicted an Academy Award nomination for him. She predicted also that Dean would be the first posthumous winner of an Oscar in the history of the Academy of Motion Picture Arts and Sciences.

The studio, meanwhile, had not yet received the grim specifics of Arthur Watkins' letter of October 17. Steve Trilling wrote a letter to Ray in London, hopeful that the British board would pass the film, but reminding Ray how adamant the board was about the knife fight's removal. Trilling reported on the results of the latest preview, in Westwood, and a favorable audience reaction, but he tempered his praise with the suggestion that more cuts were needed to speed the film's pace, especially the alley love scene, which "just laid there" and made the audience restless. Trilling was pleased, however, that Dean's untimely death had not put a damper on enthusiasm for the film. Warner and Trilling had discussed holding back the film's release, "but publicity had already been planted and it was impossible to stop the forward movement without creating comment and possibly unfavorable reaction."

On October 19, a full page ad for *Rebel Without a Cause* appeared in *Variety*, including a reprint of Jack Warner's letter to Ben Kalmenson praising the press screening at the Downtown Paramount. From Chicago came good news: the Chicago Board of Censors had passed *Rebel Without a Cause* "without eliminations." The next day, The Legion of Decency, moral guardian for the nation's Roman Catholic audience, awarded *Rebel Without a Cause* an A-II rating, meaning that the picture was morally unobjectionable for adults. The Legion's highest rating was A-I (Morally Unobjectionable for All). Its B-rated films were Morally Objectionable in Part for All. Films rated C (Condemned) were forbidden to Catholics.

The New York press was gearing up for the premiere of *Rebel* at the Astor Theater. Irene Thirer of *The New York Post* featured Natalie Wood in her column, with James Dean as the main topic. Wood explained that Dean might have been difficult and moody when working with other actors, but "he was sweet, kind and considerate to me...I found myself constantly hoping to grow up to him so that we might start dating." Wood also praised Nicholas Ray's low-key directing style and plugged her next picture, *A Cry in the Night*, with Raymond Burr.

On October 21, Ray's difficult negotiations continued with the British Board of Censors. He wired Jack Warner and Steve Trilling that the meetings had been "satisfactory" and that he would update them on his return to New York in three days. Privately, his fears about deep cuts in the British version were growing. His depression over Dean's death worsened. After three years "on the wagon," he had started drinking again.

Two important trade publications, *The Hollywood Reporter* and *Daily Variety*, presented reviews of *Rebel Without a Cause*. *Daily Variety* reported:

> "Rebel Without a Cause" is a tense, exciting melodrama, camera-probing the particular problems of a small group of the young, rather than an overall looksee at juvenile delinquency.

James Dean's performance won the reviewer's praise and prompted the observation that "under Nicholas Ray's sock[o] direction, the Marlon Brando mannerisms displayed in [*East of Eden*] are gone and the role here carries much greater audience sympathy and response as a result." The review also praised the film's two minors:

> Miss Wood, fast maturing as a young lady, and a constantly improving actress, is splendid. Exceptionally fine is Mineo's sensitive study of lonely youth. Story smartly does not go into detail about the other teenage characters, leaving development uncluttered in concentrating on the lead trio.

Jack Moffitt of the *Reporter* saw the picture more in terms of box office potential:

> The exhibitor can expect this story of juvenile delinquency to capture the "Blackboard Jungle" type of audience and be a real money picture.

His opinion of the film's dramatic qualities was less positive. He found the switchblade fight "reckless" and "silly" and the picture overall "a superficial treatment of a vital problem that has been staged brilliantly."

On October 24, Sal Mineo was the center of attention in Frank Quinn's *New York Daily Mirror* column. According to Quinn, the "17-year-old Bronxite whose acting career has a bright future" was also considering college and a career in business. He might even follow in his father's casket-making business.

Mineo had high praise for his late co-star, James Dean: "He had improved greatly since his first role in 'East of Eden.' It is a tragedy that such an acting talent was destroyed." About his own acting success, Mineo said, "The boys are okay and treat me like one of the mob. It's the girls who are okay, too, until they find out I act, then they get silly."

In Los Angeles, Natalie Wood had been making the rounds on local television. She had appeared on *Juke Box Jury*, *Teen-age Trials* and *See Hear* over the past weekend. On the 24th, she appeared on *Beat the Record* to plug *Rebel Without a Cause* once more. She would appear on two more teen-oriented shows on the 26th, one more on the 27th, and one on the 31st.

Nicholas Ray returned from London on October 25. Roger Donoghue met him at the airport in New York and was disappointed to find him drunk. Ray's arrival coincided with more bad news from the censors. This time the trouble was domestic. Memphis, Tennessee, with one of the toughest local codes in the country, had banned the showing of *Rebel Without a Cause*. The Memphis board had also banned *Blackboard Jungle* the previous March. Its notorious 88-year-old censor, Lloyd Binford, who had called *Blackboard Jungle* "the vilest picture I've seen in 26 years as censor," was not on hand to pass judgment this time; but the three remaining censors agreed that *Rebel Without a Cause* was "inimical to the public welfare."

The decision took local distributors by surprise, since they had scheduled the picture to open the next day. Warner Bros.' New York office assigned Memphis a last-minute substitute, *Three Stripes of the Sun*, about a Japanese-hating GI who falls in love with a Japanese orphanage worker.

47

PREMIERE

On Wednesday, October 26, 1955, *Rebel Without a Cause* had its world premiere at the Astor Theater in New York, the same theater where *East of Eden* had opened eight months earlier. *Variety* called it a "strong action picture." Like *Blackboard Jungle*, it had "shock value" that might "draw upon itself…outcries from academic, ecclesiastic and civic bodies." The picture's emphasis on middle-class delinquents increased its shock value, said *Variety*, but it also strained its credibility. That well-bred, advantaged children could behave as violently as their lower-class counterparts would be difficult for audiences to accept. Despite its violence, however, the picture did "bring out redeeming touches of human warmth."

Variety made the obligatory reference to James Dean's death, praised his performance and gave credit to the rest of the cast. The reviewer apparently took Plato's nickname too literally, however, describing him as "the abandoned child of a big Greek tycoon." The other gang members, *Variety* complained, were only "briefly and surfacely depicted, often hardly more than a cardboard cutout." However, "they serve well as the symbol of hostility against which the suspense develops."

The chickie run sequence earned special praise for "driv[ing] home the insanity of frightened youth lest the stigma of 'chicken' go uncontradicted." *Variety* observed that both the switchblade fight and the chickie run were "rooted in ghastly reality." The review concluded: "Adults may well come away from 'Rebel Without a Cause' as from 'Blackboard Jungle' and 'The Wild One' and other films which spotlight the compulsive cruelties of youth, with a need to believe the facts hideously exaggerated and a silent prayer that they never meet such youths except upon the motion picture screen."

Meanwhile, in Milwaukee, Wisconsin, Warner Bros. had avoided another censorship battle over *Rebel Without a Cause*. The Motion Picture Committee of Milwaukee had demanded a number of cuts, including the title sequence where a drunken Jim Stark plays with a windup monkey. The Committee had also objected to all scenes involving switchblade knives. Legal representatives for the studio had apparently convinced the Committee to abandon some demands and modify others: the opening credits remained, and the studio agreed to remove only those shots of knives that did not affect the story's continuity.

In his letter to the New York office, however, studio attorney Steven E. Keane argued that Warner Bros. might have made unnecessary concessions. The film was neither lewd, obscene, nor immoral, and those were the only grounds on which it could be prosecuted. Keane argued that if the studio had released the picture uncut, in defiance of the local censors, it was unlikely that any legal action (ie. revocation of theater licenses) would have succeeded. "The next time one of these censorship cases comes up," he suggested, "we may not have a picture which we may be as proud of."

On October 27, the New York film critics responded to *Rebel Without a Cause*. Bosley Crowther of *The New York Times* had not been a fan of James Dean in *East of Eden*. Although he still criticized the late actor for imitating Marlon Brando, he was more kind in evaluating Dean's performance in *Rebel*. He was also more positive in his evaluation of the film, noting that "there are excruciating flashes of accuracy and truth" in it. It was, however, "violent, brutal and disturbing." Like *Blackboard Jungle*, it was "a picture to make the hair stand on end." One of Crowther's major objections to *Rebel* was its shallow depiction of adults, especially Jim Stark's parents as played by Jim Backus and Ann Doran. He also found the film's "pictorial slickness" and its CinemaScope-and-Warnercolor format at odds "with the realism in the direction of Nicholas Ray."

Wanda Hale, the critic of *The New York Daily News*, also faulted the film for its cardboard adults. In *Rebel*'s view, Hale complained, "fathers should all be under psychiatric treatment, [and] mothers should be killed after childbirth." She also found a lack of credibility in the film's attempt to show middle-class teenagers as hoodlums. "As an honest, purposeful drama of juvenile hardness and violence," she argued, "the film just doesn't measure up." But James Dean's performance did: "With complete control of the character, he gives a fine, sensitive performance of an unhappy, lonely teenager, tormented by the knowledge of his emotional instability." She, too, saw a macabre quality in the film, finding it "double grim, horrendous in text, because it is a constant reminder of the tragic death of the star, James Dean." She awarded the picture three stars on a scale of one to four, an average film except for Dean's extraordinary work.

Alton Cook, the film critic of *The New York World-Telegram*, praised the acting of Dean, Wood, and Mineo, but he also believed that the story went to "unacceptable extremes."

William K. Zinsser of *The New York Herald-Tribune* was even less kind to the picture. After summarizing the plot through most of his column, he concluded, "All this takes two hours, but it seems more like two days. The movie is written and acted so ineptly, directed so sluggishly, that all names but one will be omitted here." The one name, of course, was James Dean, "the gifted young actor who was killed last month. His rare talent and appealing personality even shine through this turgid melodrama."

The Sunday after *Rebel*'s premiere, Bosley Crowther had more to say about *Rebel Without a Cause*. He believed strongly that *Rebel*, like *Blackboard Jungle*, went to extremes in presenting the subject of juvenile delinquency. The picture, he argued, "is a desperate and dangerous distortion of another aspect of modern disturbed youth." The other "aspect" was the film's attempt to place most of the blame for what the teenagers do on their parents and police. The police were to blame "for 'not understanding,'" and the parents "for being dull and dumb." Even though the film accurately reflected "the attitudes of certain teen-age elements," the over-emphasis on the failure of adults (including teachers) "render[ed] this picture's likely influence upon real youngsters with emotional disturbance questionable. There is a deception in its pretense of 'understanding' that can gravely mislead."

Philip K. Scheuer of *The Los Angeles Times* had a different view of *Rebel*. He saw it as "another in a succession of powerful films that lately have attempted to come to grips with sociological and psychological problems—a kind of 'Blackboard Jungle,' but of the 'solid' middle class, so that its exposure of some of the horrifying things that go on makes even more of an impact on us." Scheur agreed with Crowther about the film's attitude toward adults, and especially parents: "The grown folks depicted here are too stupid or too stiff to be quite real." Scheur concluded that "as melodrama, in color and CinemaScope, 'Rebel Without a Cause' is smooth moviemaking, taut enough to elicit gasps in such sequences as the fatal hot rod race, the switchblade knife duel...the descent of the gang upon a spooky and abandoned mansion, leading to wild gunfire...and the attractive—and affecting—climax at the Griffith Park Planetarium, where the principals, young and older, converge for 'the end of the world at night.'"

Most adult moviegoers were attentive to the critics' concerns. To many of *Rebel*'s younger viewers, however, the reviews were irrelevant. They came to see James Dean cheat death as Jim Stark. As the film played itself out in the darkness of theaters around the country, the ironies of life and death, fantasy and fact, compounded themselves with almost every action and line of dialogue: Jim tells Ray Framek of his father, "I don't know what to do anymore, except maybe die on him." Buzz tells Jim after the switchblade fight, "You're dead, Jack. You're cold." After Jim Stark survives the deadly game of "chicken" at the Millertown bluff, he says to Judy in the alley, "You saw where I jumped. What do I have to do, kill myself?" Plato asks if the world will end "at nighttime." Out of these freakish circumstances, a mystique was coming to life and spreading among the nation's youth. The cult of James Dean had begun, barely a month after his death.

48

BOX OFFICE

The emerging Dean cult was partly responsible for *Rebel*'s stunning success in America's movie houses. Playing in 39 cities its first week, it was 25 percent ahead of *East of Eden*'s first week of business the previous March.

At New York's Astor Theater, after 5 days, *Rebel* had grossed a "very big $40,122," according to *Variety*. The estimated gross from the first full week was $52,000. In Albany, New York, the Grand Theater had taken in $10,728 in five days. The picture would hold for a second week and then move over to the Ritz. At the Stanley in Baltimore, the picture had grossed $11,463 in only four days. It would hold for a second week. In Boston, playing four days at both the Paramount and Fenway, *Rebel* had grossed $18,766. It would play a second week in both theaters. In Buffalo, after four days at the Center Theater, the picture had taken in $14,160. It would play a second week. At the Allen in Cleveland after five days, $13,812; held over. At the Roger Sherman in New Haven, after five days, $11,485; held over. At the Majestic in Providence, $13,771 after five days; held over. At the Stanley in Pittsburgh, $13,585 after four days; held over. *Rebel* would also play a second week in Reading, Pennsylvania; Utica, New York; Springfield, Massachusetts; Madison, Wisconsin; and Washington, D. C.

In Milwaukee, legal representatives from Warner Bros. were still working out the details of an arrangement that would allow *Rebel* to play with only limited cuts. The Motion Picture Committee was to make its decision after screening the revised film. Robert Perkins, head of the New York office's Legal Department, informed the studio's attorney in Milwaukee that Steven E. Keane would sit in on the screening. It was Keane's letter of October 26 that had alerted the New York office to problems in Milwaukee.

On November 2, following the meeting with the Milwaukee censor, Warner Bros. agreed to cuts for both Milwaukee and Chicago audiences. Although Chicago had originally passed the film without eliminations, it too now demanded cuts in the switchblade fight and the scene where Jim throttles his father. The Ace Film Laboratories of Brooklyn, New York, were already altering the prints.

In *Variety*'s National Boxoffice Survey, *Rebel Without a Cause* was in third place after only a week. MGM's *Trial*, in its third week, was the number one film at the box office, followed by a travelogue, *Cinerama Holiday*.

188

With the Los Angeles area premiere only a week away, Natalie Wood was again making the rounds for the Publicity Department. Over the weekend, she expected to appear on KABC-TV's *Al Jarvis Show*. A week later, she would appear on *The Jack Owens Show* and *The Bill Gwinn Show*, both on ABC.

On November 7, good news arrived from Canada: the British Columbia Board of Censors had passed *Rebel Without a Cause* "without eliminations for adult entertainment." On the 9th, *Variety* reported that *Rebel* had dropped to fourth place in its National Boxoffice Survey, behind *Trial, Gentlemen Marry Brunettes* and *Cinerama Holiday*. However, it had had "smash" openings in Portland and Kansas City and continued to do well ($26,000) in its second week at the Astor in New York. On the same day, it opened at thirteen Los Angeles area theaters. On the lower half of the double-bill with *Rebel* was *The Warriors*, a costume drama with Joanne Dru and an aging Errol Flynn.

The Los Angeles area critics were mostly upbeat in their evaluations of *Rebel*. *The Los Angeles Examiner* saw it as "a strong, fierce young picture with Dean always in command of it." Harrison Carroll of *The Los Angeles Herald and Express* saw it as "a dramatic and challenging film, proving beyond doubt that Dean was able to sustain his bid to become one of the ranking stars of the screen." Branch Corey of the *Citizen-News* agreed, observing that the film "is distinguished by three outstanding assets—superb acting, fine directing and effective photography." He expected Dean to receive an Oscar nomination for his role as Jim Stark. Mark Tuttle of *The Valley Times* described *Rebel* as "exciting adult fare and a believable look at youth's rage to live." Dean's performance, he said, "equals, if not surpasses" his work in *East of Eden*.

Fred W. Fox of *The Los Angeles Mirror-News* struck the only note of discord. *Rebel Without a Cause*, in his opinion, fell short of *Eden* "as a vehicle for this unusual protagonist of the teenagers." Yet, he found the film a "taut and brutal drama of the jealousies, posturings, frustrations and despairs of teenster rivals." Much of Fox's praise went to Natalie Wood, who "looks like a comer" and who, "given [the] right opportunities...can develop into a first-rate performer and a popular box-office star."

The following week, in *Variety*'s National Boxoffice Survey, *Rebel* surged back into third place behind the new leaders, *Guys and Dolls* and *Cinerama Holiday*. In its first week at three Los Angeles theaters, with ticket prices ranging from ninety cents to a dollar and a half, it had grossed $52,000. According to *Variety*, it was also "robust" in Indianapolis at $12,000, "tall" in Seattle at $12,000, and $22,000 in New York.

Meanwhile, Bob Thomas, Hollywood correspondent for the Associated Press, was reporting the dark side of the growing Dean mystique. In a column in *The Los Angeles Mirror-News* he observed that Dean was "as much in the public consciousness as when he lived." Dean's death, unfortunately, was also beginning to have a frightening impact on some of Dean's more ardent fans. A woman in Erie, Pennsylvania, for example, had written a letter to Nicholas Ray, describing Dean as "the child of my heart." The letter implied that the distraught woman was contemplating suicide because of Dean.

On November 22, a month after Ray's meeting with Arthur Watkins, the British Board of Censors decided to grant *Rebel Without a Cause* an "X" certificate. Ray and

David Weisbart agreed to cut "offensive" scenes, many of which featured switch-blades. The British authorities were eager to avoid anything on the screen that would inspire its own youth gangs, known as Teddy Boys, to further violence. Teddy Boys routinely carried razors and knives. Therefore, Warner Bros. would cut the switch-blade fight in *Rebel* "to a minimum," with most of the emphasis on the spectators. The studio would also trim Buzz's death scream and the scene in which Jim chokes his father. The same day, Wolfe Cohen sent a letter to Arthur Abeles requesting details of the agreement.

After four weeks, *Rebel Without a Cause* dropped to fourth place in *Variety's* National Boxoffice Survey. *Guys and Dolls, Cinerama Holiday* and *The Tender Trap* occupied the top three spots. At the Astor in New York, *Rebel* was held over for a fifth week. Business remained brisk in Portland, Oregon; Omaha, Nebraska; and San Francisco. Its three Los Angeles bookings that week had brought in $25,000.

As *Rebel Without a Cause* succeeded at home, the studio's delicate negotiations with the British censors continued. On November 28, Arthur Abeles in London wrote to Wolfe Cohen. After eliminating the knife fight completely and "making several minor cuts here and there," the film had received an X certificate. Although an X rating would limit the film's audience and "cost us twenty or thirty thousand pounds" in lost revenue, Abeles argued that cutting the film further (to achieve an A rating) would destroy it. Abeles had booked the film for the London Pavillion, "the West End home of X certificates," and expected the film to gross a hundred thousand pounds in Britain.

Abeles apologized for allowing Nicholas Ray to become involved in negotiations with the British censors. "I did so on the off chance that he could impress Watkins, the Censor, by his sincerity about the moral tone of the film," Abeles explained, but "(Ray) cut absolutely no ice with him." Abeles also faulted Ray for leaking some details of the delicate negotiations to the press.

On December 5, Jack Warner wrote a letter to Wolfe Cohen: "Abeles did the right thing," he said. "To mutilate the film in order to satisfy the Censor for an "A" certificate would destroy the entire picture." Warner found it unfortunate that the British censors did not realize that "by showing the truth on the screen, they can correct the evils of both parents and children."

Regarding Ray's attempt to influence Arthur Watkins, Warner added, "I have never permitted Producers, Directors or Writers (sic) to interfere. Unfortunately, Ray happened to be in London and I was under the impression [that] he could be of some help. I will return to our policy of letting Producers, Directors and Writers make the films and we will sell them."

On December 6, the last day of *Rebel's* successful five-week run at the Downtown Paramount Theater in Los Angeles, James Dean won his first and only professional acting award. That night, over a thousand celebrities attended the Audience Award Polls dinner. Dean won the Best Actor award for his role in *East of Eden*. Master of ceremonies George Murphy asked the assembly to stand in a moment of silent tribute. Grace Kelly then presented the award, which Natalie Wood accepted in Dean's place.

After five weeks, *Rebel Without a Cause* held fourth place in the latest National Boxoffice Survey. On the day that *Variety* released its figures, Warner Bros. received a copy of Irving Shulman's latest novel, *Children of the Dark*, based on his script of *Rebel Without a Cause*. Henry Holt and Company would publish the book early next year. On December 8, Holt's Howard Cady wrote a letter to Steve Trilling, thanking him for his cooperation (providing still photos from the movie) in the book's advertising campaign. Although Cady did not suggest that Shulman's book would "add to the success of *Rebel Without a Cause*," he left open the hope of "indirect, long range benefits" from the book's publication.

On December 13, *Variety* reported that *Rebel Without a Cause* "ha[d] drawn one of the greatest concentrations of audience letters of any film in a considerable period." More than seventy-five percent of the letters urged that Dean be awarded a special posthumous Academy Award. The letters had come mostly "from teenagers who have identified themselves with the characters; from parents who have found [that] the film conveyed a special meaning; and from sociologists and psychiatrists who have paid tribute to the manner in which child-parent misunderstanding is highlighted." Natalie Wood had received roughly five thousand letters, Nicholas Ray more than one thousand.

On December 14, Ray flew from Los Angeles to New York. He planned to meet with executives at *Harper's* before sailing for Europe. Ray planned to write the first draft of his book, *Rebel*, during the Atlantic crossing. He had dropped his original idea of a production history and would instead do an analytical study of both the picture and his relationship with James Dean. Meanwhile, *Rebel Without a Cause* remained a top box office attraction. It was the only Warner Bros. picture to be in *Variety*'s Top Twelve for the entire month of November, finishing third overall. The picture had grossed almost $800,000 in the key cities covered by *Variety*.

As the new year began, *Rebel Without a Cause* continued to be potent at the box office, finishing fifth in the National Boxoffice Survey, behind *Guys and Dolls, Cinerama Holiday, The Tender Trap* and the new horror feature, *Tarantula*.

As *Rebel* continued to pay off for Warner Bros., Stewart Stern decided to ask a small favor from the studio. On January 12, he wrote to Steve Trilling requesting a 16mm print of the picture "for my own use and study." Stern explained that he had kept some form of visual record, such as 16mm prints and kinescopes, of everything he had done in motion pictures and television. He used these records, he explained, "to find my mistakes and keep track of my improvement as a technician." Stern understood that "most studios frown on this as a matter of general principle," but he hoped that Warner Bros. would make an exception in this case. Stern added a more personal reason: "It would mean a great deal to me to be able to have REBEL — especially since it is one of the few records of Jim." (Stern's request was eventually denied.)

Stern also reported on his most recent film, *The Rack*, starring Paul Newman. Stern praised Newman's performance and predicted that he would become "one of the most important stars we've ever had in very short order." Newman, more than any other young actor in Hollywood, had seen his fortunes fall and then rise because of James Dean. After losing numerous television roles and the role of Cal in *East of Eden* to Dean, Newman replaced the late actor in *Somebody Up There Likes Me* and *The Left-Handed Gun*.

Nicholas Ray was back in London, where he attended the premiere of the "adults only" version of *Rebel Without a Cause*. On January 21, he sent a wire to Jack Warner and Steve Trilling. Reviews of the film were "creating more sensation by quality and space than any other pic here in years," he reported.

On February 1, *Rebel Without a Cause* completed its first week at the London Pavillion, which Arthur Abeles had called the "home of X certificates" in the West End. Abele's decision to keep the film's X rating rather than butcher it had paid off handsomely. *Rebel* had grossed a hefty $11,000 in its first seven days. In its second week, it would gross $10,000 more. By the time *Rebel* completed the first four weeks of its run at the London Pavillion, it had grossed close to $30,000, well on its way toward reaching Abeles' goal for its British run. It would play a final week and then make way for *Othello*.

49

SHULMAN STRIKES BACK

On February 18, the Academy of Motion Picture Arts and Sciences released its list of nominees for the 1955 Academy Awards. *Rebel Without a Cause* received three nominations: Natalie Wood for Best Supporting Actress, Sal Mineo for Best Supporting Actor and Nicholas Ray for Best Original Story. James Dean had also won an acting nomination, for his work in *East of Eden*. Ray's Best Original Story nomination may have come as a surprise to many of those receiving ballots, since the nominating lists had given only the picture's name, not Ray's.

On February 26, Irving Shulman's attorney, Louis Naiditch, wrote to the Warner Bros. Legal Department to protest Shulman's exclusion from story credit on *Rebel Without a Cause*. Shulman claimed that he should share the credit with Ray.

On February 28, Peter D. Knecht of the Warner Bros. Legal Department responded to Louis Naiditch's letter. He reminded Shulman's attorney, "The credits...were determined within the framework of the collective bargaining agreement between all participating writers." Shulman, in effect, "agreed" to receive adaptation credit while Ray received credit for the story and Stern for the screenplay. Knecht enclosed a copy of the tentative writing credits "in accordance with the procedural requirements of said collective bargaining agreement." He added that, "Since no protests were received within the time allowed, these credits became final...It is now too late to go behind these agreements and change these credits..."

Shulman did not give up easily. On March 3, he wrote an impassioned letter to Jack Warner. Shulman claimed that although he had been denied story credit for *Rebel Without a Cause*, there was ample proof among the studio's own records that Shulman did, in fact, write the story. Shulman argued that he would never have agreed to work on the film had he known "that the authorship of the original material I was writing had been contracted away to another person *before* my arrival at the studio." Nowhere in his contract had this "arrangement" been acknowledged, and at no time during his tenure at the studio (November 1954 through January 1955) was he informed of it. Only after he had officially left the production and was writing his novelization of the film did he hear of Nicholas Ray's "The Blind Run," Shulman explained. "Furthermore, I was informed [that] nothing could be done to breach this contractual arrangement, and my raising an issue of this matter would not only embarrass the studio, but…my lack of cooperation would be remembered."

Shulman also claimed that no one at the studio had advised him of the Academy's forty percent requirement, meaning that at least forty percent of "original material purchased by the studio" had to be in the final screenplay before the writer could be eligible for story credit. "It is a matter, then, of record," Shulman argued, "that certain officials were consistently delinquent in acquainting me with certain minimum truths which could have determined my courses of action prior to assignment, during my assignment, and after my assignment."

Shulman went on to argue that, had he known of the forty percent requirement, "I most certainly would have asked for an arbitration of original story credit." He informed Warner that he had met "with the Writers Branch of the Academy" and understood that the Academy could not act until Warner Bros. agreed to settle the dispute. Shulman noted that Peter Knecht had suggested a meeting with his attorney "for whatever purpose it may serve."

In closing, Shulman said, "I am the average little citizen without power, prestige, press agents, or publicity outlets. My only strength is the truth."

50

OSCAR AND BEYOND

March 21 was Oscar night. The Academy of Motion Picture Arts and Sciences gathered to honor the actors, directors, writers, producers, artists and technicians who were the best at their crafts in 1955. Jerry Lewis hosted the ceremony at the Pantages Theater.

In the category of Writing (Motion Picture Story), the nominees were Nicholas Ray for *Rebel Without a Cause*; Daniel Fuchs for *Love me or Leave Me*; Joe Connelly and Bob Mosher for *The Private War of Major Benson*; Jean Marsan, Henry Troyat, Jacques Perrat, Henri Verneuil, and Raoul Ploquin for the French comedy, *The Sheep Has Five Legs*; and Beirne Lay, Jr. for *Strategic Air Command*. The Oscar went to Daniel Fuchs.

In the category of Best Supporting Actress, the nominees were Marisa Pavan for *The Rose Tattoo*; Peggy Lee for *Pete Kelly's Blues*; Natalie Wood for *Rebel Without a Cause*; Betsy Blair for *Marty*; and Jo Van Fleet for *East of Eden*. Jo Van Fleet won the award.

For Best Supporting Actor, Sal Mineo's competition included Arthur Kennedy for *Trial*; Joe Mantell for the popular *Marty*; Arthur O'Connell for *Picnic*; and Jack Lemmon for *Mister Roberts*. The Oscar went to Jack Lemmon.

James Dean lost his bid to win the first posthumous Oscar (he would be nominated later for *Giant*). It went to the favorite in the Best Actor category, Ernest Borgnine for *Marty*. By evening's end, *Marty* had won a total of four Oscars, including Best Picture.

Rebel Without a Cause won no honors that Oscar night. Warner Bros., nonetheless beaming with corporate pride, would measure its impact in dollars (it would make $4,500,000 and become the 11th biggest moneymaking film of 1956). Contemporary adult audiences measured it in terms of *Blackboard Jungle* and a score of similar films. Most teenagers measured it in terms of action and excitement: chickie runs and switchblade fights. Some measured it solely in terms of James Dean, who was already a legend in their eyes.

To still other teenagers, however, it began to represent a point of view, a way of looking at the world as only teenagers saw it. For the first time, a Hollywood film had shown middle-class teenagers as a separate social entity, a subculture. The film would gradually develop into a visual anthem for that subculture, just as Dean would develop into a teen icon for a larger audience several generations strong. That audience is still growing.

Rebel's actors, writers and technicians moved on to other projects with varying degrees of success. For some, *Rebel* was a first stepping stone on the path to success. For others, it was an unexpected and memorable peak on the horizon of their otherwise unremarkable careers.

For Nicholas Ray, *Rebel* marked the beginning and the end of what could have been an historic creative partnership. Dean's sudden death was also the death of Nicholas Ray's dream. Ray's career and health gradually declined after *Rebel*. Depending more and more on medications to sustain his energy, often working beyond the limits of his physical endurance, he eventually pushed himself too far. After collapsing on the set of *55 Days at Peking* in 1962, he never made a major studio film again. *Rebel Without a Cause* remains his best-known and most popular film, and one of his most admirable accomplishments as an artist: a blind run through a dark tunnel with no light at the end.

EPILOGUE:
AFTER *Rebel*...

The success of *Rebel Without a Cause*, augmented by the public's growing, if macabre, interest in James Dean, created unexpected marketing opportunities for Warner Bros. in the years following the film's release.

Less than a year after *Rebel*'s domestic run, Leonard Rosenman's musical score was already bringing in licensing agreements— and profits—from overseas markets. On May 2, 1956, J. E. Dagal, Warner Bros.' representative in Japan, forwarded a request from the Japan Victor Company to Warner Bros.' New York office. The Japan Victor Company, which released RCA Victor recordings in that country, wanted to re-record part of the sound track from *Rebel Without a Cause* and put it on the flip side of a record, "The Ballad of James Dean." The *Rebel* segment of the record would include one minute of music and one and a half minutes of dialogue from the film. Japan Victor planned to release the record to coincide with the general release of *Rebel Without a Cause* in Tokyo toward the end of May. The record jacket carried a photograph of James Dean. Japan Victor had already released a recording of the main theme song from *Rebel*, titled "Secret Doorway," prior to the picture's release, giving it air time on Japanese radio.

On August 13, 1957, barely two years after Dean's death, a documentary film, *The James Dean Story*, had its world premiere at the Paramount Theater in Marion, Indiana. Marion was the birthplace of James Dean. Martin Gabel narrated the film, which Stewart Stern had written. (A second James Dean documentary, *James Dean: The First American Teenager*, opened in New York in November, 1976. The British film, augmented by a rock music score, presented clips from Dean's film and television appearances, including *Rebel Without a Cause*.)

Warner Bros. had almost canceled *Rebel*'s production in February 1955, but by July 1962, the studio was fiercely protective of the film. When United Artists Productions tried to take advantage of *Rebel*'s success by attempting to register a title for one of their future pictures (the title was *The Rebel with a Cause*), the studio fought to protect its property. On July 11, Albert Howson of Warner Bros.' New York

197

office informed the rival studio that "Registrations of this title are...in direct and harmful conflict with Warner Bros. released feature title 'REBEL WITHOUT A CAUSE.'" Howson insisted that the registrations for the conflicting title "be withdrawn from the record." They were.

Meanwhile, Dean's popularity continued to keep the film in the public eye. *Daily Variety* reported from Paris on the dead idol's impact on the French:

> Name of the late James Dean is gaining marquee momentum in France on the strength of only two releases, *East of Eden* and *Rebel Without a Cause*. Apart from Marilyn Monroe, he has become the best-known U.S. name star in France since the war.
>
> Newspapers here recently took up a story from a U.S. mag to the effect that Dean hadn't actually been killed in his auto accident, but marred, badly, was suffering from shock and was being kept out of public life by his family. Weird tale keeps getting printed and bruited about. Actually, the Dean name keeps getting more space in the press than most of his living colleagues. As he became a symbol of disoriented youth in the U.S. (at least in his screen roles), so he has become here an idol of the teenagers who still put him at the head of popularity polls.

In early August, Dean's growing mystique created even more marketing opportunities at home. Ray Heindorf, Music Director at Warner Bros., sent a memo to Roy Obringer in the Legal Department on August 6: Columbia Records planned to release a record album featuring the sound tracks from both *East of Eden* and *Rebel Without a Cause*. On the 24th, Obringer sent a return memo confirming the record deal.

That same July, Warner Bros. was also considering a television series based on the film. In a July 13 memo, a studio official (Bryan S. Moore) outlined the problems in bringing that about. One involved awarding the writers of the original film (Stern, Shulman, Ray) "source material credit" for the series. "Depending upon the extent of our use of the various materials which were credited in connection with our 1955 theatrical feature motion picture," Moore's memo argued, "we may be obliged (or want) to give credit to one, two or all three of the writers credited." Giving credit to one or more of *Rebel*'s original writers would also mean paying them. The studio had already chosen someone else (Gloria Elsmore) to write the pilot.

There were other problems. Although the studio still held the "television motion picture" rights to *Rebel*, "a potential claim" had arisen over the film's already-famous switchblade scene. Apparently convinced that the claim could not be settled quickly enough, Moore advised that the studio "take pains to see that no such sequence is used in our teleplay."

Another problem involved the studio's original agreement with Robert M. Lindner, which stipulated that Lindner be paid $4,000 for a first *Rebel* sequel and $5,000 for each additional. The proposed pilot, however, did not plan to use any of the characters from Lindner's book, so Moore concluded that "there would appear to be no risk" in going ahead with plans for the pilot and series. There would be no threat of litigation from Robert M. Lindner in any case: the former prison psychiatrist and author of *Rebel Without a Cause: The Hypnoanalysis of a Criminal Psychopath* had died of a heart attack in 1956 at the age of 41.

The problems of adapting *Rebel* to television continued to outweigh the solutions, however. Moore's memo concluded, "I do not believe we have yet cleared 'Rebel Without a Cause' for TV series usage."

No pilot or series was ever produced.

Four years later, in 1966, the studio attempted another incarnation of *Rebel Without a Cause*, as a musical film. An inter-office memorandum of March 24 announced a production number (48786) and an uninspired title, "Rebel Without a Cause —#2." Almost a year later, on March 15, 1967, Warner Bros. changed the title of the proposed musical to "The Swinging World," but again the studio let the project die.

Warner Bros. may have given up on a *Rebel* musical, but others were still trying. On December 8, 1969, the studio granted a producer named Ted Brink a one-year option to produce a "musical stage play" based on the film. The studio expected to receive $5,000 plus two percent of the weekly gross box office receipts, plus first refusal rights on an original cast recording, plus merchandising and motion picture rights.

Brink, however, did not produce the play during the option period, and it was not until 1989 that *Rebel Without a Cause* finally reached a musical stage. The ill-fated production was called *Musical Selections from Rebel* and subtitled *The James Dean Musical*. It played at the Eighty-Eights Theater on West Tenth Street in New York and ran from May 15 through June 16.

Although *Rebel* had failed to generate successful imitations during the three decades after its initial success, it stayed alive in other forms. In a 1989 film, *Earth Girls Are Easy*, a group of aliens watch the "You're tearing me apart!" scene on television. Later, one of the aliens mimics it. A 1991 music video of singer Paula Abdul's song, "Rush, Rush," also paid tribute to *Rebel Without a Cause*. With Abdul taking the role of Judy, the video featured recreations of the film's major scenes, including the switchblade fight and the chickie run.

Rebel Without a Cause found critical success as well in the long run. It was added to the National Film Registry of the Library of Congress in 1990 and placed 56th in a Newsweek poll of the 100 best American films. It still plays frequently on television and in film retrospectives, and was re-released in 1995 to celebrate its fortieth anniversary. Warner Bros. is fiercely protective of it to this day.

Rebel's cast moved on to other projects with varying degrees of success. Natalie Wood, still enjoying the benefits of stardom, courted her public through fan magazines and the Hollywood gossip columns. Her colorful off-screen escapades included a brief but widely publicized infatuation with Elvis Presley before her marriage to actor Robert Wagner in 1957.

By 1961, however, after a series of bad films, her career was already in decline. It rebounded when Elia Kazan cast her as the female lead in *Splendor in the Grass*, with Warren Beatty. One of the scenes in that film created controversy during a private screening at Warner Bros. shortly before its release.

In his book, *The Face on the Cutting Room Floor*, Murray Schumach describes what that select audience saw:

> …It came fast. In one sequence Miss Wood was in the bathtub, in bitter argument with her mother. The girl became hysterical. Cornered by her mother, she had only one way to

escape and that was to flee the tub. The next scene was one the audience never expected. It showed Miss Wood from the rear. She was naked, running down a short hallway. The camera showed her nakedness from head to heels. Her buttocks were unmistakably bare.

Natalie Wood's nude scene would have represented the first time an American actress disrobed in a major feature film. Coming on the heels of Code-breaking films like *The Man with the Golden Arm* and *Baby Doll*, it could have signaled the end of the Production Code. Yet, when the Legion of Decency threatened to give the film a "Condemned" rating, Warner Bros. removed the offending scene.

Wood's career rose and fell periodically during the 1960s and 1970s. She was nominated twice for an Academy Award (*Splendor in the Grass* and *Love with the Proper Stranger*), while the *Harvard Lampoon* named her "worst actress of the year" for films like *Penelope* and *Inside Daisy Clover*. Her career was at low ebb again in 1981 when she attempted a final comeback in the science fiction film *Brainstorm*. On November 29, 1981, before shooting was complete, she drowned under mysterious circumstances off Catalina Island at the age of 43. Death by drowning had been one of her greatest fears.

Nick Adams also used his identification with *Rebel Without a Cause* to boost his career. On October 4, 1959, the first episode of *The Rebel*, a television Western, appeared on the ABC network. The program ran Sunday nights from 9:00 to 9:30 until September 12, 1962. Five days later, Adams started another television series, *Saints and Sinners*, playing a newspaper reporter. The show lasted only through January 28, 1963, but Adams quickly made a successful move back to theatrical films with *Twilight of Honor*. Playing a drifter accused of murder, he won an Academy Award nomination for Best Supporting Actor. Adams' career declined steadily afterward. On February 5, 1968, at the age of 35, he was found dead in his Beverly Hills home by his attorney. Adams' death was caused by an overdose of the drug he had been taking for a nervous disorder. His last films included *Die, Monster, Die* (1965), *Frankenstein Conquers the World* (1966) and *Don't Worry, We'll Think of a Title* (1966).

Sal Mineo's roles after *Rebel Without a Cause* featured him invariably as a disturbed or rebellious youth. In the 1957 film, *Dino*, adapted from a teleplay by Reginald Rose, Mineo played a delinquent befriended by a young woman (Susan Kohner) and a social worker (Brian Keith). Mineo had first played the role on television. In 1959, he played the lead role in Walt Disney's *Tonka* as an Indian brave trying to tame a wild horse. In the same year, he played the title role in *The Gene Krupa Story*, a film biography of the famous drummer. He was nominated for an Academy Award a second time for his supporting role in *Exodus*, but lost to Peter Ustinov for *Spartacus*. When Mineo's film career began to fade in the early 1970s, he turned to theater, directing *Fortune and Men's Eyes* on Broadway and the West Coast. He was rehearsing a new play, *P. S., Your Cat Is Dead*, in Los Angeles, when he was stabbed to death outside his West Hollywood apartment in 1976. He was 37.

Corey Allen's film career did not benefit greatly from his role as Buzz in *Rebel Without a Cause*. Nicholas Ray cast him as a young gangster in *Party Girl* (1958), and Allen had small roles in *Sweet Bird of Youth* (1962) and *The Chapman Report* (1962), but real success did not come until he turned to directing. In 1981 he was nominated for an Emmy award for directing an episode of *Hill Street Blues*. He lost that year, but in 1984 he won for directing an episode in the same series.

Dennis Hopper, however, more than lived up to his acting potential. As promised, Dean had tutored him on the Method during *Giant*, and Hopper quickly adopted not only Dean's acting technique, but also key elements of his personal style. Hopper already had a reputation as a renegade, iconoclast and bad boy when he produced, directed and starred in an independent feature, *Easy Rider*, in 1969. Turned down by every studio, he financed the picture with money he had raised himself. *Easy Rider* became one of the most popular films of that year, proving that an independent production could succeed without help from the established studios. In the years since *Easy Rider*, Hopper has remained both a popular actor (*Apocalypse Now, Blue Velvet, Hoosiers*) and a persistent free spirit within the film industry.

Frank Mazzola, the young gang member who played Crunch in *Rebel*, continued in films. After appearing in small roles in films like *The Way to the Gold* (1957), he became a film editor on such features as *Stiletto* (1969), *Macho Callahan* (1970) and *The Hired Hand* (1971). In recent years he has been called upon for his re-editing and film restoration abilities.

William Hopper, who played Natalie Wood's father in *Rebel*, turned a reasonably successful career in films into a gold mine when he signed to play private detective Paul Drake on the *Perry Mason* television series in 1957. The program ran for nine seasons before going into perpetual syndication. Hopper, who virtually retired from acting after the *Perry Mason* series, died in 1970 at the age of 55.

Jim Backus was another of Rebel's featured players who parlayed a fairly successful film career into television immortality, playing stranded millionaire Thurston Howell III in *Gilligan's Island*. The popular program ran from 1964 through 1967. On January 24, 1983, Backus was among those attending an Academy of Motion Picture Arts and Sciences tribute to James Dean at the Samuel Goldwyn Theater in Beverly Hills. Also honoring the late actor were Stewart Stern and Leonard Rosenman. The evening's activities included a screening of *Rebel Without a Cause*. Backus died in 1989. He had been one of the few in Hollywood to remember James Dean with genuine fondness, writing an entire chapter about him in his autobiography, *Rocks on the Roof*.

Ann Doran, who played Dean's shrewish mother, continued to work successfully in both films and television. Her film credits included *The Explosive Generation* (1962), *Kitten with a Whip* (1964) and *Topaz* (1969). Her television credits included *National Velvet* (1960), *The Legend of Jesse James* (1965), *Longstreet* (1972) and *Shirley* (1979). On November 1, 1988, when sculptor Kenneth Kendall unveiled his bronze bust of James Dean as part of a permanent monument at Griffith Park in Los Angeles, Doran (along with several of *Rebel*'s cast) was present. She died in Carmichael, California, under this writer's nose, on September 19, 2000.

Marsha Hunt, who had been signed to play Dean's mother before being replaced by the more politically correct Ann Doran, gradually returned to film and television work despite the blacklist. In 1960, she appeared in a TV situation comedy, *Peck's Bad Girl*, with Wendell Corey and Patty McCormack. In 1971, she had a role in Dalton Trumbo's film, *Johnny Got His Gun*. Many in the cast and crew, including Trumbo, had been victims of the Fifties witchhunt. As of this writing, Marsha Hunt is 86 years old.

Edward Platt was yet another of *Rebel*'s alumni whose reputation was gained in television rather than film. *Get Smart*, a secret agent spoof starring Don Adams as Agent 86, ran from 1965 through 1970 and featured Platt as Thaddeus, the Chief. Platt, who also had film roles in *Written on the Wind* (1956), *North by Northwest* (1959) and Disney's *Pollyanna* (1960), died at the age of 58 in 1974.

Rochelle Hudson, (Judy's mother in *Rebel*), whose later film credits included *Straight-Jacket* and *The Night Walker* (1964) and *Dr. Terror's House of Horrors* (1967), died in 1972 at the age of 57.

Stewart Stern continued a successful writing career after *Rebel Without a Cause*. He wrote the screenplays for *The Ugly American* (1963) and *Rachel, Rachel* (1968) and won an Emmy award for his teleplay of *Sybil* in 1977. He lives in Seattle, where he teaches screenwriting. He is also a creative advisor at the Sundance Institute Screenwriters' Lab.

David Weisbart had moved to 20th Century Fox by 1956, producing, among others, *April Love*, *The Way to the Gold* and *These Thousand Hills*. He also produced two films starring Elvis Presley, *Love Me Tender* and *Flaming Star*. In 1967, after just finishing work on *Valley of the Dolls*, he suffered a fatal stroke while playing golf. He was 52.

Leon Uris survived his dismissal from *Rebel Without a Cause* and went on to become one of America's most popular fiction writers. He died in 2003.

For Irving Shulman, *Rebel Without a Cause* was a lost opportunity, a cruel trick perpetrated by Ray and Warner Bros. that robbed him of his rightful place in *Rebel*'s credits. He fought, unsuccessfully, to regain that place until his death in 1995.

When Nicholas Ray's Hollywood career came to an end, he continued with independent projects and for a time was a visiting lecturer at the State University of New York at Binghamton. His last film projects included acting, rather than directing, roles: *The American Friend* (1977), which also featured Dennis Hopper, and *Lightning Over Water* (1980). He died in 1979 at the age of 67.

Jack L. Warner died in 1978 at the age of 86. One of the last of the all-powerful studio moguls, he had sold Warner Bros. to Kinney National Service (later Warner Communications) in 1969. Warner Bros. is now a part of the huge entertainment conglomerate known as Time-Warner.

APPENDIX

Letter from Stewart Stern to
Nicholas Ray (May 19, 1955)

1372 Miller Drive
Hollywood 46, California
19 May, 1955

Mr. Nicholas Ray
Warner Brothers Studio
Burbank, California.

Dear Nick:

I think one of us must bring this up eventually and it looks as if it's going to be me. There's no point avoiding discussion of it the way the topic of death is avoided at condolence calls. Also, I don't want you to interpret all the calls that have been flying back and forth between the Studio and myself as in any way "behind your back." *They* called *me*, asked for my reaction and I gave it — over the phone and in a letter to Dave Weisbart in which I simply outlined what had been explained to me by the Guild. I have purposely not brought the subject up with you before because, as I explained to Finlay and to Dave, I know the battle you are fighting to let this film see daylight with all its limbs intact and did not want to contribute to your anxiety. I asked repeatedly if discussion of this subject of credits could not be delayed till after you had finished shooting. The last thing I want to do is to harrass you now.

It appears that discussion will not wait and decisions have to be made. For this reason I am writing to you personally to outline my reasoning in the matter which has apparently taken on qualities of personality, which it should not.

In the first place, I had no notion that you would want any credit whatsoever for the writing of this film, any more than Arthur Loew wanted credit for TERESA which sprang directly from his idea and was later developed by Alfred Hayes and then by me. It simply did not occur to me that you would want it. Despite this, when Finlay asked me for my own credit expectations the day I left the Studio, I told him that while I thought you might not want credit, I felt you should be asked to take it. I felt that all three of us—you and Irving and I—had made substantial contributions to the story-line and I frankly had no idea at that time than an actual "story" per se ever existed, since none was ever shown to me. It seemed a perfectly logical thing that in lieu of the existence, to my knowledge, of an "original story"—that particular credit should include the three of us. I further requested that your name appear first in the listing and that the credit read: "Story by Nicholas Ray with Irving Shulman and Stewart Stern." I tell you this only to inform you of a long-standing attitude on my part which I am sure you do not know about.

To my way of thinking, the final shooting script *represents* and actually *created* the original story. Although I did the actual writing of the screenplay, I was influenced and aided to an indispensible degree by both your ideas and Irving's in the formulation of my own, so in a real sense the original story really came into being during my phase of the writing, strongly and fluidly influenced by all three minds. I know you will agree with this morally. What your practical considerations are become quite another thing and I have no way of guessing them or the reasons behind them.

Insofar as the screenplay itself is concerned, I have been told that you were surprised that I expected sole credit, feeling that you should share in it. I believe I do deserve solo credit. My writing made a worthy project which might possibly not have been made, a practical reality and allowed the picture to be made. Your contribution was a very large one and gave impetus to the project, but it was made in terms of story and our discussions decided the course and path of the story—often phase by phase. Also, I know of no worthy director who really cares about his project who does not, if permitted, work on the story with the fullest possible involvement with his writers, and without expecting writing credit. They want the story to be as perfect as possible before shooting starts so that what appears on the screen will be an expression of their intent and a full interpretation of it. Your aim in working with me and helping to guide my writing was to have a film you could be proud of. And I think you have it.

Further, I feel that Irving, while his actual writing does not occur in the screenplay except in brief dialogue between the planetarium Guide and the Kids, deserves recognition for having taken an important transitional step. It is for this reason that I feel he should have an adaptation credit of his own and whatever credit he deserves for any contribution he made to the original story which changed or influenced the course of the film.

If the original story you wrote and registered with the Guild before the time Irving and I came onto the project is so much like the final screenplay that there can be no argument about whose story it is; if it is so uninfluenced by my own particular contribution to it that it remains now what it was then, I would certainly not suggest sharing story credit with you. As I say, I have never seen your story. I can only surmise from the nature of our discussions that we have gone a long and winding way since then and that the two pieces of writing—your story and what appears on the screen—are very far apart and very different.

This then is my reasoning. I feel that it is fair reasoning. I feel that whether you agree with it or not, you must be given the opportunity to understand it before any steps are taken whereby the question of credit distribution may have to be tested and arbitrated by a neutral body dedicated to preserving *all* our interests.

Believe me, Nick, there is no personal bitterness or vindictiveness anywhere in my feelings, nor any intention to rob something which is not justifiably mine. There couldn't be. The writing of this film, as I have told you before, stands as one of the happiest and most challenging episodes of my creative life and my personal feelings for you are untarnished. They are full and warm and grateful and they shall remain so, regardless of what the outcome may be. I hope, more than hope, that you will not take my professional stand as a personal affront, any more than I do yours. I want and need your friendship and I trust and believe that you want mine. We have the fullest creative contact and that is a rare thing to come by and it would be very ridiculous to deny ourselves a continuance of it. There will be, I am sure, other projects ahead for us.

I am only thinking now of what I consider the rightful recognition I deserve in a professional area and so are you. We have different opinions about it. Because of our differences I am willing that, if we cannot agree, someone who is no more your friend than mine would play the role of Solomon and make the final decision.

Best,

Stewart Stern

Letter from Stewart Stern to Marcus and Ortense Winslow (October 12, 1955)

Hollywood 46, California
1372 Miller Drive
12 October, 1955

Dear Marcus and Mrs. Winslow:

I shall never forget that silent town on that particular sunny day. And I shall never forget the care with which people set their feet down — so carefully on the pavements — as if the sound of a suddenly scraped heel might disturb the sleep of a boy who slept soundly. And the whispering. Do you remember one voice raised beyond a whisper in all those reverential hours of goodbye? I don't. A whole town struck silent, a whole town with love filling its throat, a whole town wondering why there had been so little time in which to give the love away.

Gandhi once said that if all those doomed people at Hiroshima had lifted their faces to the plane that hovered over them and if they had sent up a single sigh of spiritual protest, the pilot would not have dropped his bomb. That may or may not be. But I am sure, I am certain, I know — that the great wave of warmth and affection that swept upward from Fairmount has wrapped itself around that irresistible phantom securely and forever. Wandering or cradled as he may be, Jimmy will never be lonely again.

Nor shall I forget the land he grew on or the stream he fished, or the straight, strong, gentle people whom he loved to talk about into the nights when he was away from them. His great-grandma whose eyes have seen half of America's history, his grandparents, his father, his treasured three of you—four generations for the coiling of a spring—nine decades of living evidence of seed and turning earth and opening kernel. It was a solid background and one to be envied. The spring, released, flung him into our lives and out again. He burned an unforgettable mark in the history of his art and changed it as surely as Duse, in her time, changed it.

A star goes wild in the places beyond air—a dark star born of coldness and invisible. It hits the upper edges of our atmosphere and look! It is seen! It flames and arcs and dazzles. It goes out in ash and memory. But its after-image remains in our eyes to be looked at again and again. For it was rare. And it was beautiful. And we thank God and nature for sending it in front of our eyes.

So few things blaze. So little is beautiful. Our world doesn't seem equipped to contain its brilliance too long. Ecstasy is only recognizable when one has experienced pain. Beauty only exists when set against ugliness. Peace is not appreciated without war ahead of it. How we wish that life could support only the good. But it vanishes when its opposite no longer exists as a setting. It is a white marble on unmelting snow. And Jimmy stands clear and unique in a world where much is synthetic and dishonest and drab. He came and rearranged our molecules.

I have nothing of Jim's—nothing to touch or look at except the dried mud that clung to my shoes—mud from the farm that grew him—and a single kernel of seed corn from your barn. I have nothing more than this and I want nothing more. There is no need to touch something he touched when I can still feel his hand on me. He gave me his faith, unquestioningly and trustfully—once when he said he would play in REBEL because he knew I wanted him to, and once when he tried to get LIFE to let me write his biography. He told me he felt I understood him and if LIFE refused to let me do the text for the pictures Dennis took, he would refuse to let the magazine do a spread on him at all. I managed to talk him out of that, knowing that LIFE had to use its own staff writers, but will never forget how I felt when he entrusted his life to me. And he gave me, finally, the gift of his art. He spoke my words and played my scenes better than any actor of our time or of our memory could have done. I feel that there are other gifts to come from him—gifts for all of us. His influence did not stop with his breathing. It walks with us and will profoundly affect the way we look at things. From Jimmy I have already learned the value of a minute. He loved his minutes and I shall now love mine.

These words aren't clear. But they are clearer than what I could have said to you last week.

I write from the depths of my appreciation—to Jimmy for having touched my life and opened my eyes—to you for having grown him all those young years and for having given him your love—to you for being big enough and humane enough to let me come into your grief as a stranger and go away a friend.

When I drove away the sky at the horizon was yellowing with twilight and the trees stood clean against it. The banks of flowers covering the grave were muted and grayed by the coming of evening and had yielded up their color to the sunset. I thought—here's where he belongs—with this big darkening sky and this air that is thirst-quenching as mountain water and this century of family around him and the cornfield crowding the meadow where his presence will be marked. But he's not in the meadow. He's out there in the corn. He's hunting the winter's rabbit and the summer's catfish. He has a hand on little Mark's shoulder and a sudden kiss for you. And he has my laughter echoing his own at the great big jokes he saw and showed to me — and he's here, living and vivid and unforgettable forever, far too mischievous to lie down long.

My love and gratitude, to you and young Mark.

/s/ Stewart.

NOTES

Part I: Preliminaries

Chapter 1: Nicholas Ray

11. **Ray's options should have been...:** Bernard Eisenschitz, *Nicholas Ray: An American Journey*, p. 231. For a full account of Ray's difficulties on *Johnny Guitar*, see Eisenschitz, pp. 198–213.

11. **When asked what subject...:** Eisenschitz, p. 231. Eisenschitz states that Ray went to the studio "the next day," but it is unclear whether Wasserman provided Ray with all the information about the *Rebel* property during their dinner party or followed up before Ray visited the studio.

11–12. **Warner Bros. had owned the film rights...:** *Rebel Without a Cause* file, Warner Bros. Archive, Cinema-Television Library, University of Southern California. Letters dated February 8 and February 14, 1946. *All further references to letters, telegrams, memos, scripts, publicity releases and production information, unless otherwise noted, are from this file.*

12. **Between 1946 and 1949...:** Geisel's 28-page draft is dated June 6, 1946; Viertel's incomplete script is dated April 9, 1947, replaced by a revised script on June 4, 1947; the Lindner/Fishel script is dated May 1, 1949; memos re: Shulman are dated August 12, 1947 and January 16, 1948 (Irving Shulman file #2519).

12. **Wald supported each effort with...:** Jerry Wald, "a dynamic, indefatigable worker," is said to have been "a part model" for the main character in Budd Schulberg's play, *What Makes Sammy Run?* (in Ephraim Katz, *The Film Encyclopedia*, p. 1201)

12. **Perhaps the right actors were unavailable...:** The memo regarding Brando is dated May 26, 1947; Homeier's is dated May 16, 1947. David

Dalton gives a brief account of Brando's screen test in *James Dean: The Mutant King*, p. 224.

13. **Now, almost six years later...:** Sperling signed out the script on July 27, 1954, MacEwen five days earlier; Weisbart signed out Lindner's script on September 10, 1954, only a week before Ray wrote "The Blind Run," and almost certainly after Ray's visit with Steve Trilling.

13. **If there was a dark side to Ray's talent...:** Eisenschitz, *Nicholas Ray*, p. 114.

13. **Ray was also at odds...:** Houseman is quoted in John Francis Kriedl, *Nicholas Ray*, p. 76.

14. **The motion picture industry, of course...:** Eisenschitz, "Biographical Outline," in *I Was Interrupted: Nicholas Ray on Making Movies*, p. xlv.

14. **Ray's directing style...:** A number of people who worked with or knew Ray have described his method: Joe Hyams in *James Dean: Little Boy Lost*, p. 205; Beverly Long in Randall Riese, *The Unabridged James Dean*, p. 421; Sumner Williams and Robert Ryan in Eisenschitz, *Nicholas Ray*, p. 156.

14. **Ray's background *was* somewhat radical...:** Eisenschitz, *Nicholas Ray*, pp. 22–32.

15. **Ray did not understand the phenomenon...:** Eisenschitz, *Nicholas Ray*, pp. 231–232.

15. **Later that same day...:** Kriedl cites the $5000 figure in *Nicholas Ray*, p. 78. His account of the negotiations roughly parallels a press release from the Warner Bros. Publicity Dept. dated March 18, 1955.

Chapter 2: "The Blind Run"

16. **In selecting the material for...:** The *Newsweek* article is from the September 6, 1954

issue. A stomping scene was to have opened the film. Ray also referred to an interview with Richard Clendenen (executive director of the Senate Subcommittee on Juvenile Delinquency) in the September 17, 1954 issue of *U.S. News and World Report*. The article was titled "Why Teen-Agers Go Wrong."

18. **The decision to change the title…:** Kriedl, *Nicholas Ray*, p. 77.

18. **Because of his recent success…:** The writer most affected by this clause was Irving Shulman, one of two who tried to develop "The Blind Run." Eisenschitz touches on this subject in *Nicholas Ray*, p. 232; Stewart Stern, who wrote the final screenplay for *Rebel* based in part on Shulman's story, wrote a three-page letter to Ray dated May 19, 1955 regarding story credit for Shulman and himself; Shulman protested the awarding of sole story credit to Ray in a letter to the Academy of Motion Picture Arts and Sciences dated February 20, 1956. The author did not see a copy of Ray's contract for *Rebel Without a Cause* at the Warner Bros. Archive.

18. **For Ray, winning an Oscar meant…:** Ray planned to form a production company with James Dean in 1956.

18–19. **Warner Bros. was making a blind run of its own…:** David Dalton cites the budget figure in *James Dean: The Mutant King*, p. 233 ($600,000 for the film, plus 40% for studio overhead, which would include a publicity campaign).

Chapter 3: James Dean

20. **Ray had undoubtedly heard…:** Ray discusses the revolver and the motorcycle in "From *Rebel — The Life Story of a Film*," (in *Hello, Hollywood!: A Book About the Movies and the People Who Make Them*, by Allen Rivkin and Laura Kerr, p. 515). Hyams describes Dean's fast driving through the Warner Bros. soundstages in *James Dean: Little Boy Lost*, pp. 197–198. He also discusses a group known as The Night Watch, of which Dean was a member (pp. 161–166).

20. **He had heard also…:** John Howlett, *James Dean*, pp. 85–87.

20. **Dean scoffed at such conventions…:** Hyams, p. 133.

20. **Dean was oblivious to…:** Val Holley, *James Dean: The Biography*, p. 217.

20. **He was also openly contemptuous…:** Jim Backus, who played Dean's father in the film, recalled an incident at the studio in which Dean crossed paths with Warner and two "obviously very important distributors or exhibitors." Warner was praising Dean as the studio's newest sensation. Dean stopped, observed Warner's expensive suit and said, "Have it cleaned and burned." (in Venable Herndon, *James Dean: A Short Life*, p. 191)

21. **Dean himself did not seem to believe it …:** Dean's reaction to his screen persona changed little over his brief career; he behaved similarly at a sneak preview of *Rebel Without a Cause* just before his death.

21. **Ray and Dean exchanged few words…:** Ray, "From *Rebel*," in *Hello, Hollywood!*, p. 516.

21. **Ray sensed that the young actor…:** *Ibid.*, p. 514.

21–22. **He even suggested that…:** *Ibid.*, p. 516.

22. **The questions Dean and his companions…:** *Ibid.*, p. 517.

22. **The two men met often…:** *Ibid.*, pp. 517–518. Dean seemed especially impressed with Odets, whom he compared with Henrik Ibsen and George Bernard Shaw.

22. **Ray used these opportunities…:** *Ibid.*, p. 516.

22. **During one or another of their meetings…:** *Ibid.*

Chapter 4: Weisbart and Uris

23. **It was common practice at Warner Bros…:** Nicholas Ray, "Story Into Script," *Sight and Sound* (Autumn 1956), p. 70.

23. **From his work on *Johnny Guitar*, Ray had…:** *Ibid.*

23–24. **Ray had several reasons for choosing…:** *Ibid.*

24. **Weisbart, however, did not…:** *Ibid.*

24. **Choosing the right screenwriter was…:** *Ibid.*, p. 72.

24. **Ray's ideal writer…:** *Ibid.*, p. 71.

24. **Ray's first choice was…:** Eisenschitz, *Nicholas Ray*, p. 234.

24. **Uris had grown up in…:** "Leon Uris," *Current Biography* (1979), p. 412. The same teacher failed Uris all three times. As Uris later explained it, "English and writing have little to do with each other."

24. **In 1942, shortly after the Japanese…:** *Ibid.*

24–25. **Ray tried to accept…:** Kriedl refers to Uris' *Rebel Without a Cause* as a "macropicture." (pp. 91–92)

25. **At this early stage, however…:** Ray, "Story Into Script," p. 72.

25–26. **Pursuing his own line of thought…:** Kelley apparently accepted Ray's offer without hesitation, as Ray referred to him in a memo to Weisbart dated October 18. Dr. Kelley was not mentioned in the studio's publicity releases until March 10, 1955, when *Rebel Without a Cause* was in pre-production.

26. **The next morning, Uris reported…:** Ray refers to Brooks' problem in "Story Into Script," p. 72, and in a Warner Bros. memo to Weisbart dated October 18, 1954.

27. **There was little excitement gathering…:** David Dalton cites October 7, 1954 as the date of Dean's contract renewal, in *James Dean: American Icon*, p. 281.

Chapter 5: Story Into Script

28. **On October 13, Uris began…:** Eisenschitz, *Nicholas Ray*, p. 234. Ray was not amused by "Rayfield" or Uris's five pages of notes on it. The idea "made me vomit…I didn't read the rest of it," he said in 1974. Eisenschitz observes that "any working relationship (between Uris and Ray) became impossible" after the "Rayfield" incident.

28. **As Uris worked on his version…:** Eisenschitz, *Nicholas Ray*, p. 233.

29. **Gradually, a sense of trust…:** Ray discusses Dean's predicament in "From *Rebel — The Life Story of a Film*" (in *Hello, Hollywood!*, p. 516)

29. **If Dean needed further proof…:** Ray listed his expenses in the October 18 memo to Weisbart.

29. **On October 20, Leon Uris…:** Leon Uris's treatments and outline are dated from October 20, 1954 through November 1, 1954. His contract period was from October 6, 1954 through November 2, 1954.

30. **The situation is not much better for…:** Kent R. Brown's synopsis of Uris's story gives "menopause" as the reason for the poor housekeeping habits of Amy's mother (in *The Screenwriter as Collaborator: The Career of Stewart Stern*, p. 88).

31. **When Ray read Uris's final outline…:** Ray, "Story Into Script," p. 72.

31. **Ray now had the "ungrateful task"…:** *Ibid.*

Chapter 6: Lindner and Shulman

32. **On Monday, November 1, 1954…:** The Hacker Foundation announcement appeared in the *Los Angeles Times* on October 31, 1954.

32. **They had a polite but uncomfortable…:** Ray, "Story Into Script," p. 74.

32. **Lindner argued that the conflict…:** *Ibid.* Robert Lindner also discussed the subject in a magazine article, "Rebels or Psychopaths?," *Time*, December 6, 1954.

32. **Ray left the cocktail party with mixed emotions…:** Ray, "Story Into Script," p. 74.

32–33. **Lindner had already begun to…:** Lindner's call was the subject of a November 19 memo from McDermid to R.J. Obringer of the Legal Department.

33. **On November 10…:** Irving Shulman file (file # 2519), Warner Bros. Archive, USC.

33. **Shulman had also been a teacher…:** One of Shulman's projects at Warner Bros. in 1947 was titled "Teacher Story."

33. **Three days after Shulman's hiring…:** Ray, "Story Into Script," p. 73.

33. **That same night…:** John Parker, *Five for Hollywood*, p. 87.

33. **The other was sixteen-year-old…:** *Ibid.*, p. 88.

Chapter 7: Changes

34. **Shulman's work on a new script…:** Ray, "Story Into Script," p. 73.

34. **One discussion involved…:** *Ibid.*

34. **Ray and Shulman also planned to…:** *Ibid.*

34. **Ray had other suggestions…:** *Ibid.*

34. **Ray and Shulman were also reshaping…:** *Ibid.*

36–37. **One of Shulman's strengths…:** *Ibid.*

37–38. **Elsewhere in the city…:** In a segment of the television program, *Warner Bros. Presents*, aired in October, 1955, Backus publicly thanked the studio for giving him the part of Jim's father. The segment is preserved on a special re-release video of *Rebel Without a Cause* (Warner Home Video, 1996). David Dalton quotes Backus on the casting of Backus and Ann Doran in *James Dean: The Mutant King*, p. 230.

38. **The Wynns extended their hospitality…:** Hyams, p. 157.

38. **At the Wynns'…:** Jim Backus, *Rocks on the Roof*, p. 152.

38. **As Ray explained it…:** Ray, "Story Into Script," pp. 73–74. Ray's memoranda, Shulman's outline and treatments, and, later, Stewart Stern's script, all use the term "Planetarium" in referring to both the planetarium theater and the larger observatory building that houses it. The author, in referring to the Griffith Observatory and its planetarium theater, will use the words "observatory" and "planetarium," respectively.

38. **On December 2…:** Eisenschitz, *Nicholas Ray*, p. 236.

39. **Soon after he and Weisbart…:** Ray, "Story Into Script," p. 74.

39. **After discussing the new scene…:** *Ibid.*

Chapter 8: Stewart Stern

40. **During the first week of December…:** Stewart Stern, correspondence with the author, November 1993.

40. **Stern, 32, was a talented…:** Stern and co-writer Alfred Hayes were nominated for an "Orig-

inal Story" Oscar for *Teresa*, and Zinnemann's documentary, *Benjy*, scripted by Stern, won an Oscar. These were impressive credentials, and were bound to be noticed by Nicholas Ray.

40. **Stern, a veteran of the Battle of the Bulge...:** Stewart Stern, correspondence with the author, September 1993 and December, 2003.

40. **Stern had never met James Dean...:** Stewart Stern, correspondence with the author, September 1993 and December 2003. Stern believes he won the contest: he could imitate three pigs at once! He later incorporated the mooing into *Rebel Without a Cause*: Jim moos during the first planetarium scene; Buzz later refers to him several times as "Toreador."

41. **That same day...:** Jack L. Warner gauged the success or failure of a preview (and the length) by the number of times people from the audience made trips to the bathroom. He once referred to a bad preview as a "two-piss picture" (in Michael Freedland, *The Warner Brothers*, p. 75).

41. **Despite the rumors of his greatness...:** Hyams, pp. 174–175.

41. **The conversation quickly turned to...:** Kent R. Brown, *The Screenwriter as Collaborator*, p. 94.

41. **After reading Shulman's script...:** *Ibid.*

Chapter 9: Dead End

42. **Irving Shulman was as eager as...:** Telephone conversation with Allan L. Alexander (Irving Shulman's son-in-law), November 29, 1993. In David Dalton's *James Dean: The Mutant King*, Shulman describes his experience with Ray as "nightmarish" (p. 226).

42. **As he labored over the final version...:** Shulman's book was titled *Children of the Dark*.

42. **On December 4, Ray put his idea...:** Eisenschitz, *Nicholas Ray*, p. 236.

44. **Shulman's outline left the ending still open...:** This part of Shulman's outline reads as follows:

> XXXVII EXT. OBSERVATORY — NIGHT
>   A. The arrival of Jim.
>   B. The attack of Plato on Judy.
>   C. Jim repulses the attack.
>   a. Judy is rescued.
>   b. Does Plato die?

44. **On December 11...:** Shulman's more "overtly psychotic" character was toned down in Stewart Stern's script.

45. **Shulman's final scene took the...:** Ray, "Story Into Script," p. 74.

45. **Ray observed later...:** *Ibid.*

45. **The continuing dispute over...:** *Ibid.*

Chapter 10: A Critique

46. **On December 16, Ray's Shulman problem...:** Dean would not actually report to *Giant* until June.

46. **That same morning...:** Although Ray suggests in the memo that Shulman review MacEwen's suggestions in a meeting with Ray and Weisbart, there is no indication in the studio records that he actually did.

47. **MacEwen had offered one final thought...:** In "The Blind Run," Ray suggests a similar narration, which should follow the three opening vignettes: "[S]ome...public figure who is still likely to be in the news six months from now...appears and informs the audience that what they have seen has actually happened, that what they are about to see has also happened and is happening — and it can happen to anyone here regardless of age, income, education or profession..."

Chapter 11: Los Angeles and New York

48. **The Griffith Park Observatory...:** The Griffith Observatory opened in 1935. David Dalton, in *James Dean: The Mutant King*, erroneously refers to the structure as the D.W. Griffith Planetarium (p. 239). Actually, it was named for Col. Griffith J. Griffith (1850–1919), who donated it to the City of Los Angeles along with Griffith Park and the Greek Theatre (from "Griffith Observatory General Information" at http://www.griffithobs.org/Generalinfo.html).

48. **One of James Dean's first...:** Dalton, *James Dean: The Mutant King*, pp. 63–65.

48. **Five days later, Kenneth Cox...:** A Warner Bros. publicity release of March 24, 1955, referred to him as "Charles A. McCormick" (sic) and gave him the rank of General. Various studio memoranda refer to him as either "Colonel" or "General."

49. **Rebel itself was apparently...:** Ray, "Story Into Script," p. 74.

49. **Hoping to overcome such objections...:** *Ibid.*, p. 73.

49. **Since Ray was satisfied with only...:** Eisenschitz, *Nicholas Ray*, p. 237.

50. **As Ray said good-bye...:** Ray, "From Rebel — The Life Story of a Film" (in *Hello, Hollywood!*, p. 521)

50. **Three days after Christmas...:** Ray, "Story Into Script," p. 74.

Part II: Pre-Production

Chapter 12: A Private Hell

53. **Stern later recalled...:** Kent R. Brown,

The Screenwriter as Collaborator, p. 95. Stern describes his "emotional meeting-ground" with Nicholas Ray as follows: "Nick was in the throes of guilt about feeling that he was not a good father to [his son] Tony, and I was still in a blaming mode about my parents not understanding me" (Stewart Stern, correspondence with the author, December 2003).

54. **Meanwhile, Stern's work...:** Kent R. Brown, pp. 95–97.

54. **On January 17, 1955...:** Dean was also scheduled to perform in "The Corn Is Green," a *Hallmark Hall of Fame* program on NBC, but he died before rehearsals began in October 1955.

54. **As they had agreed in New York...:** Dean's undeniable influence in shaping the film has led to a debate. Jim Backus (*Rocks on the Roof*, p. 153) and Dennis Hopper (Eisenschitz, pp. 246–247) claim that Dean was a *de facto* co-director with Ray. Others involved in the production, including Leonard Rosenman (Dalton, p. 232), Steffi Sidney and Beverly Long (Riese, 421–422) disagree. Ann Doran argues (*Five for Hollywood*, p. 95) that "Jimmy did most of the directing. He gave us our lines; he dominated the entire thing." Randall Riese's book, *The Unabridged James Dean*, exhibits a production still from the film in which Dean is pointing at (and therefore appears to be directing) Ann Doran in the family argument scene (p. 433). However, in that scene, Jim Stark is *supposed* to point an accusing finger at his mother.

Chapter 13: Screenplay by Stewart Stern

55. **Stern later recalled...:** Kent R. Brown, *The Screenwriter as Collaborator*, p. 96.

55. **Jim, meanwhile, amuses himself...:** Stern developed Uris's single incident with the jacket into a motif: Jim later covers a sleeping Plato with Plato's coat at the mansion and gives his jacket to Plato at the planetarium climax, after which Jim's father drapes his sport coat over Jim's shoulders.

Chapter 14: Start Notice

58. **January 27 was also the start date...:** Letter from Irving Shulman to Jack L. Warner, March 3, 1956 (Jack L. Warner file, Warner Bros. Archive, USC).

58. **That night, Dean flew to...:** Kitt's nickname for Dean made its way into the film. Before the chickie run in Stern's script, Plato refers to Jim as "Jamie" in a conversation with Judy, observing that, "People he *really* likes, he lets them call him 'Jamie.'"

58. **A photographer named Dennis Stock...:** Hyams, *James Dean: Little Boy Lost*, pp. 173, 188.

58. **The columnists had announced...:** Howlett, *James Dean*, p. 102.

60. **Stern, with Weisbart's support...:** Kent R. Brown, *The Screenwriter as Collaborator*, pp. 100–101.

60. **The doomsday dialogue...:** Stewart Stern, correspondence with the author, November 1993.

60. **The return to the observatory...:** *Ibid.*

60. **This was consistent with...:** Stewart Stern, correspondence with the author, January 2004.

61. **Stern's scene, at Ray's request...:** *Ibid.*

61. **Stern's pre-race sequence...:** Stern saw this as a significant moment in the film: "My feeling about Jim and Buzz was that without so much peer pressure to follow the king and exclude the outsider, the two boys could have become really close friends. I think they admired each other, but ritual snatched them apart" (Stewart Stern, correspondence with the author, December 2003).

61–62. **Stern's version internalized the race...:** Stewart Stern, correspondence with the author, November 1993.

Chapter 15: Casting

63. **In early February...:** Dalton, *James Dean: The Mutant King*, pp. 243–244.

63. **Mazzola was familiar with...:** Mazzola's meetings with Ray on gang-related matters are itemized in a March 28, 1955 memo from David Weisbart to Steve Trilling.

63. **With James Dean in New York...:** *The Hollywood Reporter* (February 24, 1955) announced that "Warners" (not Ray) "want Debbie Reynolds to be James Dean's leading lady in *Rebel Without a Cause.*" Reynolds' casting would have enhanced the picture's marquee value.

63. **Natalie Wood had expressed a keen interest...:** Randall Riese, *The Unabridged James Dean*, p. 567.

63–64. **She was also grown-up beyond her years...:** Raymond R. Sarlot and Fred E. Basten, "Natalie Wood's Secret Life at the Marmont," *Hollywood Studio Magazine*, March 1988 (vol. 21, no. 3), p. 22 (excerpted from their book, *Life at the Marmont*).

64. **Ray Framek of the Juvenile Division...:** Ray acquires the last name "Framek" in this scene of Stern's draft. He was named after Jim Sramek, a close friend of Stern's from World War II (Stewart Stern, correspondence with the author, November 1993).

64. **Jim tries to get the phone number...:** Judy's last name is not mentioned anywhere else in Stern's script, anywhere in Irving Shulman's treatment or outline, or anywhere in the film.

65. **In Ray's initial thinking...:** Kent R. Brown, p. 103.

65. **Stern had no objections...:** Stewart Stern, correspondence with the author, September 1993.

65. **Stern wrote out the entire...:** *Ibid.*

Chapter 16: Mr. Warner

67–68. **Among Warner's more cryptic remarks...:** Michael Freedland, *The Warner Brothers*, p. 200.

68. **On another occasion, Warner...:** Bob Thomas, *Clown Prince of Hollywood: The Antic Life and Times of Jack L. Warner*, p. 210.

68. **Ray was willing to take chances...:** Dean borrowed a device called a Minifon from Joe Hyams to record the voice of his grandfather, Charlie Dean, at the Winslow farm near Fairmount in February, 1955. (Hyams, pp. 178) Hyams claims to have introduced the Minifon to Nicholas Ray during the filming of the knife fight at the Griffith Observatory (p. 207), but Ray's forays into teenage gang hangouts precede that by several weeks. Ray himself claimed (Dalton, *Mutant King*, p. 244) that he had "invented a way of concealing a mini-phone tape recorder in a shoulder holster, with a wristwatch as a microphone" when he visited the gang hangouts during pre-production. Hyams also refers to the wristwatch microphone, so it may be the same device Dean took to Fairmount, and Hyams may simply be incorrect as to the time that he (or Dean) first introduced it to Ray.

68. **On one occasion...:** Eisenschitz, p. 232.

68. **At the same time, Stern...:** Stewart Stern, correspondence with the author, November 1993.

68. **On February 14, Valentine's Day...:** Dalton, *James Dean: The Mutant King*, p. 211.

68. **Dean sat in the Winslows' kitchen...:** Hyams, pp. 184–188.

Chapter 17: Free-for-All

70. **Shortly after returning to...:** Joe Hyams estimates the number at 500 (p. 194); Corey Allen estimates the number "conservatively" at 300 (in Eisenschitz, p. 241). A Warner Bros. publicity release dated March 30 set the number at "more than 400."

70. **At sixteen, Mineo already had...:** Ephraim Katz, *The Film Encyclopedia*, p. 811.

70. **Ray asked Mineo what work he had...:** Dalton, *James Dean: The Mutant King*, p. 228.

70. **Although Ray was looking for toughness...:** Stewart Stern, correspondence with the author, September 1993.

70–71. **The survivors of that "mass improvisation"...:** Eisenschitz, pp. 241–242.

71. **Margaret O'Brien, an early favorite...:** Dalton, *James Dean: The Mutant King*, p. 227.

71. **Natalie Wood, however, made a...:** *Ibid.*

71–72. **Wood matched her persistence with ...:** *Ibid.*, pp. 227–228. According to Randall Riese (*The Unabridged James Dean*, p. 567), Wood visited Ray's office every day for a month after her initial interview.

73. **Convinced that Mansfield's test was...:** Dalton, *James Dean: The Mutant King*, p. 227.

Chapter 18: Locations

75. **Stern also made name and character changes...:** "Crunch" and "Buzz Gunderson" evolved from a single name, "Crunch Gunderson," that Stern admired. The character named "Mil" was named after one of Stern's favorite cousins, and "Cookie" Wolfsheim was one of his mother's "best and funniest friends."

Chapter 19: Mr. Warner Returns

77. **Warner also suggested Lois Smith...:** Elia Kazan had "discovered" Smith on Broadway in the play, *Time Out for Ginger*. *East of Eden* was her first film. She made a second film for Warner Bros., *Strange Lady in Town*, but she remained primarily a stage actress.

77. **As part of his critique...:** According to Bob Thomas in *Clown Prince of Hollywood*, Warner's observations were generally astute: "Younger producers and directors were amazed by his memory for rushes he had seen weeks before and by his grasp of cinematic style." He was apparently as attentive to the details of B pictures as to those of prestige pictures (p. 252).

78. **The censors would probably not appreciate...:** Ray refers to Trilling's comments in the March 1 memo to Weisbart.

Chapter 20: Majors and Minors

79. **Despite his positive reaction to...:** The records at the Warner Bros. Archive are unclear as to when and why Mineo eventually won the role from the apparent front-runners Gray and Silver. Ray's choice of Mineo probably had as much to do

with Mineo's easy rapport with Dean as his suitability for the role.

79–80. **For the role of Judy's friend, Helen...:** Long and Grinnage discussed this subject on a local Los Angeles cable program, "Talk of the Town" (courtesy Robert Rees video collection).

80. **Gloria Castillo's name had also...:** Castillo's later films included *The Vanishing American* (1955), *Invasion of the Saucer Men* (1957), *Reform School Girl* (1957), *Teenage Monsters* (1958) and *You've Got to Be Smart* (1967).

80. **He was looking at the same actresses...:** Conspicuous by her absence in Stern's script, the role of Plato's mother was never cast.

Chapter 21: The Excitement Gathers

81. **By early March, the gossip columnists...:** Val Holley observes in *James Dean: The Biography* that the true function of the Hollywood columnists was not reporting news, but "inducing public curiosity" (p. 221).

81. **When Ray learned that Weisbart had failed...:** Weisbart's snappish exchange with Ray was apparently rare. According to Stewart Stern, Ray and Weisbart "fought about (the fantasy scenes) but not much else." Stern also refers to Weisbart as a "friendly ghost," who "was not a major part of the collaborative effort" (Kent R. Brown, *The Screenwriter as Collaborator*, p. 104). Hyams reports that Weisbart "was probably the best-liked person on the set" (p. 213).

81. **In a follow-up memo...:** "Garmes, Lee," in Ephraim Katz, *The Film Encyclopedia*, p. 468.

81. **The same day, the studio heard...:** Letter from Irving Shulman to Jack L. Warner, March 3, 1956 (Jack L. Warner file, Warner Bros. Archive, USC).

81–82. **Meanwhile, James Dean was preparing...:** Hyams, p. 190.

82. **Before flying back to Los Angeles...:** Thompson described how he came to interview Dean in Dalton, *James Dean: The Mutant King*, pp. 172, 174. The article appeared in *The New York Times*, March 16, 1955, under the title, "Another Dean Hits the Big Leagues." The article is reprinted in the *New York Times Encyclopedia of Film*.

Chapter 22: Cold Feet

84. **That same day, March 9, 1955...:** Hyams, p. 190.

84. **The next morning, the critics...:** *Ibid.*, pp.

191–192. According to Hyams, Dean's response to Crowther's review was, "The stupid cunt."

84. **Ray later recalled...:** "From *Rebel: The Life Story of a Film*," in *Hello, Hollywood!*, p. 516.

85. **On March 11, only two days...:** Rochlen was one of the few columnists (Hyams was another) whom Dean liked and trusted. Val Holley discusses Dean's relationship with the Hollywood press corps in depth in *James Dean: The Biography*, pp. 217–233.

85. **Yet, as Dean "deliberated"...:** The dates of Mazzola's meetings with Dean, as listed in the March 28 memo from Weisbart to Trilling, verify Dean's pre-production activities the week of his return from New York and afterward, indicating that he *was* working while publicly "deliberating."

85–86. **Although the studio and the gossip columnists...:** One of the persistent myths regarding Dean and *Rebel* involves his alleged "disappearance" from the picture. Dalton uses the term (p. 232) and quotes Stern as saying, "No one knew where he (Dean) was." Dalton also quotes Stern as saying that Dean "was gone about ten days." Dalton states that this disappearance occurred "a few days before shooting began." Hyams states that Dean disappeared "two weeks before *Rebel* was scheduled to begin" (p. 199). Both Dalton and Hyams discuss Dean's "out-of-the-void" telephone call to Stern in close proximity with Dean's "disappearance." Randall Riese, in *The Unabridged James Dean*, states that Dean "fled" to New York twice during pre-production, "leaving Nick Ray and producer David Weisbart in limbo" (p. 429). Since production on *Rebel Without a Cause* did not begin until March 30, 1955, and since the studio records indicate that Dean was working with Frank Mazzola on gang research on March 8 (the day Dean flew back to Los Angeles from New York), and also on March 11–12, March 15, March 23 and March 25, Dalton, Hyams and Riese seem to be in error regarding the dates of Dean's "disappearance." Their error appears to be a confusion between the start of production on March 30 and Dean's *start notice* ordering him to report to the production by March 15. Since Stern himself asserts that Dean's early-morning call was from New York (correspondence with the author, November, 1993 and December 2003), it was at *that* time, before March 8, and almost a month before the start of production, that Dean threatened not to report. According to the terms of Dean's contract, he could have been called to appear a week earlier, which would have been March 8, the day he *did* report (at 7:00 P.M.). Assuming that Dean spoke to Stern on or before March 1, he was only two weeks, and possibly only one week, away from possible suspension. At the time that Dalton and Hyams suggest that the studio was contemplating Dean's suspension (between March 17, which was two weeks before production, and

March 20, ten days before), Dean would *already* have been placed on suspension. Dean may have been hiding from public view the weeks before the start of production, but he was at no time in violation of his contract.

86. **Warner Bros. had taken Dean's threat seriously…:** The names "Tab Hunter," "John Kerr," and "Rob Wagner" are penciled in on a list of casting possibilities dated March 2. There is another copy of this same list in the Warner Bros. Archive, with the same date, but without the penciled-in names. Solly Baiano, in charge of casting at Warner Bros., appears to have written his initials on the amended list. The names appear to be in the same handwriting as the initials. If Baiano wrote in the names on March 2, when Dean was still in New York and still under threat of suspension, this would further confirm that the time period in question was at least two weeks before either of the ones suggested by Dalton and Hyams.

86. **Hedda Hopper, meanwhile…:** Both events were reported in *The Valley Times* (March 14 for Hopper's column, March 18 for the meeting with Don Pursuit).

86. **For Stewart Stern, the answer…:** Dalton, *James Dean: The Mutant King*, p. 233; Hyams, p. 200.

Chapter 23: Rehearsals

87. **The day after Dean visited…:** Hyams, p. 200.

87. **Stewart Stern, David Weisbart and…:** Stewart Stern, correspondence with the author, September 1993.

87. **Recalling his own experiences with gangs…:** Hyams, p. 200.

87–88. **As Dean improvised…:** Eisenschitz, pp. 243–244.

89–90. **Steve Trilling, Jack Warner's assistant…:** Trilling's handwritten notes appear in Stern's script dated March 18, 1955. The handwriting is identical to notes written on a typed March 28 memo regarding Frank Mazzola's hours as gang consultant. Each of the handwritten notes on the Stern script is separated from the others by a pencil line across the page, matching a similar but undated set of handwritten notes with the word "Trilling" written at the top. A typewritten document titled "Notes from Mr. Trilling," dated March 24, 1955, covers different points than the handwritten notes.

90. **Trilling wrote "process — Star Is Born"…:** For more about the carhop sequence in *A Star Is Born*, see Ronald Haver, *A Star Is Born: The Making of the 1954 Movie and Its 1983 Restoration.*

90. **Unknown to Dennis Hopper…:** Sarlot and Basten, "Natalie Wood's Secret Life at the Marmont," p. 21. On another occasion, Adele Rosenman, Leonard Rosenman's wife, apparently saw Ray and Wood taking a shower together at a poolside cabana (Hyams, p. 210).

90. **While Ray was having his affair…:** Eisenschitz, p. 242.

90–91. **Ray had them read a key scene…:** Dalton, *James Dean: The Mutant King*, p. 228. Mineo also describes the session at Ray's in the documentary film, *James Dean: The First American Teenager* (1976). The studio did not announce Mineo as Plato until March 31, 1955.

Chapter 24: Blackboard Jungle

92. **On Monday, March 21…:** Howlett, *James Dean*, p 108. Howlett is the only source this author could find for the reference to a stabbing of a teacher the day the film opened.

94. **The exterior that they used…:** A photograph taken at Ray's bungalow shows a blueprint tacked to the wall. Ray had asked for an exact replica of his living room and stairway. The photo is reproduced in Eisenschitz, *Nicholas Ray*, p. 240.

94–95. **One especially zealous supporter…:** For a good overview of the censorship issue and the impact of the Production Code, see Murray Schumach, *The Face on the Cutting Room Floor.*

96–97. **Beymer, 16, was a former…:** Beymer did not win the role of Plato, but six years later, he played Tony in Robert Wise's film of *West Side Story*. Natalie Wood played Maria.

97. **Elsewhere, W. F. Fitzgerald…:** In an apparent cost-cutting measure, the "exterior" of Jim's house was filmed on a sound stage at Warner Bros. Mr. Hass's home was apparently never used in the filming.

97. **On March 24, Steve Trilling added to…:** These are typewritten notes with the heading, "Notes from Mr. Trilling."

97. **Hunt, who was also performing in an upcoming play…:** The Carthay Circle Theater, which could seat 1,500 people, was a "legitimate" theater only briefly during the 1950s. It was much better known as a movie palace. *Gone with the Wind* had its West Coast premiere at the Carthay Circle. The theater was torn down around 1970. "Cinema Treasures/Carthay Circle Theater," http://cinematreasures.org/theater/1158.

98. **The studio also officially cast…:** The Publicity Department cited the following dates for signing the cast of *Rebel Without a Cause*: Dean, March 17; Wood, March 25; William Hopper, March 26; Jim Backus, March 26; Corey Allen, March 30; Dennis Hopper, March 30; Beverly Long, March 31.

98. **The Publicity Department observed…:** The author, after searching several sources, was unable to identify the specific television programs in which Hopper played Dean's father or Backus played Wood's.

Chapter 25: Exit Stern

99. **He later recalled…:** Charles Nafus, "Screenwriter Stewart Stern Remembers Writing Rebel," *The Austin Chronicle*, June 16, 2000 (taken from the online edition at www.austinchronicle.com).

99. **Meanwhile, James Dean left to spend…:** Hyams, p. 201.

99. **Before Stern left for New York…:** Stern's official period of employment was from December 30, 1954 through March 29, 1955.

100. **Jack Grinnage would play Moose, even though…:** Dalton, Eisenschitz, Howlett, Holley, and Robert Headrick Jr. (*Deanmania*) all list Grinnage as "Chick" rather than "Moose." Dalton lists Jack Simmons as "Moose"; Donald Spoto (*Rebel: The Life and Legend of James Dean*) also assigns the role of "Moose" to Nick Adams (p.221).

100. **Dean's friend, Jack Simmons, would play Cookie…:** Hyams briefly describes Simmons' screen test (p. 195); Holley also describes the Simmons test and Dean's attempt to secure the role of Judy for Christine White (pp. 261–262). Hyams states that Dean and White met in September of 1952 (p. 55).

100. **Away from the track, he had also scored…:** Hyams discusses Dean's two meetings with Hedda Hopper (pp. 141–142, 170). Hopper's column featured Dean on March 27, 1955.

100–101. **Despite Hedda Hopper's attention…:** Although Halperin's note is addressed only to "Jack," it is safe to assume he meant Jack Warner, who was the final arbiter of any such problems at the studio. The head of the Publicity Department at the studio, Halperin's immediate supervisor, was Bill L. Hendricks.

101. **That evening, he drove to Arthur Loew Jr.'s house…:** Hyams, p. 202.

101. **On Monday, March 28…:** *Rebel*'s Daily Production and Progress Report sheets from March 25 through March 31 list Moore as the "cutter." William Ziegler's name first appears in the Daily Production and Progress Report sheets on April 1, the day before the film switched to color. (See the "Production" section of this book for the circumstances leading to color and Ziegler.)

101. **March 29, the day before production began…:** The announcement appeared in *Variety* the next day with the headline, "First Cinema-Scoper in Black-and-White."

Part III: Production

Chapter 26: On Location

105. **Venable Herndon, one of James Dean's many biographers…:** Venable Herndon, *James Dean: A Short Life*, p. 188–189.

105. **That first day…:** Warner Bros. kept track of a film in progress through a Daily Production and Progress Report and Production Camera Sheets. The Daily Production and Progress Report listed the cast and crew for each day, the physical resources employed (i.e., number of vehicles used), the numbered scenes filmed, etc.). The Production Camera Sheets provided the content of the numbered scenes. *All further references to production details, unless otherwise stated, are from these documents. All references to dialogue are from Stewart Stern's final script or the film's dialogue transcript.*

106. **In the next shot…:** Long's line was cut from the final film. She had another line, also in French, "Les jeux de combat!" It, too, was cut (Dalton, *James Dean: The Mutant King*, p. 247).

107. **After lunch, Ray filmed the…:** Ray wanted to stage the fight like a form of ballet, to "preserve the choreographic rhythms of a familiar ritual." He had directed two musicals on Broadway and felt that he "wouldn't be worth a damn as a director" if he could not incorporate dance into a dramatic film (Dalton, *James Dean: The Mutant King*, pp. 246–247). Hyams also describes the scene in *James Dean: Little Boy Lost*, pp. 207–208.

107–108. **Neil Rau, a newspaper columnist…:** Rau's column, titled "The Fight Was for Blood—and They Got It!" appeared May 22, 1955. David Dalton mistakes the date of the column as coming the day after the filming of the switch-blade scene (*James Dean: The Mutant King*, p. 246). On May 21, the day before Rau's column appeared, and on May 22, the date of Rau's column, Ray's company was shooting part of the chickie run scene on Stage 7 at Warner Bros. The black-and-white switchblade scene was filmed April 1, the re-take in color on April 28.

108. **For a moment, Dean did not answer…:** Dennis Hopper contends that Dean responded with an outburst of profanity when Ray stopped filming because of Dean's wound. David Dalton reports this version of Hopper's story in *James Dean: The Mutant King* (p. 246), while Eisenschitz quotes Hopper as saying, "I remember, in the knife fight, Corey Allen cut Jimmy's shirt or something. Nick called, 'Cut! Cut!, and Jimmy said, 'Don't you ever say fucking Cut, man, I'm the only one who says Cut here'" (p. 247). Hyams offers a slightly different wording of the quote (*Little Boy Lost*, p. 208). Hyams also states that he was present "with some other press spectators on one of the days that the knife fight between Jim and Buzz at

the Planetarium was filmed" (p. 207). He claims that, "if memory serves, it was on the eighth or ninth take before they started to get into the spirit of battle." At that point, according to Hyams, Ray yelled, "Cut," and Dean made his outburst (p. 208). Neil Rau, however, made no mention of an outburst in his column, and neither Beverly Long nor Jack Grinnage, who were also in the scene, recalls hearing any such outburst from Dean. Long's and Grinnage's version of events were aired in a cable television program, "Talk of the Town," honoring Dean's 50th birthday (Robert Rees collection).

108. **The switchblade scene was not made any easier…:** Riese, *The Unabridged James Dean*, p. 435.

108. **During one of the many breaks in the action…:** Dalton, *James Dean: The Mutant King*, p. 244.

109. **Cast and crew had worked eleven hours…:** Randall Riese confuses Dean's and Wood's sunburn and Wood's fainting spell during filming outside the Griffith Observatory with another occasion when Dean sunned himself on the front lawn at Warner Bros. to develop a tan for his role in *Giant*. Riese states that Dean "spent as much time as he could in the sun…to obtain the weather-beaten look of Jett Rink. Natalie Wood once attempted to join Jimmy in the sun but became faint from overexposure…" (*The Unabridged James Dean*, p. 436). A publicity release dated April 2 reported Wood's light-headedness, an undated publicity release (probably April 7 or 8) reported Wood's and Dean's sunburn. Columnist Sheilah Graham reported Dean's efforts to get a tan for *Giant* in her March 23 column.

Chapter 27: Transformation

111. **Warner, as the story goes…:** Eisenschitz (p. 245), Hyams (p. 203) and Dalton (pp. 233–234) all report the meeting with Warner, Ray's offer to buy the rights, and Trilling's visit to the projectionist. Eisenschitz observes that Ray's story "can neither be confirmed nor denied from other sources," while Hyams and Dalton report it as fact. In *I Was Interrupted*, Ray says only about the meeting with Warner: "I'd already shot five days of *Rebel Without a Cause* in black-and-white when Warners realized their contract with the man who invented scope required that everything be shot in color" (p. 57).

111. **A more compelling reason for the upgrade…:** It is apparent that when Warner Bros. publicized *Rebel Without a Cause* as an "untinted C'scoper" in their March 29 publicity release, the licensor of CinemaScope, 20th Century–Fox, im-

mediately informed Warner Bros. (and also MGM) that all CinemaScope productions had to be filmed in color. An article appearing in *The New York Times* on April 5 stated that MGM had opted to drop the CinemaScope format for *Trial* before the picture started filming on April 1, only two days after the Warner Bros. publicity release. William Ziegler, a film editor who presumably had more experience with color than James Moore, replaced Moore on April 1, the day after *Trial* dropped CinemaScope, and two days into *Rebel*'s production. Since Ziegler reported on April 1, Jack L. Warner probably met with Ray on March 31.

112. **Ray substituted a red windbreaker…:** Dalton, *James Dean: The Mutant King*, p. 234. Ray is apparently the only source of this information. It is not recorded in any of the studio's publicity releases.

112. **The Wardrobe Department also re-dyed…:** *Ibid*. Dalton cites Beverly Long. The overnight switch from black-and-white to color was probably less traumatic on the Wardrobe Department than might be expected. Although Wardrobe would have had to test Wood's green dress, it wouldn't have had to re-dye the 400 pairs of jeans for the Dawson High sequence: in 1955, blue jeans were unacceptable dress in most public high schools.

112. **In Stern's script, a school monitor…:** In 1949, when James Dean attended Santa Monica City College, the college shared some facilities (including the cafeteria) with the adjacent Santa Monica High School. One day, Dean and another student, Gordon Hein, accidentally walked on the insignia for Santa Monica High School and were chastised by "a couple of burly lettermen" (in Val Holley, *James Dean: The Biography*, pp. 37–38).

113. **Meanwhile, Joe McLaughlin…:** The fee a studio paid for a copyrighted song depended on how much of the song was used, and whether the song was performed on screen by actors or served as background music. A "partial visual vocal" would thus be a song performed on screen, but not in its entirety.

Chapter 28: Red Channels

114. **Marsha Hunt should have…:** *Daily Variety* also carried the announcement, on April 6.

114. **There was another, more likely explanation for…:** John Cogley, *Report on Blacklisting* (vol. 2), pp. 149–155. The reasons behind Marsha Hunt's decision to choose a stage play rather than *Rebel* are still unclear. None of the press releases, naturally, mentions Hunt's blacklisting as having any part in her decision to give up the role of Jim Stark's mother. Eisenschitz argues that, despite the

opportunity to break back into films, Hunt simply chose the play (p.528). Yet, the role of James Dean's mother would have been a career-builder (or re-builder) for any middle-aged actress. Perhaps Hunt thought it would have directed too much attention toward her. She returned to the screen inconspicuously a year later in *No Place to Hide*, which was filmed in the Philippines. Had Hunt chosen to stay with *Rebel*, she would not have found much support from Jack L. Warner. Warner, who would have had the final say in Hunt's hiring, was an enthusiastic supporter of the blacklist and had testified before the House Un-American Activities Committee in 1947. Although Warner had joined in the Red-baiting at least partly as penance for making *Mission to Moscow*, a pro–Russian wartime film, he was equally eager to assert his loyalty to the American mainstream. Bob Thomas, in *Clown Prince of Hollywood*, sees Warner as a willing participant in the witchhunt: "Without being asked, Warner named a dozen screenwriters he had detected and fired for being 'communists.' Thus he destroyed the filmwriting careers of the men, some of whom had no communist ties whatever" (p. 165). Marsha Hunt could have expected just such a reception from Jack L.Warner had she not opted out of *Rebel*.

114. **Ann Doran, to the contrary…:** "Three cited for Battling Alleged Red-Line Movie," *The Los Angeles Times*, November 5, 1954, p. 27. ("Pedro Gonzales Gonzales" really *is* the actor's name.)

114–115. **Although Ann Doran's Mrs. Stark…:** According to an undated publicity release, the two earlier films were *Here Come the Nelsons* and *Destination Space*.

115. **Ray rehearsed quietly with his actors…:** The Photo Masterbook for *Rebel Without a Cause* (at USC) includes a production still showing Ray, the children, and the comic books.

Chapter 29: Hard Work, Hard Feelings

117. **The next day, Mrs. Maria Gurdin…:** Sarlott and Basten, p. 22.

117. **As Nick Adams observed…:** Nick Adams is quoted in "Natalie Wood," by Kevin Lewis (*Films in Review*, December 1986, p. 581). Another source, *Natalie & R.J.*, a biography of Wood and Robert Wagner published in 1988, attributes the quote to Dennis Hopper, in reference to her dating Nicholas Ray (p. 32). It is unlikely that Mrs. Gurdin would simply chaperone her daughter on the set if she knew she was sleeping with Ray. Since Wood was a minor, and had Mrs. Gurdin believed

Hopper, Ray could have been charged with statutory rape. In Hopper's version of the incident, it was Ray who informed on *him* to Mrs. Gurdin: "[T]he studio came down on me," Hopper contends, "and (Ray) came out of it as pure as snow" (Eisenschitz, p. 246).

117. **Tension between Ray and Hopper…:** Sarlott and Basten, p. 22. The authors do not identify the cast member.

117. **Hopper's action also upset…:** *Ibid.*

117. **The animosity between Ray and Hopper…:** *Ibid.*

118. **Meanwhile, the Los Angeles Police Department…:** Nearly all the studio memoranda regarding the Getty mansion suggest a sense of urgency consistent with its imminent demise. Randall Riese, however, states that the mansion was not torn down until 1957 (*The Unabridged James Dean*, p. 516). He does not list a source.

119. **When some of the *Rebel* cast began openly mocking…:** Eisenschitz, p. 246.

Chapter 30: Lost Time

120. **At least one member of the cast…:** Randall Riese, in *The Unabridged James Dean*, erroneously attributes the malaria to James Dean (p. 251). The studio's Publicity Department lists the 11th as the day of Adams' illness. However, the film's Daily Production and Progress Report lists him as present on that date, which was a Monday.

121. **Almira Sessions' character was not the only…:** The notation for 9:55–10:00 in the Daily Production and Progress Report reads: "Corey Allen and Dennis Hopper left set—could not find in time to complete shot—Co.(mpany) required to move to Ext.(erior) due to lecture scheduled for 10:45 A.M."

121–122. **Ray's approach to filming stressed collaboration…:** Beverly Long discusses the improvised scene in "Talk of the Town" (Robert Rees video collection).

122. **As Ray's young gang members…:** According to Randall Riese (p. 436), Dean was also reading Edna Ferber's *Giant* on the set; Dean started his Director's Notebook while filming *East of Eden* and kept it through the filming of *Giant*.

122. **He especially enjoyed…:** Dalton, *James Dean: The Mutant King*, p. 247.

122. **At other times…:** Hyams, p. 213–214.

122. **Dean also offered…:** *Ibid.*, p.212.

122. **Dean also enjoyed boxing between takes…:** Alan and Art Sacks, twins, were Dean's other stand-ins for *Rebel* (Riese, *The Unabridged James Dean*, p. 504).

122. **In Dean's absence…:** Val Holley claims that Dean was absent "for three days in mid–April" due to laryngitis (p. 262). Army Archerd's

column of May 2, 1955, confirms the fact of Dean's lost voice, but not the dates of any absence from the production.

123. **Dean had both the physical skills and the…:** Backus, *Rocks on the Roof*, p. 155.

123. **Three Warner Bros. executives…:** Kriedl, *Nicholas Ray*, pp. 76–77.

Chapter 31: The Mansion

124. **Maila Nurmi and Jack Simmons of the Night Watch…:** The pool location, where much of *Rebel*'s mansion sequence was played out, was also a significant setting in *Sunset Boulevard*. It symbolized the ambitions of the film's main character, Joe Gillis, and it is where his body falls after Norma Desmond shoots him.

125. **To Judy's question about babies…:** Dalton, *James Dean: The Mutant King*, p. 257.

Chapter 32: Fury and Sound

127. **After lunch, Ray planned to shoot…:** Backus, *Rocks on the Roof*, pp. 154–155.

127. **Ray later recalled…:** Ray, *I Was Interrupted*, p. 131.

127. **Then, Nicholas Ray took Dean to…:** The studio's Publicity Department issued a release on April 23 claiming that Dean was taken to the hospital. Nicholas Ray, in *I Was Interrupted*, claims to have taken Dean there himself and learned that Dean had broken a knuckle (p. 131). Val Holley, in *James Dean: The Biography*, claims that Dean "was transported no further than the Warners first aid station" (pp. 262–263). Holley cites a studio accident report reprinted in Leith Adams' and Keith Burns' book, *James Dean: Behind the Scene*, which describes Dean's injury as a contusion to his right hand. The same studio document indicates that a Dr. Hiatt examined Dean. In *James Dean: The Mutant King*, David Dalton quotes Jim Backus as saying that Dean broke two bones in his hand (p. 238). Randall Riese states in *The Unabridged James Dean* that: "Fortunately, legend aside and despite Jim Backus's claim…, x-rays revealed no broken bones" (p. 256). Donald Spoto, in *Rebel: The Life and Legend of James Dean*, cites the studio's April 23 press release verbatim (p. 225).

128. **As Ray and Weisbart studied the dailies…:** Jack L. Warner file, Warner Bros. Archive, USC.

128. **Later in the day, Stacey sent a directive…:** *Ibid.*

128. **Wood felt justifiably nervous…:** Dalton, *James Dean: The Mutant King*, p. 256. Dalton claims this off-screen exchange took place in the alley scene, where Jim meets Judy when he returns home after unsuccessfully trying to give himself up to the police. However, in that scene, Jim only kisses Judy on the forehead, and she does not return the kiss. Jim and Judy do not actually kiss until the library scene at the mansion. Dalton's chronology is also incorrect, since the alley scene was filmed a month after the library scene.

Chapter 33: Looping and Ad-Libbing

130. **Using the scene ad-libbed earlier by his actors…:** Dalton, *James Dean: The Mutant King*, p. 243.

130. **In the next two shots…:** *Ibid.*

131. **McDermid wrote to Shulman…:** Irving Shulman file (#2519), Warner Bros. Archive, USC.

131. **Adams was the most brazen scene-stealer…:** Beverly Long is quoted in Riese, *The Unabridged James Dean*, regarding the stolen lines and Adams' general behavior on the set. On one occasion, Long once punched him on the bus taking the cast to a location (p. 11). Dalton also refers to Adams' aggressiveness and line-stealing in *James Dean: The Mutant King* (p. 247).

132. **On Sunday, May 1, an off-day…:** Louella Parsons' column of May 5 referred to both the race and the casualties.

133. **However, since the Production Code forbade…:** A complete copy of the Code (as of December, 1956) can be found in Murray Schumach's *The Face on the Cutting Room Floor*, pp. 279–292.

133. **Wood brought along one of her most prized…:** In dating this event, the author combined information from the production records with several photographs taken of Dean signing the jacket (see p. 569 in *The Unabridged James Dean*). In the photographs, Dean is on an interior set (the hallway outside Jim Stark's bedroom) wearing the blood-stained shirt from the switchblade fight. The Photo Masterbook for *Rebel Without a Cause* also contains pictures of Dean with the bloody shirt and Backus wearing an apron. In the film, Jim is wearing that shirt and his father is wearing the apron when they discuss what Jim should do next. Studio production records indicate May 3 as the date that sequence was filmed.

133. **The same day, Irving Shulman sent…:** Irving Shulman file, USC.

133. **Weisbart sent a second memo to…:** Jack L. Warner file, Warner Archive, USC.

Chapter 34: Stern's Argument

135. **Backus recalled the experience…:** Backus, *Rocks on the Roof*, pp. 155–156.

136. **He later recalled…:** Ray, *I Was Interrupted*, p. 115.

137. **One scene, in which Jeff…:** The scene from "The Unlighted Road" is in the documentary film, *James Dean: The First American Teenager*.

Chapter 35: Lonely Street

138. **At 7:30, Ray's cast and a second crew…:** Ray claimed that he had sent George McGonnigal, "my property man" on *Rebel*, to procure some toys for the stomping victim to carry. The twenty mechanical toys that McGonnigal brought back included the monkey that a drunken Jim Stark finds in the street (*I Was Interrupted*, p. 116). There is no record, however, that McGonnigal was ever officially attached to Ray's production. His name does not appear in the Daily Production and Progress Report for *Rebel*.

139. **Beverly Long remembered the moment well…:** Beverly Long, in Dalton, *James Dean: The Mutant King*, p. 236.

139. **Eric Stacey informed Steve Trilling…:** Bernard Eisenschitz displays two pages of storyboard frames for the dome sequence in *Nicholas Ray: An American Journey* (pp. 250–251).

140. **In the second shot, Moose, Crunch and Goon…:** Grinnage described his drive through the alley in the "Talk of the Town" cable program.

140. **According to the Publicity Department…:** The studio press release, dated May 17, cites May 16 as the date for the fog problem. On May 16, however, Ray's company was at another location. Ray's only night shooting in Baldwin Hills was on May 11 and 12.

Chapter 36: Night Work

141. **Jim Stark's car, a sleek, black…:** Riese, *The Unabridged James Dean*, p. 38.

141. **Another debate concerned…:** Dalton, *James Dean: The Mutant King*, p. 251.

142. **Concerned for her daughter's safety, Maria Gurdin…:** Lana Wood, *Natalie: A Memoir by Her Sister*, pp. 1–2.

142. **It was cold that first evening…:** Dalton, *James Dean: The Mutant King*, p. 252.

142. **Although the weather was cold…:** Eisenschitz, p. 246.

142. **Another of Hopper's passions was raging…:** Elena Rodriguez, *Dennis Hopper: A Madness to His Method*, p. 20.

142. **Sometime in the early morning hours…:** Randall Riese is apparently the only source of this information, which he attributes to Steffi Sidney (*The Unabridged James Dean*, p. 71).

143. **That night, Dean ate dinner on location with…:** Hyams, pp. 214, 215.

Chapter 37: Reckless Violence

144. **Warner Bros. executives were not likely to relax…:** Crowther used his Sunday column to expand upon a particular film he had reviewed during the week. His view on violent films was generally consistent. However, in 1967, he used his Sunday column to reverse his initial condemnation of *Bonnie and Clyde* for unnecessary violence. It was one of the few times, if not the only time, that Crowther ever reversed himself on the subject.

146. **Exhibition of "The [sic] Blackboard Jungle"…:** The title of Evan Hunter's novel was *The Blackboard Jungle*, but the film's title was simply *Blackboard Jungle*.

Chapter 38: Two Endings and an Argument

147. **(Dean's line was a creative gift from)…:** Ray once said, "An actor should always be on the verge of an explosion…Every line he says should be the first and last time he says it" (in Dalton, *James Dean: The Mutant King*, p. 239). Ray's observation seems particularly valid for the "I got the bullets!" line. Eisenschitz, who states that Ray wanted Odets to write the script (p. 234), attributes the "I got the bullets!" line to Odets (p. 239). So does Stern (in *The Screenwriter as Collaborator*, p. 111). Donald Spoto, in *Rebel: The Life and Legend of James Dean*," claims that Odets actually worked on the film: "Now, after numerous delays and several attempts by other writers (among them Clifford Odets and Leon Uris)…" (p. 200). He offers no documentation, and does not list Eisenschitz in his bibliography. If Odets did work on the script, it was unofficial, incidental, and performed as a gesture of friendship to Ray. Odets had no contract with Warner Bros. at that time, nor is he mentioned in any studio records for the film.

147–148. **The same day, Stewart Stern wrote a letter…:** Stern's letter to Ray is not at the Warner Bros. Archive. On December 9, 1993, in a telephone conversation, Stern read the letter to the author. It is reprinted in the Appendix of this book (through the courtesy of Mr. Stern).

148. **In determining story credit...**: Shulman mentioned the forty percent rule in a letter to Jack L. Warner dated March 3, 1956.

148. **On May 21, Ray moved the...**: Bob Thomas, in *Clown Prince of Hollywood*, explains how Stage 7 became the tallest soundstage at Warner Bros. In 1936, Marion Davies, mistress of newspaper tycoon William Randolph Hearst, was making *Cain and Mabel* on the Warner Bros. lot (for Hearst's Cosmopolitan Pictures). In attempting to make a movie star of Davies, Hearst spared no expense. The script of *Cain and Mabel* called for a lavish wedding scene, during which the camera was to pan up to the top of a monumental pipe organ. The film's director, Busby Berkeley, claimed that the soundstage was not tall enough for the intended shot. Hearst asked Jack Warner how much it would cost to raise it high enough, and Warner responded, "About a hundred thousand dollars." Hearst agreed immediately, put up the money to jack up the building, and the scene was completed. A new foundation made the renovation permanent (pp. 96–97).

148. **The drape, unfortunately...**: David Dalton, in *James Dean: The Mutant King*, quotes Corey Allen (p. 253).

149. **The Sunday newspapers continued to feature...**: According to Kevin Lewis ("Natalie Wood," *Films in Review*), Wood believed that behaving like a well-bred Hollywood star was more important than improving as an actress: "At this point, Wood mistakenly thought her career depended on the fan magazines and she exploited herself to the fullest" (p. 581).

149–150. **Stewart Stern did not write Ann Doran's lines...**: Box #27, which is the Jack L. Warner file at USC, contains an undated newspaper excerpt, ostensibly from *The Los Angeles Times*. The headline reads, "Youth Slain in Drag Race Fight." Below it is the parenthetical notation, "(continued from page 1)," and the text of the excerpt, which describes John Fred Brodl's death. The end of the excerpt reads as follows:

The slain youth's widowed mother, whose only other child is his twin sister, Dee, was overcome by grief when officers brought her the news of her son's death.

"I don't understand, I don't understand," she said. "You pray for your children...You read about these things happening to other families, but you never dream it could happen to yours..."

The author located an article in the *Los Angeles Times* (April 24, 1955) confirming the incident, but was unable to find the excerpt itself and concluded that it had come from a different newspaper. The names mentioned in the excerpt matched those in the *Times* article, as did the description of events. The *Times* also carried a follow-up article (April 25) in which the youths responsible gave themselves up to police. The dating of the article is significant in determining who might have written the dialogue that became part of the film. Since Stern had left almost a month before Brodl's killing and had returned to New York, he clearly did not write it. Stern, in fact, complained about the line after seeing the film, and attributed it to Ray (in *The Screenwriter as Collaborator*, pp. 110–111). Since the studio filmed the squad car process shot that contains these lines on May 23, which was within the production period, Nicholas Ray *would* be the likely author, or possibly David Weisbart. Another writer, Sam Rolfe, added dialogue for the film, but only during post-production. There is, however, a fascinating wrinkle that involves Irving Shulman, who left the project in January, 1955, three months before Brodl's death and four months before the scene was filmed. Shulman's final scene seems almost to *anticipate* Mrs. Brodl's quote, since the last line of dialogue spoken by a woman onlooker reads: "I don't understand it. Children today have everything — and look what happens." Shulman's novelization of *Rebel Without a Cause*, titled *Children of the Dark*, includes that same line, then expands upon it. The expansion sounds even *more* similar to both Mrs. Brodl and Ann Doran's Mrs. Stark. The lines in Shulman's book read as follows:

"I don't understand," the woman spoke in a hushed and anxious voice to her neighbor who now stared at the fire. "Children today have everything. And look what happens."

"You hope and pray for children," her neighbor wept a little. "Hope and pray to God for children and then when you have them what happens? Tell me," she tugged at her good neighbor's sleeve, "what happens?"

Since one of Shulman's strengths as a writer was the creative use of remembered events (like the real chickie run at Pacific Palisades), it is conceivable that he saw the same headline that must have intrigued Ray. He then independently fit it into his own book, which he still would have been writing in April. It is highly unlikely that Ray would have shared such information with Shulman, and knowing Shulman's ill feeling toward Ray, even more unlikely that Shulman would have sought him out on *Rebel*'s progress. The picture did not open until late October, two months after Shulman submitted his novel to Warner Bros. As to the final line in Shulman's script, which precedes *all* of this, sheer coincidence seems the only logical explanation.

150. **Dean, however, had a portable...**: John Parker, *Five for Hollywood* (p. 95).

150. **The man with the briefcase was...**: Dalton, *James Dean: The Mutant King*, p. 260.

152. **Nicholas Ray and James Dean were among the last...**: There are two versions of events at the end of the last day of filming, one attributed to Nicholas Ray, the other to his friend,

Roger Donoghue. In John Howlett's biography of Dean, Ray claims that only he and Dean remained behind, toured the empty sets, then drove away together, ending up at Googie's, a hamburger place across from the Marmont (p. 123). Donoghue claims that he, Natalie Wood, Dennis Hopper and Perry Lopez were also with Ray and Dean, and that the entire group went to Googie's (Eisenschitz, *Nicholas Ray*, p. 252).

Part IV: Post Production and Beyond

Chapter 39: Two Assignments

155. **Post-Production began…:** The looping sessions involved fifty-nine of *Rebel*'s numbered scenes and over one hundred individual takes. The process took over seventy-six hours, spread over thirteen days, in Projection Room 14.

156. **After Dean raced at Santa Barbara…:** Hyams, p. 216.

156. **As Dean struggled with the mounting pressures…:** *Ibid.*, p. 217.

156. **The studio's notice required…:** Although Shulman had an opportunity at this point to protest the credits, he apparently did not, and Ray received sole story credit. Shulman did eventually respond, personally, and through his attorney, but only after the Academy of Motion Picture Arts and Sciences had released the nominees for the 1955 Academy Awards on February 18, 1956. There is no record in the Shulman file, the Jack L. Warner file, or the *Rebel Without a Cause* file at the Warner Bros. Archive of Shulman protesting the story credit between May 3, 1955, and February 28, 1956, almost nine months after the June 8 deadline. It is possible that Shulman had decided to settle for adaptation credit until the Academy released the list of Oscar nominees. In any case, the question would soon be moot. The category of "Writing (Motion Picture Story)" was changed in 1957 to "Best Story and Screenplay (Written Directly for the Screen)." The Academy's decision may or may not have been prompted by Shulman's protest.

Chapter 40: Inquisition

158. **The picture was an exploitation film…:** The advertisement for *Mad at the World* appeared in *The Los Angeles Times* on several occasions, including June 18. Mr. Bobo's name appeared in an article in the June 17 issue titled, " Film Men Strike Back at Kefauver."

159. **On the first day of the hearings…:** "Impact of Movies on Youth Argued," *The New York Times*, June 17, 1955. The article is reprinted in *The New York Times Encyclopedia of Film.*

159. **Others testifying in defense of…:** "Hollywood Test: Movies Defended, Assailed in Kefauver Probe of Films' Effect on Youth," *The New York Times*, June 26, 1955. The article is reprinted in *The New York Times Encyclopedia of Film.*

159. **As Warner presented his testimony…:** *Ibid.* Warner's remarks are also cited in "Film Men Strike Back at Kefauver," *The Los Angeles Times*, June 17, 1955.

160. **But William Mooring, the editor-critic for the…:** "Impact of Movies on Youth Argued," *The New York Times*, June 17, 1955. The article is reprinted in *The New York Times Encyclopedia of Film.*

160. **On Friday, June 17…:** "Executives Doubt Films Hurt Youth," *The New York Times*, June 18, 1955. The article is reprinted in *The New York Times Encyclopedia of Film.*

Chapter 41: Rough Cut

162. **Warner's only objection to the previewed film…:** Jack L. Warner regularly spent his summers at Cap d' Antibes, in the South of France (Thomas, *Clown Prince of Hollywood*, p. 227).

163–164. **Richard Dyer MacCann's column…:** Dean himself seems to have enjoyed the article, for he soon began parroting it. During an interview at a preview of *Rebel Without a Cause* a few weeks after the publication of McCann's column, Dean responded to a question about his acting style, "…I've discovered that most young men do not stand like ramrods or talk like Demosthenes…"

Chapter 42: Final Preparations

165. **Ray also complained about Plato's interview…:** The line about Plato's birthday, delivered off-camera by Plato's nurse, was probably added during post-production. The fact that the "birthday beat" remained despite Ray's objection indicates the limited influence he had after the studio had terminated his services. Producer David Weisbart, editor William Ziegler, and, of course, Jack L. Warner, determined the picture's final shape during post-production. Even if Ray had remained on salary through the post-production period, he would not have had "final cut" approval.

167–168. **While waiting for Leonard Rosenman's score…:** David Dalton claims that the song dedicated "to Jim from Buzz" was "Milkman's Serenade" (p. 255). However, studio records do not

list it among the incidental music numbers selected for the film. A listing of the musical credits
dated November 7, 1955, shows two songs, "I'll
string Along with You" and "Five O'clock Whistle" as background instrumental music for the
alley scene.

Chapter 43: Previews

169. **Rosenman later recalled...:** Dalton,
James Dean: The Mutant King, p. 238.
170. **On September 3, two days after...:** "Mrs.
Luce Denies Censoring Movie," *The New York
Times*, September 3, 1955. The article is reprinted
in *The New York Times Encyclopedia of Film*.
170. **Studio writer Sam Rolfe...:** Sam Rolfe's
writing credits included *The Naked Spur* (1953),
for which he received an Academy Award nomination; *The McConnell Story* (1955), *Pillars of the
Sky* (1956), and *Bombers B-52* (1957). He was also
co-creator of the popular television series, *Have
Gun, Will Travel*.
171. **On September 17, James Dean took time
off...:** The highway safety message was filmed over
Dean's strong objections. (Dean was opposed to
doing *anything* extra for the studio.) William T.
Orr, then head of television production at Warner
Bros., finally strong-armed Dean into making it
(Spoto, pp. 242–243). According to Joe Hyams,
the message was to have aired Monday, October 3
(only three days after Dean's fatal accident) following an episode of the Warner Bros. television
series, *Cheyenne*. Orr had it withdrawn the same
day (p. 260). Randall Riese claims, correctly, that
the program was on Tuesday night, not Monday
(p. 550).
171. **Dean still enjoyed watching people
watch him...:** Howlett, p. 122.
172. **That same day, James Dean purchased...:** Ronald Martinetti, *The James Dean
Story*, pp. 163–164.

Chapter 44: Death in
the Afternoon

173. **People off the set who had not followed...:** Martinetti, pp. 166–167. Jack Larson,
best known for playing Jimmy Olson on the *Superman* television series, also described Dean's
surprisingly aged appearance in the documentary,
James Dean: The First American Teenager.
173. **The day after his work on *Giant* ended...:**
Alec Guinness, *Blessings in Disguise*, pp. 34–35.
173–174. **On September 25...:** Hyams, pp.
237–238.

174. **On Monday morning...:** *Ibid.*, p. 239.
174. **Dean and Lew Bracker...:** *Ibid.*, p. 240.
174. **The next night...:** Martinetti, p. 167.
174. **On Thursday, the 29th...:** Hyams, pp.
239–241.
174. **At 6:00 P.M., Dean...:** *Ibid.*, p. 242.
174–175. **At 8:00 A.M....:** *Ibid.*, pp. 242–243.
175. **At noon, Dean's father arrived...:** *Ibid.*,
p. 242.
175. **At around 3:30...:** *Ibid.*, pp. 244–
245.
175. **At around 5:45...:** Holley, p. 276.
176. **By 6:20, the police had arrived...:** Warren Newton Beath, *The Death of James Dean*, p. 50.
176. **The call, relayed through the hospital
switchboard operator...:** Hyams, p. 249–251.
176. **Ginsberg also called Stewart Stern...:**
Ibid., p. 250.
176. **Ginsberg's next call...:** *Ibid.*, p. 249.
176. **Elsewhere in Los Angeles...:** *Ibid.*, pp.
252–253.
176. **Perry Lopez was at a party...:** Riese, *The
Unabridged James Dean*, p. 307.
176. **In New York...:** Hyams, p. 248.
176. **Later that night...:** *Ibid.*, p. 254.
176. **In Brooklyn, Leonard Rosenman...:**
Ibid., 251.
177. **Nicholas Ray was in London...:** Eisenschitz, *Nicholas Ray*, pp. 266–267.
177. **Ray received the news...:** *Ibid.*

Chapter 45: Damage Control

178. **Taylor held up through...:** *Giant* file,
Warner Bros. Archive, USC Memo from Tom
Andre to Eric Stacey, October 4, 1955.
178. **On Sunday, October 2...:** Dick Sheppard,
Elizabeth: The Life and Career of Elizabeth Taylor,
p. 156.
180. **On Saturday, October 8...:** Hyams, pp.
264–265.

Chapter 46: Reaping the
Whirlwind

181. **On October 12, Warner Bros....:** Dalton
(p. 283) and Eisenschitz (p. 254) both claim that
Rebel Without a Cause opened on October 3, 1955,
only three days after Dean's death. Hyams (p. 263)
claims it opened Saturday night, October 1. Both
dates are in error, however, because the film was
still in the preview stage at that time, and the studio was still contemplating changes in the ad campaign because of Dean's death. The picture had its
world premiere in New York on October 26. It
opened in Los Angeles in November.

181. **That evening, Nicholas Ray flew to London...:** Eisenschitz, *Nicholas Ray*, p. 267.

183. **Privately, his fears about...:** *Ibid.*, p. 268.

184. **Nicholas Ray returned from London on October 25...:** *Ibid.*

Chapter 47: Premiere

186. **Wanda Hale, the critic of the...:** Stern also found fault with the way the film depicted adults: "The major failing in *Rebel* is that Nick Ray was much too hard on himself as a father, and I was much too hard on my parents as a son... The result was that much of the writing and the direction of the parents was exaggerated and heavily biased, and brought a cartoon aspect to the film..." (in Mike Steen, *Hollywood Speaks!*, p. 140).

Chapter 48: Box Office

189. **Dean's death, unfortunately...:** There is no record that the woman contemplating suicide ever carried out her threat, and there are no other suicides directly linked to Dean's death.

Chapter 49: Shulman Strikes Back

193. **On February 18...:** Letter from Irving Shulman to Mr. Valentine Davies, Chairman, Writers Branch, Academy of Motion Picture Arts and Sciences, February 20, 1956 (courtesy of Allan L. Alexander, Irving Shulman's son-in-law).

193. **On February 26...:** Irving Shulman file (File #2519), Warner Bros. Archive, USC.

193–194. **Shulman did not give up easily...:** Jack L Warner file, Warner Bros. Archive, USC.

194. **Shulman went on to argue that...:** *Ibid.*

Chapter 50: Oscar and Beyond

195. **March 21 was Oscar night...:** Riese, *The Unabridged James Dean*, p. 373.

195. **James Dean lost his bid...:** Dean had a second opportunity to win a posthumous Oscar, making him the only actor in the history of the Academy to have that distinction. He was nominated as Best Actor for *Giant* in 1956, even though Jett Rink was a supporting role rather than a lead. He lost the Oscar that year to Yul Brynner for *The King and I*. Anthony Quinn won the award for Best Supporting Actor for *Lust for Life*.

Epilogue

198. **Meanwhile, Dean's popularity...:** quoted in Randall Riese, p.187.

198. **There would be no threat of litigation...:** Robert Lindner's obituary appeared in *The New York Times* on February 28, 1956. Although Lindner did not live to see *Rebel* filmed as he would have wanted it, six years after his death his book, *The Fifty-Minute Hour*, became the basis for the movie, *Pressure Point* (1962), which starred Sidney Poitier and Bobby Darin.

199–200. **It came fast...:** Murray Schumach, *The Face on the Cutting Room Floor*, p.7.

200. **Wood's career rose and fell periodically...:** In his autobiography, *Elia Kazan: A Life*, Kazan describes how he tried to use Wood's water phobia to enhance her performance in *Splendor in the Grass* (p. 604).

200. **Nick Adams also used his...:** "Adams, Nick," in Katz, *The Film Encyclopedia*, p. 10.

200. **He was rehearsing a new play...:** H. Paul Jeffers details the circumstances of Mineo's murder in *Sal Mineo: His Life, Murder, and Mystery*. Susan Braudy offers a "fictional" account in her novel, *Who Killed Sal Mineo?*

201. **He lost that year, but in 1984...:** Corey Allen won his Emmy for "Goodbye, Mr. Scripps," an episode of *Hill Street Blues*. The episode aired on November 24, 1983.

201. **Frank Mazzola, the young gang member who...:** Frank Mazzola has a website at www.mazzolafilmco.com which profiles his successful career as an editor and "film doctor."

201. **Ann Doran, who played...:** The author has found no obituary for Ann Doran in *The Sacramento Bee*, although the paper did feature her in an article on May 4, 2000. She died on September 19 of that year. The Internet Movie Database cites 251 film and television credits and 69 "noteable tv guest appearances" for Ann Doran.

201. **Marsha Hunt, who had been signed to play...:** Although numerous sources support the idea that Marsha Hunt's absence from film and television between 1952 and 1956 was specifically due to blacklisting, the Internet Movie Database biographical sketch for Marsha Hunt states that although she and her husband, Robert Presnell, Jr., were "often identified with liberal (left-wing) causes," they were "not on any studio's blacklist." The Internet Movie Database cites this observation as "Trivia," then goes on to quote from *Leonard Maltin's Movie Encyclopedia* that, in fact, Hunt *was* blacklisted.

BIBLIOGRAPHY

Allan, Blaine. *Nicholas Ray: A Guide to References and Resources*. Boston: G. K. Hall & Co., 1984.

Backus, Jim. *Rocks on the Roof*. New York: G. P. Putnam's Sons, 1958.

Beath, Warren Newton. *The Death of James Dean*. New York: Grove Press, 1986.

Brown, Kent R. *The Screenwriter as Collaborator: The Career of Stewart Stern*. New York: Arno Press, 1980.

Cogley, John. *Report on Blacklisting*. New York: The Fund for the Republic, 1956.

Dalton, David. *James Dean: American Icon*. New York: St. Martin's Press, 1984.

_____. *James Dean: The Mutant King*. New York: St Martin's Press, 1974.

Eisenschitz, Bernard. *Nicholas Ray: An American Journey*. London: Faber & Faber, 1993.

Freedland, Michael. *The Warner Brothers*. New York: St. Martin's Press, 1983.

Guinness, Alec. *Blessings in Disguise*. New York: Alfred A. Knopf, 1986.

Harris, Warren G. *Natalie & R. J.: Hollywood's Star-Crossed Lovers*. New York: Doubleday & Company, 1988.

Herndon, Venable. *James Dean: A Short Life*. Garden City, New Jersey: Doubleday, 1974.

Holley, Val. *James Dean: The Biography*. New York: St.Martin's Press, 1997.

Howlett, John. *James Dean*. London: Plexus Publishing Limited, 1975.

Hyams, Joe with Jay Hyams. *James Dean: Little Boy Lost*. New York: Warner Books, 1992.

Jeffers, H. Paul. *Sal Mineo: His Life, Murder, and Mystery*. New York: Carroll & Graf Publishers, Inc., 2000.

Katz, Ephraim. *The Film Encyclopedia*. New York: Thomas Y. Crowell, Publishers, 1979.

Kriedl, John Francis. *Nicholas Ray*. Boston: Twayne Publishers, 1977.

Lewis, Kevin. "Natalie Wood," *Films in Review*, vol. XXXVII, No. 12 (December 1986), pp.579–592.

Lindner, Robert M. *Rebel Without a Cause: The Hypnoanalysis of a Criminal Psychopath*. New York: Grune & Stratton, 1944.

Nafus, Charles. "Screenwriter Stewart Stern Remembers Writing Rebel," *The Austin Chronicle*, June 16, 2000.

Parker, John. *Five for Hollywood: Their Friendship, Their Fame, Their Tragedies*. Carol Publishing Group, 1991.

Riese, Randall. *The Unabridged James Dean: His Life and Legacy from A to Z*. Chicago: Contemporary Books, 1991.

Rivkin, Allen and Laura Kerr. *Hello Hollywood!: A Book About the Movies By the People Who Make Them*. New York: Doubleday & Company, 1962.

Rodriguez, Elena. *Dennis Hopper: A Madness to His Method*. New York: St. Martin's Press, 1988.

Sarlott, Raymond R.and Fred E. Basten. *Life at the Marmont*. Santa Monica: Roundtable Publishing, Inc., 1987.

Sheppard, Dick. *Elizabeth: The Life and Career of Elizabeth Taylor*. Garden City, New York: Doubleday & Company, 1974.

Spoto, Donald. *Rebel: The Life and Legend of James Dean*. New York: HarperCollins, 1996.

Steen, Mike. *Hollywood Speaks: An Oral History*. New York: G. P. Putnam's Sons, 1974.

Thomas, Bob. *Clown Prince of Hollywood: The Antic Life and Times of Jack L. Warner*. New York: McGraw-Hill, 1990.

Warner, Jack with Dean Jennings. *My First Hundred Years in Hollywood: an Autobiography*. New York: Random House, 1965.

Wood, Lana. *Natalie: A Memoir by Her Sister*. New York: G. P. Putnam's Sons, 1984.

INDEX

Numbers in **bold** represent photographs.

Abdul, Paula 199
Abeles, Arthur S., Jr. 171, 181, 182, 190, 192
Academy of Motion Picture Arts and Sciences 182, 193, 195
Ace Film Laboratories 188
The Actors Studio 14, 49, 50, 54, 58, 77, 85, 163, 173
Adams, Don 202
Adams, Nick 72, 73, 79, 87, 97, 100, 117, 120, 130, 131, 148, 167, 176, 200
Air Force 98
Air Pollution Control Board (City of Los Angeles) 97
Albright, Roger 160
All I Desire 79
"All-Out for All-American Day" 114
Allen, Corey 70, 70–71, 72, 79, 97, 107, 108, 119, 121, 130, 131, 142, 150, 163, 171, 200–201
Allyson, June 180
Amateau, Rodney 13
The Amboy Dukes 12, 33, 41
The American Friend 202
Anderson, Judith 179
Anderson, Mylee 79
Anderson, Sherwood 33
Anderson, Warner 80
Andre, Tom 170, 178
Andress, Ursula 174
Angeli, Pier 38
The Angry Hills 33
Anniversary Waltz 114
Apocalypse Now 201
Applegate, Fred 139
April Love 202
Aranas, Stephanie 115
Archerd, Army 130, 132
Are These Our Children? 123
Arnold, Edward 133

Arrowhead 72
Astor Theater 84, 180, 185, 188
Audience Award Polls 190
Axmann, Hanna 181

Baby Doll 200
Back Creek Friends Church (Fairmount, Indiana) 180
Backus, Henny 37, 80, 176
Backus, Jim 37–**38**, 41, 80, 87, 98, 114, 115, 120, 125, 126, 131, 133, 166, 186, 201; on Dean's boxing skills 123; Dean's death and 176; meets James Dean 38; staircase scene and 135–136
The Bad and the Beautiful 69
Bad Day at Black Rock 144
The Bad Seed 150
Baiano, Solly 72, 80, 94
Baird, Jimmy 123
Baker, Carroll 49–**50**, 63, 176
Baker, Doyle 79
Baker, Nancy 72, 79
Bakersfield (road race) 132, 136
Baldwin Hills 88, 94, 137, 138, 139, 151
"The Ballad of James Dean" 197
Barris, George 141, 174
Barth (Officer) 28
Barton, Bruce 79
Battle Cry 21, 24, 25, 77
Battle of the Bulge 40
Bau, Gordon 98
Beatty, Warren 199
Beaumont, Hugh 80
Beavers, Louise 117
Begley, Ed 80
"Behind the Cameras" 181
Bend of the River 79
Bernard, Tom 72, 97, 100, 130
Bert, Malcolm (Mal) 68, 74, 88,

93, 102, 113, 128, 130, 136, 137, 141, 143
Bessie, Mike (*Harper's*) 143, 171
Bettger, Lyle 80
Beverly Hills Hotel 32
Beymer, Richard 96, 97
Big Brothers of America 26
Billingsley, Barbara 80
Binford, Lloyd 184
Binns, Edward 80
Black Tuesday 159
The Blackboard Jungle (book) 13
Blackboard Jungle (film) 26, 90, 92, **93**, 94, 102, 111, 112, 144, 146, 157, 159, 169, 170, 184, 185, 186, 187, 195
Blackwell's Corners 175
Blair, Betsy 195
Blanke, Henry 23
"The Blind Run" 15, 16–18, 20, 24, 25, 28, 29, 33, 58, 81, 147, 148, 156, 193
Blue Velvet 201
Blyth, Ann 133
Board of Education (City of Los Angeles) 97–98, 125, 126, 139, 144–145
Bobo, James 158
Bogart, Humphrey 58, 114
Boone, Richard 54
Borgnine, Ernest 195
Bostwick, Harold 138, 139, 150
Bosworth, Patti 49
Bowers, Hoyt 101, 125, 126, 144, 156
Bracker, Lew 41, 174
Brainstorm 200
Brando, Marlon 12, 13, 70, 84, 97, 122, 130, 149, 164, 179, 183
Brannum, Tom 49
Breen, Joseph I. 94
Brewer, Roy 114

Brink, Ted 199
Brissac, Virginia 115, 130
British Board of Film Censors 171, 181, 182, 183
British Columbia Board of Censors 189
Brodl, John Fred 149–150
Broken Lance 86
Brooks, Richard 26
Brooks, Steve 176, 180
Bruce, Edwin 49
Bryar, Paul 120
Bunnell, Ray 128
Burr, Raymond 80, 183

Cady, Howard 191
California State Juvenile Officers Association 97
California Youth Authority 179
Callahan, Mushy 122, 123
Cameron, Rod 80
Canty, Marietta 117
Carl's Drive-In 88
Carlyle, John 72, 73
Carroll, Harrison 59, 90, 189
Carthay Circle Theater 97
"Casablanca" (Warner Bros. Presents) 150
Cassavetes, John 49
Castillo, Gloria 33, 72, 80
Catalina Island 143, 200
Cavell, Butch 79
Chaplin, Charlie 122
The Chapman Report 200
The Charge at Feather River 23
Chateau Marmont Hotel 11, 22, 33, 54, 63, 68, 87, 90, 94, 96, 117, 173, 176
Cheyenne 181
Chicago Board of Censors 182, 188
Children of the Dark 191
Christian Science Monitor 162
CinemaScope 57, 72, 78, 97, 101, 111, 186, 187
Cinerama Holiday 188, 189, 190
Clark, Mae 80
Clayton, Dick 85, 99, 176
Clift, Montgomery 122
Close, John 120
The Cobweb 124
Coffee Dan's 171
Cohen, Wolfe 170, 190
Columbia Pictures 13, 69, 128, 159, 165
Columbia Records 198
Competition Motors 173, 174
Connelly, Joe 195
Connors, Chuck 80
Converse, Peggy 80
Cook, Alton 186
Cook, Elisha, Jr. 80
Cooper, Gary 167

Corey, Branch 189
Corey, Wendell 123, 201
"The Corn Is Green" 179
Coudly, Dr. 26
The Court-Martial of Billy Mitchell 167
Cox, Kenneth 48
"Crazy Rhythm" 126
Cronyn, Hume 80
Crosby, Bing 72
Crowley, Pat 29, 63, 72
Crowther, Bosley 84, 92, 144, **145**, 186, 186–187
A Cry in the Night 183
Curtis, Tony 149
Cury, Ivan 49

Dagal, J. E. 197
Daily Variety 132, 183, 198
Daly, James 80
Damone, Vic 38
Dano, Royal 80
Davalos, Richard 84, 176
Davis, Bette 116
Davis, Katherine 107
Daylight Saving Time 124
DCU (Delinquency Control Unit) 86
Deacy, Jane 58, 81, 100, 125, 149, 156, 173, 176
Deadline, U.S.A. 38
Dean, James 23, 27, 29, 33, 38, 39, 48, 54, 63, 68–69, 72, 77, 79, 81–82, 84, 85, 87, **96**, 97, 98, 99, 100–101, 110, 111, 112, 114, 119, 120, 125, 126, 130, 131, 132–133, 141, 143, 145, 146, 147, 148–149, 150, 151, 152, 155, 156, 157, 163–164, 166, **167**, 169, 170, 171, 181, 182, 183–184, 185, 186, 187, 188, 189, 190, 191, 193, 195–196, 197, 198, 199, 201; announced for *Rebel* 46; buys Porsche Spyder 172; death and aftermath 173–177, 178–180; Dennis Hopper and 142; desk-punching scene and 127; doubts about *Rebel* 84–85, 86; first meetings with Nicholas Ray 20–22; Hedda Hopper and 100; meets Stewart Stern 40–41; Natalie Wood's first screen kiss and 128; with Ray in New York 49, 50; *Rebel*'s opening sequence and 139; spare time on the set 122, 123; staircase scene and 87–88, 135–136; "start notice" for *Rebel* 58–59; switchblade fight scene and 107–108, 131; tests with Sal Mineo 90–91; "The Unlighted Road" and 136–137

Dean, Jimmy (singer) 177
Dean, Mildred 156
Dean, Winton 174, 175, 176
Dehner, John 80
Denning, Richard 80
Derek, John 174
De Sica, Vittorio 97
The Desperate Hours 114
Destry 79
Detective Story 81
Devlin, Nancy 49
Diary of a Film 143
Die, Monster, Die 200
Dietrich, Marlene 84
Dino 200
Dr. Terror's House of Horrors 202
Donoghue, Roger 177, 184
Don't Worry, We'll Think of a Title 200
Doran, Ann 80, 114, 114–**115**, 133, 149, 150, 156, 186, 201
Downtown Paramount Theater (Los Angeles) 181, 182, 190
Dragnet 11, 115
Dru, Joanne 189
Dunham, Katherine 58
Dvorak, Ann 80

Eagle-Lion (film studio) 40
Earth Girls Are Easy 199
East of Eden 20, 29, 41, 50, 59, 68, 77, 81, 84, 85, 98, 100, 111, 115, 119, 124, 157, 172, 174, 176, 177, 179, 183, 185, 186, 188, 189, 190, 191, 195
Easy Rider 201
E. C. Schirmer Company 107
The Edge of Darkness 23
The Egyptian Theater 41
Elsmore, Gloria 198
Erickson, Leif 80
Evans, Jean 49
Evert, June 49
Executive Suite 115
Exodus 33, 200
The Explosive Generation 201

Fairmount (Indiana) 58, 68, 180
Famous Artists 176
The Far Country 151
Farfan, Robert 74, 101
Farmer's Market (West Hollywood) 175
Father Knows Best 73, 79
Father of the Bride 117
Father Was a Fullback 37
Father's Little Dividend 117
Fellows, Robert 23
Ferber, Edna 97, 163
Fidler, Jimmie 112
Field, Henry 102
The Fieldston School 85

55 Days at Peking 196
First Aid Man (*Giant*) 178
First Aid Man (Mr. Hill) 107, 108, 112
Fitzgerald, W. F. 69, 72, 74, 88, 94, 97, 101
"Five O'Clock Whistle" 168
Flaming Star 202
Flying Leathernecks 13
Flynn, Errol 23, 149, 189
Ford, Glenn **93**, 101
Forever Female 72
forty percent rule 148, 194
Foulk, Robert 115
Fox, Fred W. 189
Francis, Cedric 23
Frankenstein Conquers the World 200
Fredericks, Charles 126
Freeman, Y. Frank (Paramount Pictures) 159
Fuchs, Daniel 195
Fuhrmann, F. C. 139
Fuller, Tyra 149

Gabel, Martin 197
Garland, Judy 13, 90
Garmes, Lee 81
Gary, Ben 79
Geisel, Theodor Seuss 12
The Gene Krupa Story 200
General Electric Theater 81
Gentlemen Marry Brunettes 189
Georgia Street Jail 74
Get Smart! 115
Getty, J. Paul (and mansion) 65, 67, 69, 118, 121, 124, 125, 126, 128–129
Giant 29, 46, 49, 85, 125, 126, 132, 142, 145, 155, 156, 157, 163, 170, 171, 172, 173, 174, 176, 178, 180, 195
Gilligan's Island 80, 201
Ginsberg, Henry 23, 176, 180
Goldbeck, Willis 23
Gone with the Wind 72, 81
Gonzales, Pedro Gonzales 114
Googie's 171
"Got to Be This or That" 167
Graham, Sheilah 143
Grahame, Gloria 11
Grant, Cary 133
Grant, Kathryn 73
Gray, Billy **72**, 73, 79
Graziano, Rocky 123, 143
The Green Room (at Warner Bros.) 125
Griffith Observatory 48, 67, 88, 93, 105, **106**, 107, 108, 109, 120, 121, 122, 123, 128, 130, 131, 133, 139, 145, 146, 147, 148, 187
Griffith Park 48, 150, 201

Grinnage, Jack 72–73, 79, 97, 100, 140, 167
The Group Theater 14, 24
Groves, George 133, 167
Guard of Honor 68
Guernica (Picasso) 86
Guinness, Alec 173, **174**
Gunfight at the O.K. Corral 33
Gurdin, Maria 117, 142
Guthrie, William L. 48, 69, 88, 94
Guys and Dolls 189, 190, 191

Hacker Foundation (for Psychiatric Research and Education) 32, 159
Hale, Wanda 186
Haller, Ernest 72, 93, 94, 97, 98, 101, 105, 124
Hallmark Hall of Fame ("The Corn Is Green") 179
Halperin, Jonah (Joe) 54, 100–101
The Happy Time 114
Hardy, Pat 137
Harper's (magazine) 143, 171, 191
Harris, Julie 20, 174
Harris, Lowell 49
Hass, Mr. Hugo 97
Hayes, Alfred 40
Hayes, Helen 63, 180
Hays, Will 94
Hayward, Leland 23
Heffernan, Harold 132
Heindorf, Ray 168, 198
The Hell of It 99
Hell's Island 159
Hendricks, William 179
Hennesy, Tom 98, 117, 143
Henry Holt and Company 191
Hepburn, Katharine 38
"Heroic Love" 177
Hickman, Bill 174, 175, 176
Higgs, Stewart 101
"High Green Wall" 81
High Sierra 159
Hill Street Blues 201
The Hired Hand 201
His Kind of Woman 37
Hitchcock, Alfred **12**, 13
Hohler, Howard 101
Hollywood High School 88
Hollywood Motion Picture Alliance 114
Hollywood Police Station 74, 88, 118
The Hollywood Reporter 183
The Hollywood Ten 114
Homeier, Skip 12
Hoosiers 201
Hope, Bob 123, 126
Hopper, Dennis **53**, 54, 72, 79,

97, 99, 167, 170, 201; James Dean and 142; Natalie Wood and 71–72, 90; problems with Nicholas Ray 90, 117, 121, 142; reaction to Dean's death 176
Hopper, Hedda 46, 50, 63, 86, 98, **100**
Hopper, William 80, 98, 123, 133, 150, 201
Hoshelle, Marjorie (Mrs. Jeff Chandler) 88
Houseman, John 13, 22
How to Build Character (book) 122
Howson, Albert 181, 197–198
Hudson, Rochelle 80, 123, 139, 202
Hudson, Rock 149, 174
Huerta, Skipper 115
Hunt, Marsha 80, **96**, 97, 114, **115**, 201
Hunter, Evan 13, 92
Hunter, Tab 24, 77, 86
Hupfeld, Herman 121
Hussey, Ruth 80
Hutton, Brian 49
Hyams, Joe 41, 99, 174

I Am a Camera 174
I Died a Thousand Times 159
I Love Lucy 150
"I'll String Along with You" 167
Illegal 81
"I'm a Fool" 33
In a Lonely Place 58
Indiscretion of an American Wife 97
Inside Daisy Clover 200
Interrupted Melody 73

James Dean: The First American Teenager 197
The James Dean Story 197
Japan Victor Company 197
Johnny Belinda 23
Johnny Got His Gun 201
Johnny Guitar 11, 13, 18, 23
Johnson, Arte 49
Johnson, Claude 102
Johnson, Erskine 157
Johnson, Russell 80
Johnson, Victor (Vic) 93, 102, 128
Jones, Stanley 101

Kalmenson, Ben 162, 166, 181, 182
Kardell, Lilli 99
Kazan, Elia 13, 14, 20, 21, 23, 84, 86, 97, 122, 132, 143, 199
Keane, Steven E. 186, 188
Kefauver, Estes (Senator) 158–**159**, 160, 162, 165

Keith, Brian 200
Kelley, Dr. Douglas M. 25–26,
    26, 28, 73, 74, 78, 85, 139, 157,
    179
Kelly, Gene 22, 41, 63
Kelly, Grace 190
Kennedy, Arthur 101, 195
Kerr, John 86
Keyes, Evelyn 80
Kilgallen, Dorothy 122, 167, 182
Kinney National Service
    (Warner Communications)
    202
Kitt, Eartha 58, 174
Kitten with a Whip 201
Knecht, Peter D. 193, 194
Knock on Any Door 14
Kohner, Susan 200
Kramer, Stanley 114
Kuehl Funeral Home 176

Ladd, Alan 89, 180
Lady Godiva of Coventry 73
La Jolla Playhouse 54
Lancaster, Burt 89
Lane, Louise 116
Leave It to Beaver 80
Lee, Peggy 195
The Left-Handed Gun 191
The Legend of Jesse James 201
The Legion of Decency 94, 182,
    200
Lemmon, Jack 195
"Let's Put Out the Lights" 121,
    123
Letter to an Unknown Woman
    81
Lewis, Jerry 195
Liberace 125
Life (magazine) 84
"The Life of Emile Zola" 85
Lightning Over Water 202
Lindner, Robert M. 11–12, 13,
    14, 15, 159, 198; meets
    Nicholas Ray 32–33; threat of
    litigation over Rebel, 32–33,
    37
Little Nelly Kelly 121
Loew, Arthur, Jr. 37, 40, 41, 101,
    174, 176
Loew, Marcus 42
Logan, Joshua 148
Logue, Betty 49
London Pavillion 190, 192
Long, Beverly 79–80, 97, 108,
    122, 139, 150, 167, 176
Longstreet 201
Loomis, Edward 177
Lopez, Perry 21–22, 29, 122,
    148, 176
Los Angeles Board of Education
    see Board of Education (City
    of Los Angeles)

The Los Angeles Citizen-News
    189
The Los Angeles Examiner 189
The Los Angeles Herald and Ex-
    press 189
The Los Angeles Mirror-News
    85, 157, 166, 180, 189
Los Angeles Police Department
    118
The Los Angeles Times 112, 114,
    160, 168, 178, 187
Love Me or Leave Me 195
Love Me Tender 202
Love with the Proper Stranger
    200
Lovejoy, Frank 158
Luau Restaurant 90
Luce, Claire Booth 170
Lupino, Ida 13
The Lusty Men 13, 81
Lux Video Theatre 85

Mabry, Moss 85, 102
MacCann, Richard Dyer 162–
    163, 163–164
MacEwen, Walter 13, 46–47, 48,
    49, 90
Macho Callahan 201
Mad at the World 158, 160
Magnificent Obsession 174
The Maltese Falcon 98
"Man in the Moon" 75, 85, 107,
    113, 121, 123, 139, 168
The Man with the Golden Arm
    95, 200
Mandiberg, Myrtle 26, 29
Mansfield, Jayne 59, 63, 67, 73,
    79, 81
Mantell, Joe 195
Marfa, Texas 157, 163
Marlowe, Scott 49
Marsan, Jean 195
Marshall, Gregory 96
Martinez, Leonard 115
Marty 195
Massey, Raymond 20, 84
Matthau, Walter 80
Mature, Victor 144, 166
Mazzola, Frank 70–71, 72, 79,
    87, 97, 99–100, 107, 167, 171,
    201; as gang consultant 63, 68,
    84, 85, 101, 141
Mazzola, Tony 72, 79
McCarty, Floyd 101
The McConnell Story 180
McCord, Ted 139
McCormack, Col. Charles H.
    48
McCormack, Patti 150, 201
McDermid, Finlay 25, 33, 37,
    58, 94, 108–109, 130–131, 156,
    158
McGuire, Dorothy 54

McKesson, Judge William B. 26,
    179
McLaughlin, Joseph 107, 113,
    123
McMahon, Dave 150
Medic 53, 54
The Method 14, 49
MGM 13, 37, 40, 69, 92, 101, 111,
    123, 124, 143, 159, 188
Midwestern Street (Warner
    Bros.) 139, 150
Miller, Janette 174
Miller, Ken 79, 97
Miller, Peter 72, 79, 120
Milliken, Carl 25, 37, 93
Mineo, Sal 71, 79, 96, 125, 125–
    126, 133, 139, 141, 144, 145,
    155, 156, 167, 176, 200; Bronx
    accent of 118, 166; on Dean's
    self-consciousness 171; limita-
    tions as a minor 80, 124; 1955
    Oscars and 193, 195; at open
    audition for Rebel 70; opinion
    of Dean 183–184; tests with
    Dean 90–91
The Miracle of Morgan's Creek
    121
Miramar Hotel (Santa Monica)
    97
Mr. Magoo 38, 114, 125
Mister Roberts 72, 148, 195
Mitchell, Georgette 79
Mitchum, Robert 13, 33, 38
Mocambo Restaurant 148
Moffitt, Jack 183
Moise, Nina 108
Monroe, Marilyn 84
The Moon Is Blue 94
Moore, Bryan S. 198–199
Moore, James 101, 112
Mooring, William 160
Morris, Cliff 107
Morrison, Marilyn 148
Mosher, Bob 195
Moss, Thelma 173
Motion Picture Association of
    America 94, 160, 162
Motion Picture Committee of
    Milwaukee 185, 188
Motion Picture Magazine 149
Mueller, William 118, 170
Murphy, George 159, 190
Musical Selections from Rebel:
    The James Dean Musical 199
"Must We Conform?" 32
"The Mutiny of Adolescence"
    32
Mutiny on the Bounty 100
My Three Angels 150

Naiditch, Louis 81, 193
Nall, Adeline 85
National Safety Council 171

National Velvet (television series) 201
Nelson, Lori 79
Nelson, Norma Jean 79
New Dramatists Committee 40
New Orleans Uncensored 159
New York Board of Censors 181
The New York Daily Mirror 183
The New York Daily News 186
The New York Herald-Tribune 186
The New York Post 180, 183
The New York Times 82, 84, 85, 92, 144, 162, 186
The New York World-Telegram & Sun 186
Newman, Paul 40, 191
Night of the Hunter 70, 80
The Night Walker 202
The Night Watch 22, 124
Nightmare Alley 81
No Sad Songs for Me 123
Nolan, Jeanette 80
Nolan, Kathy 49
Noonan, Bruce 112, 171
North by Northwest 202
Nuell, Faye 71, 142, 143, 166
Nurmi, Maila **21**, 22, 124

O'Brien, Margaret 58, **59**, 63, 71
Obringer, R. J. 33, 37, 58, 81, 155
O'Connell, Arthur 195
Odets, Clifford 14, 22, 24, **25**, 147
O'Donnell, Cathy 158
The Office of Naval Intelligence 123
O'Hara, Maureen 133
Olken, Jerry 79, 97
On Dangerous Ground 13, 100
On the Waterfront 144
One Touch of Venus 81
Orr, William T. 48, 49, 155
The Ox-Bow Incident 121

Pacific Coast Highway 88, 94
Pacific Palisades 36–37
Page, Don 74, 88, 93, 97, 98, 101, 121, 125, 126, 128, 136, 139, 161
Palm Springs (road race) 99, 100, 121, 122
Palos Verdes 145
Pantages Theater 195
Paramount Pictures 40, 69
Parks and Recreation Department (City of Los Angeles) 48, 88, 101
Parsons, Louella 81, 88, 122–123, 136, 143
Party Girl 200
Paso Robles 175, 176

Pat and Mike 38
Pavan, Marisa 195
Peck, Gregory 133
Peck's Bad Girl 201
Penelope 200
Perian, (Mr.) 158
Perkins, Sgt. Ray 26
Perkins, Robert 188
Perrat, Jacques 195
Perry Mason 201
Persson, Gene 49
Pete Kelly's Blues 195
Peter Pan 65
Philco TV Playhouse 40
Photography Magazine 126
Picnic 148
Pidgeon, Walter 115
Pinkson, (Officer) 29
Planer, Franz 81
Platt, Edward 80, 115, 202
Player's Ring 150
Plews, Herbert 101–102
Ploquin, Raoul 195
Poitier, Sidney **93**
Pollyanna 202
Poppy 123
Porsche Spyder 141, 172, 173, 174, 175
Porsche Super Speedster 125
Postal, Charles 107
Preminger, Otto 94–95
Presley, Elvis 199, 202
Prince Valiant 86
The Private War of Major Benson 195
The Prodigal 159
Production Code (Motion Picture Production Code) 47, 94–95, 133, 144, 200
Projection Room 14 (Warner Bros.) 155, 156, 163, 167, 168, 171
P. S., Your Cat Is Dead 200
The Public Enemy 15
Pursuit, Don 86

Quinn, Frank 183

Rachel, Rachel 202
The Rack 191
Randell, Chris 72
Rau, Neil 107–108, 132, 135
Ray, Johnnie 148
Ray, Nicholas 11–15, **17**, 18, 20, 23–27, 28–29, 31, 34, 53, 54, 55, 57, 58, 60, 61, 62, 63, 65, 74, 77, 78, 81, 88, 89, 90, 91, 92, 93, 94, **96**, 97, 98, 99, 100, 101, 102, 112, 113, 115, 116, 117, 118, 119, 120, 121, 122, 123, 124, 125–126, 127–128, 129, 130, 131, 132, 133, 134, 135, 138, 139, 140, 141, 141–143, 144, 145,

146, 147–148, 149–150, 151–152, 155, 158–159, 161–162, 165, 166, 171, 180, 181–182, 183, 184, 186, 189, 190, 191, 191–192, 193, 195, 196, 198, 202; affair with Natalie Wood 90, 117, 142; artistic differences with Leon Uris 24–25, 28, 29, 31; "The Blind Run" and 11–15; casting for *Rebel* and 79–80; "chickie run" and 36–37; concerns over editing of *Rebel* 156–157, 158; differences with Irving Shulman 38–39, 45; ensemble rehearsal for *Rebel* and 87; first day of production and 105–110; first meetings with James Dean 20–22; gang research 68, 69, 84, 85, 86; Jack Warner's critique and 67; meets Stewart Stern 40–41; open auditions for *Rebel* and 70–71, 72, 73; planetarium sequence and 38–39, 42; reaction to Dean's death 177, 181; Robert M. Lindner and 32–33; secret clause in contract 18–19, 54; talent search for *Rebel* 48–50; upgrading to color and 111–112; Walter MacEwan's critique of *Rebel* and 46–47
Ray, Tony 49, 50, 70
"Rayfield" 28
Reagan, Ronald 159
Rear Window 72
The Rebel 200
The Rebel with a Cause 197–198
Rebel Without a Cause 13, 19, 23, 27, 47, 48, 49, 50, 57, 61, 65, 68, 69, 78, 81, 88, 90, 93, 98, 101, 105, 106, 107, 115, 118, 123, 125, 130, 132, 135, 139, 143, 145, 149, 150, 162, 164, 166, 180, 196, 197, 198, 200, 201, 202; animosity on the set of 117, 119, 122; *Blackboard Jungle* and 26, 92, 94, 102, 111, 144, 157, 169, 170; box office 188, 189, 190, 191, 192; British censor and 177, 181–182; casting for 72, 80; censor's objections to 95; chickie run, planetarium scenes 38; David Weisbart's concerns about 24; Dean's death and 178, 179; Dean's uncertainty about 84, 85, 86; domestic censorship and 184, 185; editing of 163, 165; firing of Uris 31; Irving Shulman's novelization of 42; J. Paul Getty mansion and

121, 124; James Dean's interest in 21–22; Jayne Mansfield and 59, 63, 67; last day on the set of 151–152; Leon Uris's concept of 28; Lindner, legal threat from 32–33, 37; locations for 74; Marsha Hunt and 97; musical production of 199; Nicholas Ray's concept of 28, 41; night filming and 128, 133, 136; odds of signing Dean for 46; open auditions for 70; Oscar night and 195 ; Oscar nominations for 193; post-synchronization of 151, 155, 167; rehearsals for 87; release date of 171; reviews 183, 186, 187; Robert M. Lindner and 11–12; *Romeo and Juliet* theme 34; screen tests for 96; Shulman and 53, 54, 58; Stern leaves the production 99; Stewart Stern replaces Shulman 53; title chosen 18; trailer for 168; U.S. Senate investigation of 158, 159, 160; upgrade to color 111, 112; writing credits for 147–148, 156
Rebel Without a Cause (television series) 198–199
Rebel Without a Cause: The Hypnoanalysis of a Criminal Psychopath 11–12, 32
Red Channels 114
Reeves, George 80
Remick, Lee 49
Republic Pictures 18
Reynolds, Debbie 63
Ride of the Valkyrie 127
The Rifleman 80
Riverside Drive Emergency Hospital 127
RKO Pictures 11, 69
Roberts, Bruce 97
Roberts, Leon 102
Robinson, Edward G., Jr. 81
Rochlen, Kwendis 85
Rocks on the Roof 135, 201
Rolfe, Sam 170
Romanoff's Restaurant 58
Rooney, Mickey 13
Rose, Reginald 200
The Rose Tattoo 195
Roseanna McCoy 81
Rosenberg, Frank P. 23
Rosenman, Leonard 20, 39, 41, 86, 124, 130, 162, 163, 166, **167**, 168, 169, 176, 179, 197, 201
Roth, Sandy 174, 175, 176
Royce, Marguerite 102
The Ruggles 73
Ruggles, Charles 80
Run for Cover 11

Russell, Jane 59, 165
Ryan, Robert 13

Sabra 40
Saint, Eva Marie 84
Saints and Sinners 200
Salinas (road race) 173, 174
Salt of the Earth 114
Sande, Walter 80
Santa Barbara (road race) 156
Santa Monica City College 88, 94
Santa Monica High School 88, 94, 108
Saxon, John 72, 73
Schaefer, Carl 171
Schaefer, Natalie 80
Schary, Dore 159
Schenectady, New York 146
Scheuer, Philip K. 112, 187
Schlitz Playhouse of Stars 54, 136–137
Schoen, Helen 107, 123, 126, 166
Scott, Martha 80
"Secret Doorway" 197
Sessions, Almira 120–121
The Seven Little Foys 123
Seventeen (magazine) 179
She Done Him Wrong 123
The Sheep Has Five Legs 195
Shirley 201
Shulman, Irving 12, 37, 41, 46–47, 49, 50, 53–54, 58, 60, 61–62, 81, 131, 191, 202; disagreements with Nicholas Ray 38–39; dispute over *Rebel*'s writing credits 133, 147–148, 156, 167; hired to write *Rebel* 33; impasse with Ray 42, 44, 45; letter to Jack Warner 193–194; story line for *Rebel* 34–37
Shurlock, Geoffrey M. 94, 95–96, 99, 108–109, 111, 133, 139, 144, 145, 159–160
Shurr, Bill 101
Sidney, Steffi 63–64, 79, 97, 117, 131, 142, 167
Sidney, Sylvia 80
Silver, Jeff 79
Simmons, Jack 22, 87, 97, 100, 124, 180
Sincerely Yours 125
Singin' in the Rain 63
Skolsky, Sidney 79, 119
Sloane, Everett 80
Smith, Joel 126, 167
Smith, Lois 77
Smog Control Board (City of Los Angeles) 121
So Big 97
Somebody Up There Likes Me 123, 143, 191
"Song of the Moon" 121, 123, 126, 168

Spartacus 200
Sperling, Milton 13
Splendor in the Grass 199–200
Spokesman Review 180
Stacey, Eric 48, 74, 78, 80, 88, 93, 97, 98, 118, 121, 125, 126, 128, 131, 136, 139, 156, 163, 167, 170
Stage 1 (Warner Bros.) 94, 96
Stage 5 (Warner Bros.) 149, 150, 151
Stage 6 (Warner Bros.) 113, 114, 115, 118, 120, 123, 127, 143, 145
Stage 7 (Warner Bros.) 148, 150, 151, 161
Stage 8 (Warner Bros.) 130, 131, 134, 136, 137
Stage 22 (Warner Bros.) 132, 163
Stapleton, Maureen 80
A Star Is Born 68, 90
Starriett, Tillie 102
State University of New York at Binghamton 202
Statler Hotel 114
Stein, Lorrie 72
Steinbeck, John 24, 84
Stern, Stewart 40–42, 50, 57, 63, 85, 87, 95, 96, 97, 101, 105, 107, 109, 112, 118, 124, 125, 128, 130, 132, 133, 138, 139, 142, 144, 149, 166, 169, 191, 197, 198, 201, 202; Dean's doubts about *Rebel* and 86; death of James Dean and 176 180; dispute with Ray over film's credit, 135, 147–148, 156; Dr. Kelley's critique and 73; first meeting with Nicholas Ray 41; Jack Warner's critiques and 67–68, 77–78; leaves the production 99; meets James Dean 40; *Peter Pan* theme and 65; *Rebel* script 55–57; script revisions 59–62, 64–66, 74–76, 82–83, 88–89; Revised Estimating Script of 68; working sessions with Ray 53
Stevens, George 13, 29, 84, 132, 155–156, 173, 176, 178
Stiletto 201
Stock, Dennis 58, 68, 84, 87, 99, 180
Straight-Jacket 202
Strange Lady in Town 115
Strasberg, Lee 14, 173
Strasberg, Susan 54
Strategic Air Command 195
A Streetcar Named Desire 23, 97
Sullivan's Travels 121
Sunset Boulevard 65, 124
Sunset Plaza Hotel 85
Superman (television series) 80

Susan Slept Here 80
Sweet Bird of Youth 200
"Sweetheart Ball" 58, 68
The Swinging World 199
Sybil 202

Tambourine (Hot Blood) 165
Tarantula 191
Taylor, Elizabeth 46, 174; meets James Dean 125; reaction to Dean's death 176, 178, 180
Taylor, Kenneth 93
Tea and Sympathy 86
Technicolor 112
Teddy Boys 190
The Tender Trap 190, 191
Teresa 40, 41
Them! 23, 107
These Thousand Hills 202
They Live by Night 14, 100
Thirer, Irene 183
Thomas, Bob 189
Thompson, Howard 82, 85
Those Whiting Girls 150
Three Stripes of the Sun 184
"Thunder of Silence" 40
Time-Warner 202
Tonka 200
Topaz 201
Track of the Cat 98
Tracy, Spencer 38
Tranqueda, Ernest A. 126
A Tree Grows in Brooklyn 20
Trial 101, 111, 188, 189
Trilling, Steve 49, 58, 98, 99, 101, 111, 112, 118, 128, 139, 144, 155, 156, 158, 161, 162, 163, 170, 181, 183, 191, 192; British censors and 182; critiques *Rebel* script 78, 89–90, 97; first meeting with Nicholas Ray 14–15; letter from Stewart Stern to 135; problems with the censor 108–109; at *Rebel* preview 171; response to Stern's letter 169
Troyat, Henry 195
Trumbo, Dalton 201
Turner, Robert "Red" 101–102
Turnupseed, Donald 175
Tuttle, Mark 189
20th Century–Fox 69, 81
Twilight of Honor 200
"Two Sleepy People" 90, 123

UCLA Medical Center 178
The Ugly American 202
Underwater 59
United Artists 69, 197–198
Universal Studios 69
"The Unlighted Road" 54, 136–137
Uris, Leon 26–27, 28, **30**, 32, 33, 34, 45, 50, 54, 156, 202; concept of *Rebel* 24–25; story line for Rebel 29–31
Ustinov, Peter 200

Valentino, Rudolph 179, 180
Vallee, Rudy 133
Valley of the Dolls 202
The Valley Times 112, 132, 179, 189
Van Fleet, Jo 195
Variety 102, 146, 151, 172, 179, 182, 185, 188, 189, 190, 191
Venice Film Festival 170
Verneuil, Henri 195
Viertel, Peter 12, 13, 33
A View from the Bridge 176
Vilardo, Henry 102
Villa Capri Restaurant 173, 174
Violent Saturday 144

Wagner, Robert 86, 199
Waite, Maggie 176
Wald, Jerry 12, 159
Walker, Clint 181
Wallace, William 102
War Memorial Hospital 176
Warner Bros. 11, 13, 14, 19, 20, 23, 24, 25, 41, 42, 49, 53, 54, 70, 77, 79, 84, 85, 86, 89, 95, 98, 107, 117, 122, 123, 125, 126, 132, 141, 148, 151, 156, 169, 171, 172, 173, 176, 181, 184, 191, 193, 195, 197, 198, 199, 200, 202; censorship issues 144, 185–186, 190; Dean's racing and 136; Dean's start notice for *Rebel* and 58; doubts about *Rebel* 29; early attempts to film *Rebel* 12; "hasty" editing of *Rebel* and 158; J. Paul Getty and 72; James Dean's contract and 27; legal problems with *Rebel* 32–33, 37; purchase of Nicholas Ray's story 15; reaction to *Blackboard Jungle* 92; reaction to Dean's death 178; secret agreement with Ray 18; threat to cancel *Rebel* 111; underage actors and 80
Warner Bros. Presents 150, 181
Warner Bros. Ranch (Calabasas) 74, 141–143,
WarnerColor 112, 120
Warner, Jack L. 13, 14, 18, 20, 69, 74, 75, 84, 89, 90, 94, 96, 100–101, 108, 123, 156–157, 165, 166, 169, 181, 182, 183, 190, 191, 202; the censor and 144, 190; critiques *Rebel* 67–68, 77–78; Irving Shulman's letter to 193–194; Kefauver investigation and 158, 159, 160; at previews of *Rebel* 162, 171; racial prejudice of 67–68; upgrades *Rebel* to color 111–112
The Warriors 189
Wasserman, Edie 11
Wasserman, Lew 11, **12**, 13, 14, 171
Watkins, Arthur 171, 181, 182, 189
Wattles Park 138, 145
The Way to the Gold 201, 202
Wayne, John 13
"We Are the Girls of the Institute" 56, 90
Webb, Clifton 100
Weisbart, David 13, 25, 26, 28, 29, 41, 46, 48, 49, 50, 54, 60, 63, 74, 78, 79, 80, 81, 85, 86, 87, 88, 92–93, 97, 98, 101, 107, 108, 110, 111, 121, 124–125, 128, 133, 141, 145, 149, 155, 161, 166, 170, 179, 190, 202; changes in *Rebel*'s ending and 147; cost-cutting procedures and 139; "hasty" editing of *Rebel* and 156, 157; Nicholas Ray and planetarium scenes 38, 39; qualities as producer for *Rebel* 23–24; *Rebel*'s sound problems and 131; Robert M. Lindner and 37
Werthman, Bernie 85
Wessel, Dick 107
Westwood Village Theater 171
Weutherich, Rolf 174–175, 176
White, Christine 100
White, Gordon S. 162
White, Jesse 80
White Heat 15
Whitmore, James 85
Whitney, Susan 72
The Wild One 13
Wilde, Cornell 165
Wilder, Billy 65, 124
Williams, Bob 150
Williams, Sumner 26
Wilson, George 102
Winslow, Ortense and Marcus 68
Winter Meeting 116
Winthrop Theatre (Massachusetts) 151
Wolfe, Ian 100, 107, 120, 168
Wood, Lana 142
Wood, Natalie 33, 37, 58, 79, 80, 87, **96**, 108, 109, 112, 118, 123, 125, 133, 138, 139, 141, 142, 143, 148, 149, 155, 156, 166, 167, 171, 180, 181, 186, 190, 191, 193, 195, 199–200; affair with Nicholas Ray 90, 117, 142; Board of Education and

126, 144–145; crying scene in *Rebel* 115–116; Dean's death and 176; delinquent behavior of 63–64, 71–72; first screen kiss 128; publicity work for *Rebel* 183, 184, 189; wins role of Judy in *Rebel* 97
Wright, Frank Lloyd 14

Written on the Wind 202
Wyatt, Jane 133
Wyman, Jane 174
Wynn, Keenan 37–38
Wynn, Sharley 37

Young, Carleton 80
Young, Gig 171, 181

Ziegler, William 112, 145, 148, 152, 156, 162, 163, 165, 168, 170
"Zing Went the Strings of My Heart" 167
Zinnemann, Fred 40, 41
Zinsser, William K. 186
Zukor, Adolph 40